Let Mutual Love Continue

Report of the Third Global Gathering
Bogotá, Colombia, 24–27 April 2018

Edited by Larry Miller

Preface and Postscript by Casely Baiden Essamuah

WIPF & STOCK · Eugene, Oregon

Wipf and Stock Publishers
199 W 8th Ave, Suite 3
Eugene, OR 97401

Let Mutual Love Continue
Report of the Third Global Gathering; Bogota, Columbia, 24-27 April 2018
By Miller, Larry and Essamuah, Casely B.
Copyright © 2021 Verlag für Kultur und Wissenschaft All rights reserved.
Softcover ISBN-13: 978-1-6667-1959-8
Hardcover ISBN-13: 978-1-6667-1960-4
Publication date 4/28/2021
Previously published by Verlag für Kultur und Wissenschaft, 2021

Contents

Preface ii
Introduction v
Programme xi
A Message to the Churches xv

Day One
Morning Prayer 1
Opening Plenary: Welcome! 9
Plenary Session: Let Mutual Love Continue! 35
Afternoon Interchurch and Evening Confessional Groups 59

Day Two
Morning Prayer 63
Plenary: Relationships Old and New 73
Plenary: Facing Common Challenges Together
in Mutual Love 103
Afternoon Interchurch Groups 131
Plenary: Together in the Global Church 133

Day Three
Morning Prayer 161
Plenary and Morning Meetings: Envisioning the Journey Ahead. 169
Plenary: The Future of Global Christianity:
Identifying Hopes and Challenges 203
Afternoon and Evening Meetings 219

Day Four
Morning Prayer 223
Plenary: Forward Together in Faith and Hope 233
Plenary: Facing Common Challenges Together in Faith and Hope .. 245
Plenary: Where Is the Spirit Leading Us? (1) 271
Closing Plenary: Where Is the Spirit Leading Us? (2) 283
Closing Prayer and Commissioning Service 293

Postscript and Appendices 307
Participants, Churches, Organisations and Roles 331

Revd Dr Casely
Baiden Essamuah

Preface

The palpable excitement and expressive dynamism we experienced at Bogotá, Colombia, in April 2018 were unforgettable. Most of us could sense that we were a part of something greater than our own church family or denominational affiliation. We were indeed the bride of Christ, the global church gathered from the ends of the earth.

The Global Christian Forum's uniqueness lies in who it can invite to the table. Beyond what we call the Forum's 'four pillars' (the World Evangelical Alliance, World Council of Churches, Pentecostal World Fellowship and Roman Catholic Church through its Pontifical Council for Promoting Christian Unity), we had several other participants from independent and unaffiliated churches as well.

It may very well have been the most diverse assembly of global church leaders ever, framed in authentic spirituality. And yet we always ask: who is missing at the table? Who is not yet a part of this fellowship and needs to be invited?

For those of us who were privileged to be at the table, this publication will be a reminder of a veritable feast where we experienced the wholeness of the global body of Christ. My predecessor, Larry Miller, called it a 'station on the way' to Christian unity, and indeed it was a memorable and pleasant station.

For those who have not yet experienced the Global Christian Forum in any of its formats, I would invite you to read carefully, noting not only what was shared but who shared it, and you will soon realize that there is a lot more that unites us than divides us. I believe you will be touched by this publication and that, like me, you will return to read portions of it again and again.

A global gathering of such scope first dwells in the hearts and prayers of a few before it becomes reality. The person on whose shoulders the giant share of this responsibility rested was my predecessor, Larry Miller. In addition to his six and a half years of service as Secretary to the Global Christian Forum (which we joyfully celebrated on the last day of the conference), Larry has also painstakingly completed the task of collecting, collating and, together with Eleanor Miller, transcribing where necessary all that is in this publication. We owe Larry an unpayable debt of gratitude. Bruce Barron and Eleanor are to be credited with the English-language copy-editing, no small task when English is not the first language of some of those who spoke at Bogota. We are grateful to them too. Kim Cain, who served as Communications Assistant for the GCF and has a very astute eye for impactful photography, and designer Jesse Cain have added much beauty to the content of this publication. Magali Moreno Sancho, whose title is GCF Events Coordinator but who does much more than this, invests her hard-working spirit and diligence in all that we do behind the scenes; in addition, she transcribed where necessary and translated the presentations delivered in Spanish for this book.

The Gathering was substantially underwritten by those who contributed to the Jubilee Fund, supported by churches, organizations, and individuals from all over the world, which enabled us to cover the cost of participation for about half the participants. Our heartfelt thanks go to the sponsors as well. Finally, we are grateful to the Gebende Hande Foundation (Germany) which has underwritten financially and overseen administratively the publication of this book.

We give thanks to God that the wind that blew in Bogotá continues to call churches together in collaboration and partnership, for the sake of the gospel, in response to our Lord's prayer that all may be one, and in a world that so desperately needs reconciliation. Indeed, let mutual love continue …

To God be the glory!

        Casely Baiden Essamuah
        Global Christian Forum Secretary from July 2018
        Annapolis, MD
        September 2020

Introduction

Revd Dr Larry Miller,
Secretary, Global
Christian Forum
(January 2012-
June 2018)

According to its Guiding Purpose Statement, the Global Christian Forum's calling is to be 'an open space wherein representatives from a broad range of Christian churches and inter-church organizations (...) can gather to foster mutual respect, to explore and address together common challenges.' A primary instrument for the realization of this vocation is the occasional 'global gathering' of international church leaders. After global gatherings in Africa (November 2007) and Asia (October 2011), the Forum's Third Global Gathering took place in South America (Bogotá, Colombia, 24-27 April 2018), under the theme, 'Let Mutual Love Continue', a quote from the New Testament book of Hebrews (13:1).

The specific objectives of the Gathering were:

- To nurture existing relationships and facilitate new ones between 'older' churches (Anglican, Catholic, Orthodox, Protestant) and 'younger' ones (Evangelical, Independent, Pentecostal) both globally and in Latin America and the Caribbean.

- To highlight and give thanks for progress in relationships between the 'younger' churches and the 'older' since the Forum process began in 1998.

- To identify common challenges the churches should address together in the years ahead.

This book contains the proceedings of the Third Global Gathering, as well as its Message, list of participants, and significant supporting documents. This introduction provides context for understanding the composition, theme, programme, and spirituality of the event.

Participants

Since the Global Christian Forum focuses on relationships between churches but has no membership, participation is the foundation of all Forum events. The intention is that approximately half of the participants at any Forum event be leaders of 'older' churches and half leaders of 'younger' churches. To ensure authentic ecclesial representation rather than only individual interest, the Forum invites the churches themselves to determine their participants or at least who from their communities should receive an invitation to participate. For the Third Global Gathering, this included first of all global church bodies and international Christian organisations, then also regional (continental) church bodies and forums, especially Latin American and Caribbean ones, as well as Colombian churches and organisations. The Forum encouraged each church and organisation to give attention to geographic, age, and gender balances as it composed its participant list but did not establish quotas in these regards. The Forum reviewed the invitation list thus established, asking who was still missing, and who from previous Forum events ought to be invited; one goal was that the gathering should be a first Forum experience for about half of the participants. In the end, however, the composition of the body of participants depended on which individuals accepted the invitation and which ones declined it.

This procedure led to a participant group that reflected the leadership structure of the global church itself, both its strengths and weaknesses. For the Third Global Gathering, with a goal of 250 participants, 417 invitations were issued. Approximately half went to leaders of 'younger' churches and half to leaders of 'older' churches. Invitations declined or unanswered numbered 193. Of these negative responses, nearly 60% were from 'younger' churches, approximately 35% from 'older' churches; the identity of the remainder uncertain. All leaders except one who declined the invitation gave 'schedule conflict' as the reason for doing so. 224 invited leaders accepted the invitation, 38% from 'younger' churches and 62% from 'older' churches. The Third Global Gathering Jubilee Fund, a cost-sharing mechanism established for the event, facilitated the participation of 115 leaders.

Other statistics are further revelatory of Gathering balances and imbalances. The geographical distribution of these participants from 53 countries of residence looked like this:

- Africa (7 countries) — 38 invitations issued, 20 accepted;
- Asia (4 countries)— 40 invitations issued, 10 accepted;
- Europe (18 countries) — 100 invitations issued, 66 accepted;
- Latin American and the Caribbean (15 countries) — 122 invitations issued, 66 accepted;
- Middle East (5 countries) — 14 invitations issued, 9 accepted;
- North America (2 countries) — 86 invitations issued, 51 accepted;
- Pacific (2 countries) — 10 invitations issued, 2 accepted.

Invitations went to 76 women (18%) and 341 men (82%); 56 women (74%) and 168 men (49%) accepted their invitations. Reviewing the list of representatives nominated by the participating churches and organisations several months before the Gathering, the Forum Committee noticed that it included few young leaders. Consequently, the Committee decided to itself invite as many young leaders from around the world as financially possible. These 13 'youth delegates' participated fully in the main programme of the Gathering as well as additional activities designed especially for them, where there were joined by other younger leaders in attendance.

These statistics do not include staff, interpreters, communication team members, stewards, or family members of participants. When all of these significant persons are added, the total number of those present in the Third Global Gathering rises to 267 from 64 countries.

Programme

The theme of the Global Gathering, 'Let Mutual Love Continue' (Hebrews 13:1), acknowledged the special moment at which the Gathering took place: twenty years after the call for a global Christian 'forum' had first resounded. Since then not only had mutual respect been fostered between leaders of churches and organization, as envisioned in the Forum's 'Guiding Purpose Statement,' mutual love had flourished. Since then not only were common challenges being explored, as the Statement had called for, but leaders had begun to address them together in the 'space' provided by the Forum. It was indeed time to review these developments with thankfulness and consider what might lay ahead.

During the first two days of the Global Gathering attention was given to the way that had been travelled together both in the Global Christian Forum and in the world church more broadly. Thematically, Day One centred on the general theme 'Let Mutual Love Continue,' recognizing that what had grown during the two decades called for a common future. Day Two focused more specifically on some of the 'Relationships Old and New' rooted in the journey of twenty years of growing 'mutual love.'

During the last two days of the Gathering, participants considered the way forward. Thematically, Day Three gave attention to 'Envisioning the Journey Ahead' while Day Four concentrated on moving 'Forward Together in Faith and Hope.' How should the churches live as global church not only in faith and hope but also in mutual respect and durable love? What challenges should they address together? The diversity and breadth of church leadership in the Gathering provided a unique 'space' in which to consider such questions.

Participants did so through a process of listening and conversation that included plenary sessions, primarily in the mornings, and smaller group exchanges, mostly afternoons. For the first time at a

Forum global gathering, each of the 'pillars' of the Forum—the World Evangelical Alliance, the World Council of Churches, the Pentecostal World Fellowship, the Pontifical Council for Promoting Christian Unity—prepared and led a keynote plenary on the theme of the day. All small groups were inter-church groups, either global or regional, each one composed of leaders from each confessional stream of Christianity present at the gathering. Perspectives and proposals from the small groups found their way to the full gathering through the work of reporters and the comments of individuals in plenary discussions. The first evening, confessional groups met separately. Special events enriched the next three evenings: addresses on the shape of the global church today (Day Two); a Columbian cultural presentation (Day Three); and a festive banquet (Day Four).

Common morning and evening prayer provided a framework for the relationships, conversations, and deliberations of the gathering. Morning prayer was celebrated all together, prepared and led by one of the 'pillars.' Evening prayer took place in the inter-church groups, following a common pattern of song, proclamation, silence, intercession, and thanksgiving. The closing prayer on the final day included a commissioning service for the new secretary of the Forum, Casely Essamuah. The texts of the prayer services are found at the appropriate chronological place in this book in order to give a fuller 'feel' of the spiritual rhythm throughout the gathering.

Sharing with one another in small groups the stories of participants' journeys with Jesus Christ was foundational at the Third Global Gathering as it had been at nearly every previous Forum meeting. Experience had shown that recognizing Christ in one another and one another in Christ through faith sharing can inspire mutual trust, preparing the way to identify, explore, and face common challenges together. Introduced in a morning plenary the first day, the entire afternoon of Day One was dedicated to this practice. In the same spirit, ensuing morning plenaries included time for several 'testimonies.' To enhance the process, Forum leadership had prepared guides for the 'Sharing of Faith Stories in Groups,' one for all participants and one for group facilitators. These guides are included in the appendix of this book; we recommend to all their broad use. (English, French, and Spanish versions of the guides can be found on the Global Christian Forum website.)

Message

The message of the Third Global Gathering was the relationships, the perspectives, and the words participants took home with them and shared with others. To the extent that this book serves to extend in time and space those relationships, perspectives, and words it is another part of the Gathering message. A more succinct statement, summarizing key elements of the gathered body's sense of the meeting, is found in the 'Message to the Churches' composed during and received at the end of the Gathering. It is with this 'Message to the Churches' that, following the Programme outline, we begin this record of the Global Christian Forum's Third Global Gathering.

Programme

Tuesday, 24 April
Let Mutual Love Continue!

08.30 – 09.30	**Morning Prayer** World Evangelical Alliance leading
09.45 – 11.00	**Welcome to the Third Global Gathering!**<ul><li>Welcome to Colombia! (Churches of Colombia)</li><li>Welcome to Colombia! (Government of Colombia)</li></ul>Introduction to the GCF and the Global Gathering: Our Unfolding Journey with Jesus Christ
11.00 – 11.30	*Morning Restoration: Coffee, Tea, Conversation*
11.30 – 13.00	**Let Mutual Love Continue**<ul><li>Presentation in Biblical Perspective by the WCC</li></ul>**Recognizing One Another in Christ and Christ in One Another:**<ul><li>Introduction to the Afternoon</li></ul>
13.15 – 14.45	*Lunch*
14.45 – 16.15	**Sharing the Stories of Our Journeys with Jesus Christ**<ul><li>Global Interchurch Groups</li></ul>
16.15 – 16.45	*Afternoon Restoration: Coffee, Tea, Conversation*
16.45 – 18.15	**Sharing the Stories of Our Journeys with Jesus Christ**<ul><li>Global Interchurch Groups</li></ul>
18.30 – 19.00	**Evening Prayer**<ul><li>In Global Interchurch Groups</li></ul>
19.00 – 20.30	*Dinner*
21.00 – 22.00	**Optional Meetings**<ul><li>Organized by Participants (see note below)</li></ul>

Wednesday, 25 April
Let Mutual Love Continue: Relationships Old and New

08.30 – 09.15	**Morning Prayer** World Council of Churches leading
09.30 – 10.45	**Greetings** • World Evangelical Alliance **Relationships Old and New** • Presentation in Biblical Perspective by the WEA **Testimony**
10.45 – 11.15	*Morning Restoration: Coffee, Tea, Conversation*
11.15 – 12.45	**Facing Common Challenges Together in Mutual Love** • 'Discrimination, Persecution, Martyrdom: Following Christ Together' • 'Call to Mission, Perceptions of Proselytism: a Global Conversation'
13.00 – 14.30	*Lunch* *Table Talk – open luncheon with Lorena Rios (Director, Office of Religious Affairs)*
14.30 – 16.00	**Conversations on Subjects from Previous Sessions and other Group Agenda** • Global Interchurch Groups
16.00 – 16.30	*Afternoon Restoration: Coffee, Tea, Conversation*
16.00 – 17.30	**Conversations on Subjects from Previous Sessions and other Group Agenda** • Regional Interchurch Groups
17.30 – 19.00	**Evening Prayer** • In Regional Interchurch Groups
19.00 – 20.30	*Dinner*
21.00 – 22.00	**Together in the Global Church** Presentations and Conversations • Gina Zurlo, Co-Author, *World Christian Encyclopedia* • Mike Perreau, Director General, United Bible Societies • Gabrielle Thomas, Lead Researcher, Receptive Learning between Churches

Thursday, 26 April
Let Mutual Love Continue: Envisioning the Journey Ahead

08.30 – 09.15	**Morning Prayer** Pentecostal World Fellowship leading
09.30 – 10.45	**Greetings** • The Catholic Church **Envisioning the Journey Ahead** • Panel of Perspectives & Biblical Presentation by Pontifical Council for Promoting Christian Unity **Testimony** **Future of Global Christianity** • Introduction to the Subject
10.45 – 11.15	*Morning Restoration: Coffee, Tea, Conversation*
11.15 – 12.45	**The Future of Global Christianity: Identifying Hopes and Challenges** **Regional Interchurch Groups**
13.00 – 14.30	*Lunch* *Table Talk – open luncheon with Gabrielle Thomas: 'Receptive Learning Between Churches'*
14.30 – 16.00	**The Future of Global Christianity: Identifying Challenges and Hopes** **Regional Group Reporting and Plenary Conversation** **Global Gathering Message: Introduction**
16.00 – 16.30	*Afternoon Restoration: Coffee, Tea, Conversation*
16.00 – 17.30	**Conversations on Previous Sessions and Other Agenda** • Global Interchurch Groups
17.30 – 19.00	**Evening Prayer** • In Global Interchurch Groups
19.00 – 20.30	*Dinner*
21.00 – 22.00	**Together in Colombia** • Colombian Cultural Evening

Friday, 27 April
Let Mutual Love Continue: Forward Together in Faith and Hope

08.30 – 09.15	**Morning Prayer** Pontifical Council for Promoting Christian Unity leading
09.30 – 10.45	**Greetings** • Pentecostal World Fellowship **Forward Together in Faith and Hope** • Presentation in Biblical Perspective by the PWF **Testimony**
10.45 – 11.15	*Morning Restoration: Coffee, Tea, Conversation*
11.15 – 12.45	**Facing Common Challenges Together In Faith and Hope** **Prioritizing Common Challenges** • Presentations and Conversations **Global Gathering Message – First Reading**
13.00 – 14.30	*Lunch*
14.30 – 16.00	**Testimony – Youth Message** **Where is the Spirit Leading Us?** • Plenary Conversation **Global Gathering Message – Second Reading** **Thank You for Larry & Eleanor Miller**
16.00 – 16.30	*Afternoon Restoration: Coffee, Tea, Conversation*
16.00 – 18.00	**Panel of Perspectives: What Next?** **Global Gathering Message: Final Reading and Reception**
18.00 – 19.00	**Closing Prayer and Commissioning**
19.30	*Festive Dinner*

A Message to the Churches

Global Christian Forum Third Global Gathering
Bogotá, 24-27 April 2018
'Let Mutual Love Continue'

Greetings to all who call on the name of Jesus Christ as Lord and to all people throughout the world!

The third international gathering of the Global Christian Forum met in Bogotá, Colombia, from 24–27 April, 2018. We express our thanks to our Colombian hosts who have so graciously received us. We rejoice and give thanks that 267 participants from the Eastern and Oriental Orthodox Churches, the Evangelical Churches, the Historic Christian World Communions, Independent and indigenous Christian Churches and communities, the Pentecostal Churches, and the Roman Catholic Church from 64 countries came together to engage with one another on the theme, 'Let mutual love continue' (Hebrews 13 : 1).

The theme, *'let mutual love continue'*, expresses the spirit and practice of the Global Christian Forum since its inception in August 1998, when a group of 28 visionary leaders met at the Ecumenical Institute at Château de Bossey-WCC to create a new space for broadening interchurch encounter and dialogue. The Guiding Purpose Statement of the Global Christian Forum was affirmed at the first Global Gathering in Limuru, Kenya, in 2007:

> *To create an open space wherein representatives from a broad range of Christian churches and interchurch organizations, which confess the triune God and Jesus Christ as perfect in His divinity and humanity, can gather to foster mutual respect, to explore and address together common challenges.*

1. A 'Cloud of Witnesses' (Hebrews 12:1)

The Letter to the Hebrews reminds us, 'We are surrounded by a great cloud of witnesses' (Hebrews 12). In our gathering, we listen to, and are nourished and challenged by many different witnesses of faith journeys in the mysterious and empowering presence of God.

Witnessing to Each Other Through Praying Together and Sharing Our Faith Stories

Gathered in Jesus' name, praying together has nourished and sustained us on our journey as witnesses.

Indeed Jesus has been present among us as we have praised God and prayed for peace, reconciliation and all those who suffer persecution, poverty and injustice (Matthew 18:20). Sharing stories of our journeys with Jesus Christ, which has become the hallmark of the Global Christian Forum, has helped us to recognize one another as brothers and sisters in Jesus Christ and created an atmosphere of closeness and trust so that we can address issues that are still separating us.

Gathered in Jesus' name in Bogotá, Colombia, we have listened to and been inspired by witnesses working for peace. We pray that the peace process may continue in Colombia and bring hope and reconciliation to those who are suffering and struggling.

Testimony to Repentance and Reconciliation between Christians and Churches

We have heard testimony from representatives of the Lutheran World Federation, the Catholic Church, the World Methodist Council, the

World Communion of Reformed Churches and the Anglican Communion about their Churches' respective journeys to embracing the Joint Declaration on the Doctrine of Justification (1999). Along with them, we 'give thanks to the Lord for this decisive step forward on the way to overcoming the division of the Church' (JDDJ 44). What happened in the past cannot be changed, but what is remembered and how it determines our present can. We hope and pray that retelling our histories and our stories together may lead our Churches to a fuller recognition of each other as Christians on the same journey, sharing the joy and power of the Gospel, hearing what the Spirit is saying (Revelation 2:29), and witnessing to the mercy of God through proclamation and service, so that the world may believe (John 17: 21).

2. The Way of Jesus Christ, Suffering and Sacrifice (Hebrews 12)

'Consider him who endured such hostility against himself from sinners, in order that you may not grow weary and lose heart' (Hebrews 12:3). Sharing the stories of our faith journeys testifies to our common faith in the salvific work of Jesus Christ. In sharing our faith in Christ, the participants have acknowledged that Jesus continues to call us to take up our cross and follow him (Matthew 16:24; Mark 8:34; Luke 9:23).

A readiness to follow Jesus, even to giving up our own lives as he did, is the condition of true discipleship. As such, we have honored and pray for His Eminence Metropolitan Mor Gregorius Yohanna Ibrahim, a devoted member of the GCF Committee, and the Greek Orthodox Archbishop of Aleppo Boulos Yazijy on the fifth anniversary of their abduction in Syria. We call on all Christians to remember them, as well as all of our brothers and sisters in the Middle East. We also call Christians to join with those who pray for peace and justice in Jerusalem. In the bond of Christian unity, we call on all Christian communities to remember in their daily prayers all who suffer persecution and martyrdom for living their faith throughout the world (Matthew 5: 10-12).

We encourage our fellow disciples to persevere while looking to Jesus, with hunger and thirst for righteousness, and hope and joy in the Resurrection.

3. Let Mutual Love Continue in a Life-Generating Work of the Spirit

As disciples of Jesus, we acknowledge that sharing the Good News of Jesus to all nations is a joyful calling of all Christians (Acts 1:8).

As disciples of Jesus, we pray with and lift up in prayer all peacemakers (Matthew 5:9); those who feed the hungry, give drink to the thirsty, welcome the stranger, clothe the naked and visit the imprisoned (Matthew 25: 35-36); those who defend God's creation awaiting the revelation of the children of God (Romans 8:19); those who labor to free those who have been enslaved and put an end to human trafficking; those who strive to end violence and discrimination against women; those who serve migrants and displaced people, persons with disabilities and those who care for the sick.

To let mutual love continue on our journey as brothers and sisters in Christ, we need repentance and reform, encouraged and led by the Holy Spirit. We must first critically examine ourselves rather than others. The Global Christian Forum Consultation Message from Tirana, Albania, states, 'We repent of having at times persecuted each other and other religious communities in history, and ask forgiveness from each other.' We cannot be content with 'polite ecumenism', but rather let our narratives be redeemed in the Spirit, confessing that our division openly contradicts the will of Jesus Christ, scandalizes the world and harms our mission to share the Gospel.

We implore the forgiveness of our Lord and encourage one another to be bound together in our mutual love in Jesus Christ and journey forward together. As united, we now call upon Christian Churches around the world to take courage in facing together today's challenges in various cultural and regional contexts.

As we journey together as friends of Jesus Christ, we must always make room for others by asking who is missing in our midst at the Global Christian Forum. Here in Bogotá, we yearned in particular for the gifts of more women, young people, indigenous people and persons with disabilities.

We want to share and grow the joy we have experienced in Bogotá, by extending the experience of the Global Christian Forum through regional and local initiatives rooted in the places where we live.

We are sent as disciples of Jesus out into the brokenness, pain and injustice of the world.

In our sharing the struggle of authentic Christian witness in our world, we heard and applauded strong warnings to resist the captivity of the Gospel by any national or ideological powers. We desire to hold one another in support and accountability united in one body, transcending all attempts to weaken the truth of our witness to Jesus Christ.

Conclusion

Hebrews 13:20-21 blesses us, 'Now the God of peace, that brought again from the dead our Lord Jesus...make you perfect in every good work to do in his will'. Being together and sharing stories of our faith journey, we have learned to recognize and receive one another as gifts of God. We remembered and named the stories of our brothers and sisters who bear the suffering marks of Jesus in their bodies (Galatians 6:17). Our hearts were not dismayed but wondrously lifted in hope (Romans 8:35-38). We encourage one another to press on and continue in the spirit and works of love.

In strengthening and continuing mutual love, we are called upon to be the Church in and for the world, bearing faithful witness to the love of God in Jesus Christ and embodying his truth in our ordinary practices of Christian life. Like the disciples on the road to Emmaus whose encounter with Jesus led them to recognize him as they shared together, we have gathered in a shared space praying and conversing with one another, feasting together on the Word of God. Being together, our eyes were also opened, and we recognized the living presence of Jesus Christ.

May the Spirit of God continue to gather us together in mutual love in Jesus Christ, encouraging and strengthening one another to stand firm in our shared faith and help us be the prophetic witness for the hurting world.

Bogotá, Colombia, 27 April 2018

Dr Rosalee
Velloso Ewell

DAY ONE: TUESDAY 24 APRIL
LET MUTUAL LOVE CONTINUE!

MORNING PRAYER

Prepared and led by the World Evangelical Alliance

Welcome, Greetings, Prayer:

> **Rosalee Velloso Ewell** (Brazil/United Kingdom), Executive Director, Theological Commission, World Evangelical Alliance (WEA)
>
> **David Ruiz** (Guatemala), Executive Director, Missions Commission, WEA

Music:

> **Santiago Benavides Group** (Colombia)
>
> **Brother Paolo** (France), Taizé Community

Scripture Reading: Zephaniah 3:17-18 and Hebrews 13:1
Spanish: ***David Ruiz***
Arabic: ***Esther Schirrmacher*** (Germany)
English: ***Michael Perreau*** (United Kingdom)
French: ***Joséphine Nthininyuzwa*** (Rwanda/France)

Morning Reflection

Rosalee Velloso Ewell

John 17:13–19 (NRSV)

> But now I am coming to you, and I speak these things in the world so that they may have my joy made complete in themselves. I have given them your word, and the world has hated them because they do not belong to the world, just as I do not belong to the world. I am not asking you to take them out of the world, but I ask you to protect them from the evil one. They do not belong to the world, just as I do not belong to the world. Sanctify them in the truth; your word is truth. As you have sent me into the world, so I have sent them into the world. And for their sakes I sanctify myself, so that they also may be sanctified in truth.

This is the word of God for the people of God.

I considered inviting our readers to read the gospel text all together, at the same time, in their various languages. Imagine the chaos, the noise. A little taste of Pentecost right here in Bogotá.

As we come together from all around the world for this third Global Gathering, we celebrate the mutual respect and love that mark our time together. This text from the gospel of St John reminds of that respect and that love that the triune God makes possible for us. The text also tells us of the cost of this love.

Look at your name badge. What does it say? If I ask you, 'Where are you from?' How will you answer?

In Jesus' prayer in John 17, Jesus gives us an answer to the question, 'Where are you from?' He says: 'Not from this world.' Now there's a weird identity!

Jesus' prayer is set within the context of Jesus' love and care for his disciples. It is a prayer that mixes up present and future. In John 16:33, Jesus speaks of being of good cheer because he has already overcome the world, yet this is all before the crucifixion. It is a prayer about unity and evangelism, and living as God's people in a world that does not like us.

Jesus makes four requests in this selection of verses. First, he prays that the disciples may have his joy. Second, he prays that they may be protected from the evil one. Then he prays twice that they may be sanctified in the truth. Yet in a text about love and truth and unity and complete joy, Jesus says we will be hated.

The word of Jesus is truth and light. So why is it hated? It is hated because the type of holiness for which Jesus prays, the type of love which we are to show one another, is the type of love that threatens the powers of this world.

Jesus prays that this little band of disciples will be so peculiar that those who meet them and see their love might actually think that they are not from this world.

Jesus' prayer for his disciples becomes his prayer for us. This is our story. It is an invitation that we join in God's mission, as Jesus continues with his prayer in John 17:23: 'so that the world may know'. Our gathering here in Bogotá is a sign that points to Jesus and to the love that only he makes possible between us.

More than that, we have no part in God's mission if we cannot love as God loves.

If we make Jesus' prayer our own—if we pray that God sanctify us, that God's truth and love be known in this gathering—are we really ready for God to answer our prayers?

The holiness and love that Jesus prays for are about displaying our radical difference, showing the marks of God's ownership. It is a text about answering the question, 'Where are you from?'

It is a text about belonging; about true citizenship and showing how strange to the world is the life in Christ. It is the strangeness of trusting in what God has promised. Do you trust God to answer your prayer?

If we do trust, then as Jesus says, we should expect to be hated. He had already warned the disciples of this in John 15:18: 'If the world hates you, be aware that it hated me before it hated you. If you belonged to the world, the world would love you as its own. … Because you do not belong to the world … the world hates you.'

It is distinctly uncomfortable not to belong. Perhaps you feel you don't belong here. But in this text Jesus pushes it further. It's more than uncomfortable, it means you'll be hated.

When we think of hate, joy is not the first thing that comes to mind. And yet this is the first request Jesus makes: 'I speak these things so that they may have my joy made complete' (v. 13).

Jesus is not asking them or us to laugh at hatred, to dismiss the suffering that so many Christians face for the sake of their faith. Not at all. Indeed, there is a call for mourning, for lament, for coming together alongside those who suffer and who are persecuted. Doing so has been a hallmark of the Global Christian Forum.

This is not a text that makes light of suffering or hatred. This is a text about belonging and about being joyful in our heavenly citizenship; about showing the peculiar people that we are because we have all been called by God.

If you ask me, 'Where are you from?' I might say I'm from São Paulo, Brazil. I'll say my grandmother was from the Tupi-Guarani tribe and my grandfather was half German, half Portuguese. I'm married to a north American and I live in England.

But no matter where I am—in Colombia, in the UK, in Lebanon or Tanzania last month—when I see the green and yellow of the Brazilian flag on the television for a football game, my heart is strangely warmed.

During the World Cup, I am 1000% Brazilian. It's not a thoughtful, rational decision, made under careful consideration whether ours is a good team or not. That does not matter. It is a joyful sense of belonging.

My joy in being Brazilian during the World Cup is just a very faint echo of what Jesus is saying here.

Jesus says, 'Share that excitement when it comes to your origin in God. Be thrilled because you have been chosen from above, you are not of this world, and I have brought you together in love!'

I belong to Jesus and I belong to you much more than I belong to Brazil's football team. You are my identity markers.

Where are we from? We are from another world, a world formed and chosen and redeemed by God, Father, Son and Holy Spirit. We are called to show God's light, to be the joy and love of Jesus to those we serve.

Through Jesus and the gift of the Holy Spirit, God has given us another origin, another belonging, another identity in which we are to be joyful. Jesus said to Nicodemus that it is an identity born from above, and it is an identity that we share with Jesus himself.

Verse 18: 'As you have sent me into the world, so I have sent them into the world.' Jesus sends those who share in his homeland. He has given us his word, his light and his truth. He has given us himself and as we share life in him, we shine his light.

Let mutual love continue! Through our love the world will come to know the one true God. What greater promise, what greater incentive could there be for us indeed to show that love to God and to one another?

This isn't just a global gathering. We are a light, the light of Christ—as St Paul says in Philippians, a light shining like stars in a dark world. Let us not take this gathering for granted. Let us shine the joy and love of being in Christ amidst all our diversity, difference and wonder. That is how God enables us to move forward in mutual love. May we follow God's Spirit in truth and love.

Music
Santiago Benavides Group, and *Brother Paolo*

Prayer
David Ruiz

Mr Héctor Olimpo
Espinosa Olivier,
Larry Miller

DAY ONE: TUESDAY 24 APRIL
LET MUTUAL LOVE CONTINUE!

OPENING PLENARY

Welcome!

> *Welcome to the Third Global Gathering:*
> **Larry Miller**, Secretary, Global Christian Forum

> *Welcome to the Churches of Colombia:*
> **Diana Cruz**, Coordinator, World Student Federation, Colombia
>
> **Jeferson Rodriguez**, Pastor and Professor, Assemblies of God, Colombia

> *Welcome to Colombia:*
> **Héctor Olimpo Espinosa Olivier,** Deputy Minister for Political Relations, Ministry of the Interior, Government of Colombia

> *Music:* **Santiago Benavides Group**

**Our Unfolding Journey with Jesus Christ:
The Story of the Global Christian Forum**

Moderator: **Elisabeth Matear** (UK), Secretary for International Ecumenical Relations, The Salvation Army International Headquarters; GCF Committee Member

Film (script): Twenty Years of the Global Christian Forum

Experiences on the Way: The Global Gatherings

- 'I was in Limuru' — **Daniel Okoh** (Nigeria), General Overseer, Christ Holy Church International; President, Organization of African Instituted Churches

- 'I was in Manado' — **Victoria Matthews** (New Zealand), Bishop of Christ Church, Anglican Communion

- 'I am in Bogotá' — **Marie Eugena Figueroa de Gongora** (Guatemala), President, Latin American Catholic Charismatic Council

Roll Call of Third Global Gathering Participants:

Elijah Brown (USA), General Secretary, Baptist World Alliance, GCF Committee Member;

Georgine Kengne Djeutane (Cameroon), Chairperson, World Student Christian Federation, GCF Committee Member

Welcome!

Welcome to the Third Global Gathering

Larry Miller

Ephesians 1:3–14

> *Blessed be the God and Father of our Lord Jesus Christ, who has blessed us in Christ with every spiritual blessing in the heavenly places, just as he chose us in Christ before the foundation of the world to be holy and blameless before him in love. He destined us for adoption as his children through Jesus Christ, according to the good pleasure of his will, to the praise of his glorious grace that he freely bestowed on us in the Beloved. In him we have redemption through his blood, the forgiveness of our trespasses, according to the riches of his grace that he lavished on us. With all wisdom and insight, he has made known to us the mystery of his will, according to his good pleasure that he set forth in Christ, as a plan for the fulness of time, to gather up all things in him, things in heaven and things on earth. In Christ, we have also obtained an inheritance, having been destined according to the purpose of him who accomplishes all things according to his counsel and will so that we, who were the first to set our hope on Christ, might live for the praise of his glory.*

'With all wisdom and insight, he has made known to us the mystery of his will ... as a plan for the fullness of time, to gather up all things in him, things in heaven and things on earth.' The church fathers spoke often of the 'mysteries' of the faith. John Chrysostom said that they are called 'mysteries' because what we believe about them is not the same as what we see in them; we see one thing and believe another.

The New Testament itself is the story of a mystery, a great mystery where what one sees in the beginning is not what one believes in the end. In Ephesians, the apostle Paul claims that what may have been the greatest mystery of all time is in fact no longer a mystery.

In a tweet-length theological declaration, he describes the mystery of God's plan for the entire cosmos and all of eternity. In and though Christ Jesus, Paul claims ecstatically (Eph. 1:9–10), God is drawing together *all* people in the universe and *all* things in the cosmos. Perhaps we still cannot see it clearly, but God has had a plan from the very beginning—even from before the beginning—and that plan is unity, the gathering up of all people and all things, all things on earth and all things in heaven, through and in Christ Jesus.

That is very good news, indeed. But can you believe it?

Some say 'seeing is believing.' It is my profound joy to welcome you to this Third Global Gathering of the Global Christian Forum. It is my prayer that this place of our togetherness on the way will be a place where seeing is believing. The Third Global Gathering is not the place where all things and all people are gathered up in unity in and through Jesus Christ. But it can be a station on the way.

May our time together be such that the apostle Paul would say to us what he said to the believers gathered in Ephesus:

> *I have heard of your faith in the Lord Jesus and your love toward all the saints, and for this reason, I do not cease to give thanks for you, as I remember you in my prayers. I pray that the God of our Lord Jesus Christ, the Father of glory, may give you a spirit of wisdom and revelation as you come to know him, so that, with the eyes of your heart enlightened, you may know the hope to which he has called you. (Eph 1:15–18)*

Welcome to the Colombia Churches

Santiago Benavides

We are going to sing together to introduce this special time of welcome to our country, Colombia. We will begin with a musical adaptation of Romans 5:3–5, which says that 'suffering produces perseverance, perseverance produces character, character produces hope, and this hope does not disappoint us because God has poured out his love into our hearts.'

It seems to me that this verse has much to do with our nation. Suffering produces perseverance. The national anthem of Colombia literally says that in the furrow of pain, good things germinate. Hear that phrase: 'In the furrow of pain, good is germinating'. This Bible verse reminds us of that in a very beautiful way. Maybe it will be difficult to sing for those who do not speak Spanish. But those who speak Spanish, please sing out loudly!

Text of the Spanish song:

Suffering produces perseverance, perseverance produces character, character produces hope, and this hope does not disappoint us. No, it does not disappoint us, because God has poured out his love into our hearts by the Holy Spirit he has given us.

Diana Cruz and *Jeferson Rodríguez*

Introduced by Larry Miller

One of the deepest joys for me as we prepared this 'station' for you in Colombia has been the gift of coming to know the churches of Colombia and especially the leaders of the churches of Colombia. So it is now an honour and a privilege to welcome them into our midst to tell the stories of their journey with Jesus Christ. Diana and Jeferson, welcome!

Jeferson Rodríguez (JR): It is a pleasure for us to welcome you to Colombia, to the Third Global Gathering of the Global Christian Forum, with the theme of 'Let mutual love continue.'

Diana Cruz (DC): Colombia is a diverse country and that's why we have several expressions of the Christian faith here.

JR: For this reason, the different churches and organizations invited would like to extend a warm greeting and tell you a little about who we are and what we do, so that you can have a sample of the church community of Colombia.

DC: We will present some videos of the different denominations and faith-based organizations that are present in Colombia, and representatives of these denominations will come forward carrying a distinctive symbol of each church or organization.

JR: Let's start by watching videos from the Assemblies of God in Colombia, the Anglican Church, the Baptist Church, and the Catholic Church.

Assemblies of God: The National Council of the Assemblies of God in Colombia, a Pentecostal denomination, has been in the country for 76 years. Today it is a large denomination with more than 1,300 congregations and 1,264 ministers. We are focused on the vision 'Extending the Kingdom to Generations.' Through pastoral missions we are empowering the church to respond to the needs and expectations of society today, and thus to establish the kingdom of heaven in Colombia and in the nations.

Anglican Church: Colombia is one of the dioceses of the Episcopal Church, which makes this the official church of the Anglican Communion in Colombian territory. The denomination's work here began with a chapel service for foreigners residing in Colombia; it was dependent on the missionary district of Panama and the Canal Zone. In 1963 the Episcopal Diocese of Colombia was established, with the Most Reverend David Reed as its first bishop. Our current bishop is the Most Reverend Francisco Duque Gómez. The diocese of Colombia is made up of 27 congregations with about 3,600 faithful in 20 cities and municipalities throughout the country. There are 27 priests, 10 deacons and one missionary bishop from the Dominican Republic.

Baptist churches: Baptists are a group of believers united by our faith in salvation through Jesus Christ our Lord, gathered together in churches that believe in the holy Scriptures as our rule of faith and authority, and practicing the principles established therein. The first efforts to establish Baptist work in Colombia date back to 1845 on the island of San Andrés. On the mainland, missionary efforts began in 1915 with the support of Cuban brothers and sisters. Baptist work was organized in 1940 in the Colombian Baptist denomination, which held its first assembly in 1951. 'We exist to establish and strengthen Baptist churches that fulfill the Great Commission.' This sentence summarizes our purpose, and we believe that it is the desire and commitment of each affiliated church. Today there are more than 21,000 Baptists in Colombia, with 200 established churches located throughout most of the country and nearly 100 more in development.

Catholic Church: Based in Rome, our church was established in Colombia with the discovery of America. We arrived here with the message of the Gospel. We work all over Colombia, through parishes, schools, universities, hospitals, homes for people with disabilities, and many social assistance activities. We are organized into 78 ecclesiastical jurisdictions, including archdioceses, dioceses, and apostolic vicariates, active in evangelizing the country. Many thousands of faithful bishops, priests, religious men and women, and laypersons joyfully carry out the mission entrusted to us by Jesus Christ, our founder and Savior. The church, in fidelity to its mission, is committed to peace, justice, and the good of all.

DC: We invite you to watch now the videos of the Church of God, the Lutheran Church, the Methodist Church, and the Presbyterian Church.

Church of God: We are the Church of God in Colombia. We have 150 churches throughout the country and more than 10,000 members nationwide. We are feeding stations (social work). We are also schools.

We are training seminars. We are planters of future pastors. We are leaders. More than a church, we are the Church of God in Colombia.

Evangelical Lutheran Church: The Evangelical Lutheran Church of Colombia is the fruit of 82 years of gospel proclamation and diaconal witness in the country. We are an historic Christian church of Lutheran confession, committed to the mission of God, that integrally proclaims the gospel of our Lord Jesus Christ for the liberation and salvation of human beings and creation. Currently, the church has a total of 14 congregations and 10 missions distributed across four regions nationwide, comprising more than 2,100 believers. It also has six national ministries—Pastoral, Evangelism, Youth, Women, Education, and Diakonia—that contribute to peace building, the strengthening of formal and informal education programs, the empowerment of women, and the improvement of the quality of life of communities. We implement projects that directly serve peasant families, older adults, vulnerable girls, people with disabilities, mental and sexual health, and training in human rights issues.

The Methodist Church: We are the Colombian Methodist Church, the Colombian expression of Methodism, which was founded by John and Charles Wesley in England in the 18th century and is now a worldwide church of which we are one of the youngest members. We are barely 22 years old. Initially formed by a retired Methodist pastor from the United States in Colombia's coffee region, we now have 35 congregations and about 5,000 members. As part of the body of Christ, we contribute to extending the kingdom of God, which is expressed in the building of inclusive communities that proclaim the good news, and doing good works that serve Colombian society. We also carry out a series of projects that address human rights violations, health, social welfare and the problems affecting vulnerable youth in urban slums. By addressing the various challenges, needs and aspirations of our country, we are contributing to the fulness of life in Colombia.

Presbyterian Church of Colombia: We have been in Colombia since 1856. We have three districts: Central, Costa Norte, and Urabá. We contribute to education from the perspective of our Reformed tradition. We value responsibility and autonomy, inclusiveness, and respect for diversity. We promote human dignity and social justice. We are committed to a sustainable future and to defending life. We engage in public advocacy as a testimony of faith. We value freedom and democracy. We proclaim the Word of God and His love. Under the guidance of the Holy Spirit, we give glory to God in our Colombian context.

JR: Finally, we have videos from some of our faith-based organizations that relate to all the churches present in our country. These organizations are World Vision, the YWCA, and the World Student Christian Federation.

World Vision: We are a Christian organization of development, humanitarian aid, and advocacy at the global level, focused on the welfare and holistic protection of the most vulnerable children. We are celebrating 40 years in Colombia, bringing hope to the most vulnerable communities, promoting human transformation, justice and the good news of the Kingdom of God. During 2017, we impacted more than 978,000 children in 52 municipalities across Colombia. We work to give each child life in all its fulness. We pray for each heart, asking for God's help to make this goal possible.

YWCA: We are the Young Women's Christian Association in Colombia, representatives of the global Young Women's Christian Association based in Geneva, Switzerland. We are based on Christian principles without discrimination by race, nationality, social class, political or religious creed. We carry out programmes to improve the role of women in the world. Our mission is to improve the social and economic conditions of women, teaching peaceful coexistence through sharing and respect of the basic human rights to which all people are entitled: welfare, security, dignity, freedom, justice and peace. Our vision is that the full inclusion and empowerment of women may become a reality, to promote justice, peace, education, culture, health and environmental protection through women's leadership. With your help, we will be able to carry out these and many other projects.

World Student Christian Federation: We are a global ecumenical organization that brings together students and youth in more than 90 countries. We come from different Christian faith traditions: Protestant, Anglican, Evangelical, Catholic, and Orthodox. We are gathered in more than 107 national student movements globally. Our mission in Colombia is to promote among the student community a sensitive, critical, and transforming commitment to the Latin American and Caribbean reality. In Colombia we are active in Bogotá and Barranquilla.

DC: In addition to these churches and organizations, others also wish to extend their greetings and a warm welcome including the Adventist Church, the Mennonite Church, the Salvation Army, and the Orthodox Church.

JR: We, as Colombian churches, hope that you will all have a good time here and that we can continue to build bonds of brotherhood in love.

DC: To close our presentation, we invite you to sing with us 'Tenemos esperanza' (We Have Hope).

Santiago Benavides: The following song is one of the most famous hymns written in Latin America. There are many hymns in the Wesleyan tradition, most of them from Europe. The one we are going to sing now was written by the Methodist Bishop Federico Pagura in the city of Buenos Aires. We invite you to stand up and sing it together.

> *Because he came, to enter our human history,*
> *Because he broke the bonds of silent anguish,*
> *Because he filled our world with radiant mystery,*
> *And brings his warmth and light to where we languish.*
>
> *Because his birth made rich a humble manger,*
> *Because he sowed the seeds of life and pardon,*
> *Because he shattered hatred of the stranger,*
> *And lifted up the weary and disheartened.*
>
> *(Refrain)*

Because of this, we wait with eager patience,
Persistent in our struggles toward the morning.
Because of this, our hope and expectations
Look toward the dawn when earth will know his coming.
Because of this, we wait with eager patience,
Persistent in our struggles toward the morning.
Because of this, our hope and expectations look toward the dawn.

Because he launched attacks on blind ambition,
And he denounced hypocrisy and evil;
He honoured women and he blessed the children,
But left the proud to rage at their own peril.

Because he bore the cross for our transgression,
And drank the bitter cup of sin and sorrow,
He bowed beneath the yoke of sin's oppression
And he suffered death that we might face tomorrow.

(Refrain)

Because he vanquished fear, deceit, and lying,
Because the cross could not complete his story,
He rose victorious, trampling death by dying:
And he will reign in power and in glory!

(Refrain)

Text: Frederico Pagura, trans. Mary Louise Bringle

Welcome to Colombia

Introduction by *Larry Miller*

Stations on the way to the unity of all people, including all Christians, are always 'somewhere'. We are grateful that our 'somewhere' this week is Colombia.

As we began to foresee the Third Global Gathering, the only certainty was that we knew we wanted to gather in Latin America. But the country and the city were initially a mystery. Little by little the plan, which we trust is the plan of God, unfolded. And so here we are today in Colombia.

We are honoured that His Excellency Deputy Minister Olimpo Espinosa Oliver has come to greet us this morning.

Your Excellency, these global, continental and national leaders of Christian churches from around the world have great interest in your country. Wherever we are at home in the world, we are aware of Colombia and Colombians—and not only when your football team humiliates its international opponents, as it did recently in France, the country where I live.

We follow closely the unfolding peace process. We give attention to the developments in favour of religious liberty. So today, we are grateful that you have come to spend a few moments with us.

Your Excellency, welcome!

Deputy Héctor Olimpo Espinosa Oliver

First, I thank God for allowing us to be here this morning and for allowing me to share these minutes with you. Second, I would like to thank the Revd Larry Miller for his words, for his welcome, for his heartfelt words, I felt in a very special way the comments he made. I also liked very much the song that I heard before I came up to speak, referring to hope. And I appreciate the theme, the logo and the slogan of this Global Christian Forum, referring to letting mutual love continue. It seems to me a supremely powerful message when we speak of the permanence of mutual love combined with hope.

I want to greet in a very special way all the members of this Global Christian Forum, which includes a broad representation of the Christian churches in the world. In this Christian ecumenical space, we have leaders at the highest level in world Christianity, and it's a forum whose purpose is not only the exchange of experiences but making a joint response to the challenges faced by the churches worldwide. I also wish to greet, in a very special way, the leaders gathered here from the Catholic Church, the World Council of Churches, the World Evangelical Alliance and the Pentecostal World Fellowship. To your holinesses, beatitudes, eminences and excellencies, thank you for being in Colombia, thank you for having chosen Colombia as the place of this meeting. This is the most important meeting of Christian churches in the world that has taken place in our country, the most broadly representative. We are aware of the importance and level of this meeting, so I heeded the call made by Lorena Rios, our Director of Religious Affairs in the Ministry of Interior.

First, I want to tell you that something very positive is happening in Colombia when so many world leaders come together here, attracted by a country that wants peace, reconciliation and change, and that has a desire to excel. That translates not only into a desire but also into real actions of transformation—actions towards which all the churches and religious organizations have contributed considerably through their sacrifice, as well as in building this process of peace and reconciliation. The religious institutions in Colombia were transformed into peacemakers, by means of their participation in the government's decisions and in the steps that led to the peace agreements. And they were not only peacemakers, but also harmony makers in that fundamental work of the churches to enable harmonious relationships between human beings and God, and also with our brothers and sisters and with the environment.

Here we see the three relational dimensions in which the churches contribute greatly to our community, our coexistence and our vision of society: strengthening our relationship first with God, second with our brothers and sisters, and third with our environment, our natural resources, the conservation of that great house that God has given us called nature. In those three dimensions, the participation of religious institutions and organizations is supremely important. The work of our churches is fundamental in our society in including all human beings, not only from an economic perspective but also with regard to inclusion in the possibilities of deliberation, orientation, listening, mutual support, training, dialogue and prevention, so that our brothers and sisters will walk the right path, the path of peace, the good path. In this regard, you are supremely important for us, for our society and for our government.

That is why, inspired by this example, we have wanted churches and religious institutions to have a place in government deliberations. We have created the first public policy on religious freedom, which seeks to guarantee that churches in Colombia will have a space to be able to exert influence and fulfil their calling. This is a legal and political guarantee by the state and society that churches will have space to facilitate their impact on the course of our society. We included this in the national development plan for 2014-2018, presented by the current government of President Juan Manuel Santos. The Ministry of the Interior, which I represent, created the Religious Affairs Office, consulted all religious organizations in the country over a period of almost three years. This collective work has led us to construct a public policy with three axes, one of which is cooperation and interaction with international religious organizations so that this vision that we have as a state, conceived in our constitution, is not just rhetoric but reality—that there are real spaces of participation. We have worked deeply on this.

In this environment of peace, guaranteed inclusion, and a vision of determining what should be the role of religious institutions and Christian churches in our society, you have come to Colombia, a country that welcomes you with open arms and is very grateful for your presence. Welcome!

Larry Miller

Your Excellency, thank you for your words of welcome. We pledge our support for everything and everyone who labours for justice and peace in Colombia.

Your Excellency, for you and your country, our prayer is that God will bless you and keep you. Our prayer is that God's face will shine upon you and be gracious to you, that God will give peace to you, to your country and to everyone in it.

Our Unfolding Journey with Jesus Christ: The Story of the Global Christian Forum

Elizabeth Matear

Our physical journey, for each of us, has brought us from different locations, near and far. Our journey spiritually, theologically and culturally, brings us with different perspectives, opinions and diverse gifts. As we journey together in these next days, we will strengthen our friendships and enrich our fellowship. We will embrace our family connection, as a people belonging to Christ! We will focus on what unites, rather than on what separates. I believe God will hold us accountable in this.

We will be blessed. We are better together, as a witness to the world. We are better together because we need each other. We are better together because that is how we love God.

None of us has arrived; we are part of an unfolding journey. Be ready to be surprised, inspired, challenged and involved.

We journey together. Please join the journey as we watch together the story so far and listen to testimonies of others from different places.

Film: 20 Years of the GCF

Following is the script of a video presented during the opening plenary session to summarize the history and purpose of the GCF.

Narrator: The Global Christian Forum arose within a context of major transformation affecting the contemporary religious landscape. The centre of numerical gravity in the Christian world was clearly shifting southwards and the younger churches—Evangelical, Pentecostal, charismatic, independent—were experiencing rapid growth.

Moreover, there was a desire to overcome the distance in world Christianity separating churches engaged in the ecumenical movement and those opposed to it. In 1998, at its General Assembly in Harare, Zimbabwe, the World Council of Churches, under the leadership of its general secretary, Konrad Raiser, called for a new 'space' where leaders from every tradition and stream of world Christianity could meet and talk with one another. This ultimately became the Global Christian Forum.

The beginning and development of the Global Christian Forum

Narrator: In the years that followed the WCC Assembly in Harare, many conversations in many places led to the creation of the Global Christian Forum. The one that took place in June 2002, at the famous Fuller Evangelical Faculty of Theology in Pasadena, California, with 60 leaders from many church traditions and geographical regions, proved to be foundational.

Larry Miller: The people who were there speak of a kind of revelation where they came to one mind to say 'Yes, the time has come for us to enter into a continuing conversation with one another,' and they were able to craft a three-sentence purpose statement which affirms the full humanity and full divinity of Jesus Christ and the Trinitarian nature of God, and on that basis then we were able to move forward through a series of other meetings in the following years.

Narrator: It was at this meeting that the 'Guiding Purpose Statement' was first crafted; it remains to the present the basic statement of GCF self-understanding. From that moment, regional meetings began in Asia, Africa, Europe, Latin America and the Caribbean—each a building block for the new global Christian platform.

The first truly global gathering took place in 2007 in Limuru, Kenya, with the participation of leaders from an unprecedented diversity of Christian families worldwide. This gathering 'launched' the GCF and endorsed continuing pursuit of the vision. It was to be followed by another series of regional and sub-regional meetings—in the Middle East, Africa, Europe, Asia and Latin America—which led finally to a second global gathering, in Manado, Indonesia in 2011.

In the period following the Second Global Gathering, the Forum continued to convene regional consultations, notably in the Middle East and Latin America. Also during this period, a number of local, national, and regional forums emerged. The phenomenon was not new. Already before the Second Global Gathering, national forum-like initiatives had arisen in several places. In each case, the development took place spontaneously and independently of the GCF, though usually at the initiative of church leaders who had participated in a GCF continental or global event.

The Global Christian Forum: a new space for new challenges

Narrator: The Global Christian Forum's objective is to bring to the same table, and into the same conversation, the whole spectrum of contemporary Christianity. From the start it was envisioned that the new 'forum' would be based on participation, not membership, and would be more like a continuing conversation than a permanent institution.

A 50-50 principle has been established, always trying to have about 50 percent of the participants in a Global Christian Forum event from the older churches (Orthodox, Catholic, Protestant, Anglican) and 50 percent from the younger churches and movements (Evangelical, Pentecostal, Charismatic, Independent, migrant churches, mega churches).

An international committee composed of representatives appointed by Christian world communions and related global Christian organizations guides the work of the Forum. The Catholic Church, the Pentecostal World Fellowship, the World Council of Churches, and the World Evangelical Alliance each have two permanent seats in the committee.

Sharing one's faith story

Narrator: One of the characteristics of the Global Christian Forum as a movement of unity is the emphasis upon relationship: relationship with Jesus Christ and through that relationship, and because of it, relationship with one another. The Forum's vocation is not first of all to be an instrument of doctrinal unity. It is primarily an instrument for greater relational unity—relationships between churches through relationships between leaders of churches, each of whom is already on a journey with Jesus Christ and discover that they can journey together.

Anne-Cathy Graber: At Manado, I witnessed a meeting between two church leaders of the Middle East and the effect that the methods employed by the Global Christian Forum, i.e. the sharing of the faith testimony, could have on them. The charismatic pastor asked the Orthodox priest, 'How long have you been Christian?' to which the other replied, 'For two thousand years.' Naturally, for the charismatic pastor, it was not easy to hear this, and naturally, it was not easy for the Orthodox priest to hear the language used by the Pentecostals, who refer to a language of conversion or breaking with the past: when we encounter Christ, there is a before and an after. Ultimately, both sides reached the point of accepting and understanding the other's way of speaking and its legitimacy.

Facing common challenges

Narrator: The Guiding Purpose Statement of the Global Christian Forum names two main objectives: to foster mutual respect between churches and leaders of churches, and to explore and address together common challenges.

The participants in the Second Global Gathering said that it is time to begin work on the second objective. 'The Spirit (is) calling us,' they said in their message from Manado, 'not only to foster respect for one another, but now also to move forward together in addressing common challenges.'

After wide consultation and careful discernment, it was decided to focus first on two painful topics affecting Christian churches globally: the discrimination and persecution of Christians, and problems related to perceptions of proselytism between churches. The first initiative concluded with a global consultation on the theme of 'Discrimination, Persecution, Martyrdom: Following Christ Together'. This historic meeting—the first of its kind to embrace nearly all streams and traditions of world Christianity—took place in Tirana, Albania, from 1 to 5 November 2015.

The second initiative, 'Call to Mission, Perceptions of Proselytism: A Global Conversation', is drawing to a conclusion. It has included a global consultation in Accra, Ghana, hosted by the Church of Pentecost, and is leading to a common statement on this important and sometimes church-dividing issue.

And now, coinciding with its 20th anniversary, the Global Christian Forum convenes the Third Global Gathering. After Africa and Asia, it's the first Global Gathering in the Americas, the first in a Spanish-speaking nation, and a place for fostering deeper mutual respect while exploring together the common challenges that lie ahead.

Words on screen:

> ***Let Mutual Love Continue***
> **Relationships Old and New**
> **Envisioning the Journey Ahead**
> **Forward Together in Faith and Hope**

'I Was in Limuru': The First Global Gathering

Daniel Okoh

All my life I have been a member of an African Independent Church—a church tradition that is largely misunderstood and one that has suffered various levels of persecution and stigmatization by Christians of other church traditions. Much of the persecution and stigmatization came as a result of misinformation about the activities of these churches. Though there have been attempts by the AICs to get involved in ecumenical meetings in their local settings for mainly political reasons, there was a need for a platform that would enable more and deeper interaction among members of all church traditions, at a global level, for a better understanding of who we are, what we are called to be in Christ and how to respond to issues that confront the body of Christ.

This platform was provided by the GCF Global Gathering at Limuru in Kenya, East Africa in 2007. For the first time, the AICs were actively involved in the preparation for a large global Christian gathering and a large section of AIC leaders attended on invitation. As a matter of fact, leaders of AICs identified with the practice of telling stories of our faith journeys, because in Africa storytelling is a major means of communication in all spheres of life. It gave members of all the Christian traditions the opportunity to interact with one another in an atmosphere of fraternal love. The Bible study groups and the discussion groups gave church leaders opportunities to listen to each other telling their stories of our journey with Jesus Christ, our reconciler. During the conversations that took place over meals and during coffee and tea breaks, I observed that participants were happy to share experiences and opinions on matters of common concern. Mutual suspicion was beginning to give way to mutual understanding, mutual trust and mutual love among leaders.

One of the high points at the Limuru gathering was the day that the AICs were asked to lead the morning worship. On that day, hearing the sound of African drums and standing at the pulpit in the midst of leaders of a cross-section of Christian traditions to share the word of God, I came to a conclusion that things have changed—for good and forever. A miracle had just happened! As we all happily celebrated our Lord Jesus Christ together, all our differences seemed to have disappeared. I prayed that this type of fellowship should continue for the disappearance of our differences to become a reality.

My discussion with some leaders in that gathering that brought together more than 240 church leaders revealed that all Christian traditions have a lot to contribute to the expansion of the kingdom of God. We only needed to sustain what happened in Limuru and even improve on it. The experience of Limuru raised the hope of a deeper fraternal engagement and support on issues of common concern in this broken world.

On a general note, the Global Christian Forum is the widening of the space that we all hoped for. I see it as a genuine and concerted effort to bring about healing, reconciliation and mutual love in the body of

Christ. It is a move that broke away from the period of exclusion, superiority/inferiority complexes and name-calling. May I, at this time, salute the deep insight, the wisdom and the courage of people like Hubert van Beek, the Founding Secretary of the Global Christian Forum, and many others who worked very hard to organize the first Global Gathering in Limuru.

Finally, the Limuru gathering was a wakeup call for all of us to see what is left for us to do. There, I saw the willingness of leaders to work together with mutual respect and a great sense of inclusiveness. I therefore left Limuru with the resolve to get ready for a more engaging relationship with our brethren in other church traditions.

'I Was in Manado': Reflections from the Second Global Christian Forum in Indonesia

Victoria Matthews

It has been my great privilege to attend both the Kenyan and Indonesian meetings of the Global Christian Forum. They stand out in my memory as the best Christian gatherings I have attended over my lifetime, and like many of you, I have had my share of Christian gatherings and meetings.

What made the second Global Christian Forum stand out for me? It was the generosity of spirit that prevailed throughout. We talk about open space, but at the Indonesian meeting we also had open hearts and open minds. The presence of Christ was very much in evidence as was the guidance of the Holy Spirit.

The theme was 'Life Together in Jesus Christ, Empowered by the Holy Spirit.' Churches that rarely communicate, often because of a history of mistrust, were together and as the individual journeys in Christ were shared, conversations began to flow and trust deepened. A number of papers were delivered or shared.

Dr Dana Robert of the theological school of Boston University called on churches to reflect across ecclesiastical boundaries and to not only recall but actually live our identity as the 'one holy catholic and apostolic church'.

Fr Dr K. M. George of the Malanakara Orthodox Syrian Church brought his learning in patristics to the topic of the unifying power of the Holy Spirit and how ecclesiological roadblocks have been smoothed by the leading of the Holy Spirit.

The emerging questions were: where does unity and mission meet and foster each other, and what is the Spirit saying to the Church, locally and globally? In prayer, Bible study and worship we experienced a growing hunger for unity across the whole body of those in attendance.

At the end of the meeting we gave profound thanks for the leadership of Hubert van Beek as the GCF Secretary from its inception and welcomed the Rev Dr Larry Miller to lead us forward as the Global Christian Forum, which brings us to today.

'I am in Bogotá': The Third Global Gathering

Marie Eugenia Figueroa de Gongora

Now we are in Bogotá with great expectations, after all the journey that our history has entailed, and which has been recounted to us with great hope. I will share three specific expectations with you.

First, a mutilated body is not so beautiful. I would ask you to think of us as a mosaic. If the pieces are not in their proper place, the mosaic is not complete, clear or beautiful. Here we come from many places, but the great thing about that is not that there are 100, 200 or more of us, but that in Christ we are one, as Ephesians 4:4 says.

The second expectation that I would propose to you is as follows. May each one of us prepare to receive our brother or sister in our heart, as if our heart is an empty chalice, ready to contain the brother with his own history, with his experience. Let us receive him with admiration, respect and tenderness and learn from him. In other words, let Jesus

Christ come to speak to us and enrich us through him, putting aside any suspicion or preconceptions.

Third, may we come out of this third Global Gathering like a new Pentecost. May we ask here that the Holy Spirit of our risen Lord Jesus Christ, which is the Spirit that is love, will invade and fill us, because only with that Spirit can we recognize the other person as my brother or sister and love him or her reciprocally. And this is ultimately the sign by which the world will recognize that we are his disciples, if we love one another.

To conclude I would like to request that you stand up for a moment, and asking the Lord that our face might be like the face of Jesus, may we embrace those to our left and right, those in front of and behind us. Let us only look to him, so that our gaze may be the look of Jesus immersing and embracing those around us, and so that when we leave this third Forum we may be more connected in brotherly love and loving him more.

Roll Call of Participants

Elijah Brown and *Georgine Kengne Djeutane*

We thank you for your presence today. We are now going to acknowledge the continents, countries, and churches represented in this global gathering.

Gathered from 64 different countries, we welcome one another.

We welcome one another from Africa, including from the countries of Cameroon, Gabon, Ghana, Kenya, Liberia, Nigeria, Rwanda, Senegal, Sierra Leone, South Africa, Swaziland, Togo, Uganda, and Zambia.

We welcome one another from Asia and the Pacific, from Australia, China, India, Indonesia, New Zealand, South Korea, and Taiwan.

We welcome one another from Europe, including the countries of Albania, Austria, Belgium, Denmark, Finland, France, Germany, Greece, Ireland, Italy, Latvia, The Netherlands, Norway, Poland, Russia, Sweden, Switzerland, United Kingdom, and Vatican City.

We welcome one another from Latin America and the Caribbean, from Argentina, Bolivia, Brazil, Chile, Colombia, Costa Rica, Cuba, Ecuador, Guatemala, Jamaica, Mexico, Paraguay, Peru, Puerto Rico, Uruguay, and Venezuela.

We welcome one another from the Middle East, from Cyprus, Israel, Jordan, Lebanon, Oman, and Syria.

We welcome one another from North America, from Canada and the United States.

Gathered from 24 different church families, we welcome one another. Please stand as we acknowledge your church family: African Initiated; Anglican; Baptist; Catholic; Church of Christ; Disciples of Christ; Evangelical; Holiness; Independent; Lutheran; Mennonite; Messianic Jew; Non-denominational; Old Catholic; Orthodox; Oriental Orthodox; Pentecostal; Quakers; Reformed and Presbyterian; Salvation Army; Seventh-day Adventists; United and Uniting; Waldensian.

In the name of the Father, the Son, and the Holy Spirit, we greet one another with the peace of Jesus Christ.

Prof. Dr Dimitra Koukoura

DAY ONE: TUESDAY 24 APRIL
LET MUTUAL LOVE CONTINUE!

11.30 PLENARY SESSION

Introduction

Dimitra Koukoura (Greece), Session Moderator, Professor of Homiletics, Aristotle University of Thessaloniki; GCF Committee Member for the World Council of Churches and the Ecumenical Patriarchate

Let Mutual Love Continue: Biblical Perspective

Olav Fykse Tveit (Norway/Switzerland), General Secretary, World Council of Churches;

Text read by ***Odair Pedroso Mateus*** (Brazil/Switzerland), Director, Faith and Order Commission, WCC)

Recognising One Another in Christ and Christ in One Another: Telling Our Faith Stories

Why Do We Tell Each Other Our Faith Stories? —
Kathryn L. Johnson (USA), Director, Ecumenical and Interreligious Relations, Evangelical Lutheran Church in America; GCF Committee Member for the Lutheran World Federation

Glimpses of Four Faith Stories
- ***David Sang-Ehil Han*** (Republic of Korea/USA), Professor of Theology and Pentecostal Spirituality, Pentecostal Theological Seminary; GCF Committee Member for the Church of God (Cleveland)
- ***Rosemarie Wenner*** (Germany), Bishop, Evangelisch-methodistischen Kirche in Deutschland; Geneva Secretary, World Methodist Council; GCF Committee Member for the World Methodist Council
- ***Ioan Sauca*** (Romania/Switzerland), Deputy General Secretary, World Council of Churches
- ***Richard Howell*** (India), General Secretary, Asia Evangelical Alliance; GCF Committee Member for the World Evangelical Alliance

Sharing Faith Stories in Global Interchurch Groups

Pirjo-Liisa Penttinen (Finland), GCF Committee Member for the World Young Women's Christian Association

Andrzej Choromanski (Poland/Vatican City), Ecumenical Officer, Pontifical Council for Promoting Christian Unity, GCF Committee Member for the PCPCU

Introduction

Dimitra Koukoura

As announced by the programme, I represent both the Ecumenical Patriarchate and the World Council of Churches. In my first capacity, I would like to greet you in the 'resurrectional' way because in the Orthodox calendar we are still celebrating the Resurrection. So I will say to you:

> *Christ is risen!*
> > *He is risen, indeed!*
>
> *Christ is risen!*
> > *He is risen, indeed!*
>
> *Christ is risen!*
> > *He is risen, indeed!*

as a member of the Central Committee of the World Council of Churches and as a member of the Global Christian Forum Committee. The World Council of Churches is strongly and highly represented here. Unfortunately our General Secretary, Revd Dr Olav Fykse Tveit, was not able to come due to health issues with a family member. Therefore, he sent a high-level delegation composed of the Director of the Faith and Order Commission, Revd Dr Professor Odair Pedroso; Prof Dr Angela Berlis, who is a member of the Faith and Order Commission; and Revd Dr Katalina Tahaafe-Williams, Programme Executive for the Commission on World Mission and Evangelism, as well as me and three members of the World Council of Churches media team, who are here to take the best possible photos and write the best reports about the meetings.

Father Ioan Sauca is the leader of the delegation. He is 'the one after the one', which means he is the Deputy Secretary of the World Council of Churches. Revd Professor Dr Father Ioan Sauca is one of the pillars of the World Council of Churches, of whom as Orthodox we are very proud. So, Father, you have a lot of tasks on behalf of the World Council of Churches to do here. Remember that!

Now, since we lack the presence of Olav, our friend Odair Pedroso will read his speech. But before that, as a good traditional and modern lady, I would like to invite you, from your heart and from your mind, to give thanks and express our gratitude to two persons.

The first person is Emeritus Professor Dr Konrad Reiser, who was the General Secretary of the World Council of Churches at the time when the Global Christian Forum was conceived. He was a visionary and we would like to give thanks to him. I would like to invite you to also give thanks to Huibert van Beek, who was the coordinator of this vision and has worked very hard up until the last years when our friend and beloved brother, Revd Larry Miller—or, in the French way, 'Laurent Muller'—took his place.

'Let Mutual Love Continue': Biblical Perspective

Olav Fykse Tveit (read by **Odair Pedroso Mateus**)

Mutual love

'Let mutual love continue.' The theme of our gathering points to the spiritual heart of the Global Christian Forum. Mutual love has been the motivation, shared attitude and practice of those participating in the GCF. Respecting and recognizing each other as sisters and brothers in Christ has been the basis of our togetherness and has sustained us on our way that has both its origin and goal in the love of the Triune God. Mutual love flows from the fact that we are all created in the image of God; we are called and sent by Jesus Christ; and we are empowered by the Holy Spirit to participate in God's mission.

'Let mutual love continue.' The theme shall accompany us when we go home to our communities and workplaces as disciples of Christ. Mutual love must affect our behaviour and attitudes as we continue our journey together in different directions.

Hebrews 13 combines mutual brotherly and sisterly love (in Greek, *philadelphia*) immediately with love of the stranger and hospitality (in

Greek, *philoxenia*): 'Do not neglect to show hospitality to strangers, for by doing that some have entertained angels without knowing it' (Heb. 13:2). Mutual love cannot be reserved to my community, to my faith tradition or nation. It flows out of God's love for this world like the rivers of life in the beautiful image of the new creation in the book of the Revelation to John. The bond of love that unites us as disciples of Christ in one body has its horizon in the unity of one human family and of God's creation.

Jesus says in chapter 17 of the Gospel of John, 'As you, Father, are in me and I am in you, may they also be in us so that the world may believe that you have sent me' and 'that the world may know that you have sent me and have loved them even as you have loved me.' We betray the love of God and the gift of unity in Christ if we continue to witness and act separately instead of walking, praying and working as pilgrims together. We betray the love of God and the gift of unity in Christ if our witness and mission remain untouched by the suffering of marginalized and poor people around us and deaf to the silent cries of creation.

I will unfold now this praise of mutual love in three dimensions:

- let us remember the first steps to create the Global Christian Forum and the vision that brought it to life;
- let us recall that oneness in Christ means participating in God's mission to reconcile and heal the world;
- let us look around and remind ourselves of the relevance of a common witness of Christians for reconciliation and peace here in Colombia.

The 20th anniversary of the first steps to create the Global Christian Forum

2018 is a year of anniversaries for the World Council of Churches. We are celebrating the 70th anniversary of the founding of the WCC in Amsterdam. We are remembering the 50th anniversary of the 1968 Uppsala assembly. This assembly responded to the calls especially of WCC member churches from the Global South to address more actively poverty, marginalization, racism and other forms of violence. Taking a stance in the divisions and conflicts of this world was costly for the fellowship of churches in the WCC. The WCC was heavily criticized. But at the same time, the fellowship grew together in a more truthful engagement for justice, reconciliation and peace. We are remembering also the Decade of the Churches in Solidarity with Women, which was initiated 35 years ago at the 1983 Vancouver assembly and culminated 20 years ago at the 1998 Harare assembly. Churches were challenged to show what it means to be just and inclusive communities of women and men.

It was also in August 1998 before the Harare assembly that a group of 28 visionary and committed people met at the Ecumenical Institute at Château de Bossey, near Geneva, to develop a proposal for a 'forum of Christian churches and ecumenical organizations'. They represented the WCC, Christian world communions, regional ecumenical organizations, national councils of churches, international ecumenical organizations, and churches that were not associated with ecumenical structures, from Evangelical, Pentecostal and Charismatic traditions. They recognized that fellowship in Christ transcends membership in a fellowship of churches such as the WCC.

They took steps to create a new space of encounter and dialogue. The intention was to broaden the circle beyond existing structures, but not to create a new movement. The constitutional basis of the WCC was to become the common ground for participation in the forum they envisaged. They declared: 'Participation will be based on confessing the Lord Jesus Christ as God and Saviour according to the Scriptures and seeking to fulfil together the common calling to the glory of the one God, Father, Son and Holy Spirit.'

They presented their vision in the form of goals and objectives. They said:

> *The proposed forum is* **possible** *because of the unity which is already given in Christ. It is* **called** *for because of our common faith in a reconciling God whose church knows itself summoned to become God's reconciled and reconciling people. …*

The forum will not speak for the participating bodies, but will provide a way for them, transcending the limitations of existing frameworks, to think new thoughts, dream new dreams, and glimpse new visions.

Seeking to be open to the charisma the Spirit gives to Christ's people, the forum's style will be open, expectant and relying on a minimum of rules and structures. One condition for participation (not membership), therefore, is a willingness to accept other participants as bona fide partners in dialogue, the aim of which is to strengthen the obedience of all to Christ.

The occasional gatherings of the forum will provide opportunities for worship, exploration of matters of common Christian concern and development of enhanced mutual understanding. They are not conceived as decision-making, programme-initiating or document-producing events. However, they might lead to new forms of cooperation.

I am quoting this proposal because it already contains all the elements that were later spelled out with a stronger emphasis on mission in the purpose statement of the GCF that was shared tentatively with the 2006 WCC assembly in Porto Alegre and endorsed by the first GCF global gathering held in Limuru, Kenya in 2007.

The story of the GCF is a remarkable success story of building trust among participants and opening ways for new forms of cooperation. This was visible for a worldwide audience in the greetings shared with the delegates at the 2013 WCC assembly in Busan. Never before was such a wide range of Christian leaders present at such an event. The effect of the GCF has been seen in notably improved and more extensive relations and cooperation between partners that had few or difficult relations before. The need to address our common challenges and our common call to witness and service has been strongly affirmed. One of the most exciting results of broadened participation encouraged by the GCF was the document on 'Christian Witness in a Multi-religious World' that was jointly presented to the public by the leadership of the

Roman Catholic Church, the WCC and the World Evangelical Alliance.

Together on the way, we encountered also certain challenges, particularly in the understanding of the tasks of this Forum, and the limits of those tasks. Representatives of the Pontifical Council for Promoting Christian Unity (PCPCU), the World Evangelical Alliance (WEA), the World Pentecostal Fellowship (WPF) and the WCC met last year in Bossey to take stock of our journey together in the past two decades. They affirmed the character of the GCF as a shared space, a forum, gathering people to build relations, to address issues of common concern and interest and to stimulate better relations between partners involved. It would be utterly misleading to look at it as an organization or a group with the mandate to pursue alternative ecumenism or make statements on behalf of the partners.

I am confident that we will experience again here in Bogotá the great gift of the GCF for building trust, renewing the commitment to cooperation and experiencing the bond of mutual love in Christ through the presence of the Holy Spirit.

Being one in Christ, called to common witness and service

Being one in Christ, we are called to common witness and service. I would like to recall the experience of the pioneers of the ecumenical movement.

'Let mutual love continue' (Heb. 13:1) corresponds to Romans 15:7, 'Receive one another as Christ received you, for the glory of God.' Those Christians who began more than a century ago to call the churches to unity in the faith once delivered to the apostles and saints (Jude 3) made a precious spiritual experience as they gathered together. They realized that in spite of their past church divisions, they found each other in a real though imperfect communion in and through the Spirit of God who is the giver of life and communion (*koinonia*). They rediscovered in a new way that Christ is not divided (1 Cor. 1:13); and because Christ is not divided there can be but one body of Christ, one holy, catholic, and apostolic Church. Not two. Not many.

They started moving together, ready to share their own experience of communion in the love of Christ amidst division. They followed their vision, making the gift they experienced visible by crossing denominational borders and calling Christians and their communities to repentance from persistent divisions among them. This was the beginning of the ecumenical movement.

They could have been satisfied with the experience of mutual love among themselves at the personal and individual level, but they went beyond that. The love of Christ compelled them (2 Cor. 5:14) to call the churches to overcome isolation and to begin encountering each other in dialogue, mutual intercession, mutual support and mutual accountability as expressions of mutual love.

In this spirit, they began to move forward and realized their common calling. They became pilgrims of justice and peace in the world. Christ prayed for the unity of his disciples not only for their own sake but for the sake of the world (John 17:21). According to the Scriptures, Christ in his reign will bring a broken and fragmented world into a just peace. If the head of the one body is also the firstborn of all creation (Col. 1:15), and if he is the one who will lead creation to its fulness (Eph. 1:10), it follows that the search for church unity is inseparable from the struggle against the systemic forces that cause poverty, racism, sexism and marginalization.

These have been some of the basic theological convictions that led 70 years ago to the fellowship of churches which is the WCC. In parallel, however, world Christianity was changing and growing especially in the Global South. New expressions of Christian faith emerged; new churches and communions developed that did not share the same experience and convictions. In the process that led to the GCF, we were reminded that the fellowship in Christ exists beyond those who were committed to the fellowship of churches in the WCC.

Keeping all this in mind, we realize that the calling of the GCF is to celebrate the blessing of being gathered in Christ by the Spirit in such a way that we can embrace each other and the communities and churches we belong to, regardless of our views on each other's churches and on visible church unity. We cherish the gift of mutual love; we reject proselytism; we refrain from condemning each other; we welcome mutual support and admonition, because we are not our own. We belong to Christ, and by belonging to Christ we belong to each other. The calling of the GCF is to help Christians from very different cultural and confessional traditions to discern the urgency of manifesting the unity in Christ and the fundamental unity of humanity in a world increasingly separated by walls.

Praying and working for reconciliation and peace in Colombia

If mutual love is the spiritual heart of the GCF, being one in Christ and being called to common witness and service to the world are our shared convictions. Since we are gathering in Bogotá, I would like to explore what this practically means in the context of Colombia.

We hope and pray that the peace process in Colombia will continue and will lead to just peace for the people of this country who have suffered from violence and war for more than 60 years. Colombia is a priority country for the WCC in Latin America. We are working closely together with our member church, the Presbyterian Church of Colombia (PCC), and our local partners Justapaz of the Mennonite Church and the ecumenical platform DiPaz, the Interchurch Dialogue for Peace.

We recently organized together with them four pilgrim team visits to different regions of the country to learn from community and church leaders, government officials and other people how they experience the present situation. The visits have shown that this is a very critical moment in the Colombian peace process. We also organized meetings of our Pilgrimage of Justice and Peace Reference Group in Bogotá and of the WCC Commission on International Affairs in Cartagena with the presence of Colombian President Juan Manuel Santos.

Although the peace accord has been signed by the FARC (Revolutionary Armed Forces of Colombia) after six years of negotiations in Cuba, the negotiations with the National Liberation Army (ELN) are still in process, and other smaller guerrilla groups have not been directly addressed. Additionally, responsibilities for paramilitary groups have not been adequately upheld. Various reports have demonstrated that violence is still prevalent in many areas with the killing of community leaders. Displaced people who want to return to their land are being threatened and attacked. The current post–peace accord context in Colombia sees a unique 'Truth Commission' (TC) that seeks to examine the root causes of complex situations of violence. But other points of the peace accord are only partially implemented, and the government does not deliver on all of its promises.

Solidarity has to be demonstrated along with the need to give hope to those who are struggling. The Presbyterian Church and the Mennonite Church support the peace process because many of their members and congregations have suffered, especially those in the countryside and within entire communities that were victims of war. In these communities, people were displaced and persecuted. Families and pastors were overwhelmed by the conflict at the hands of different actors. The war went on without discriminating between the civilian population and armed actors. These communities are longing for peace and the fulfilment of the prophecy of Micah: God 'shall judge between many peoples and shall arbitrate between strong nations far away; they shall beat their swords into ploughshares and their spears into pruning hooks; nation shall not lift up sword against nation, neither shall they learn war anymore; but they shall sit under their own vines and under their own fig trees, and no one shall make them afraid, for the mouth of the Lord of hosts has spoken' (Micah 4:3–4). This is the Micah-challenge today in Colombia.

We are extremely grateful that DiPaz includes many different churches and church-based organizations in Colombia, among them the ecumenical officer of the Roman Catholic Conference of Bishops of Colombia and the Pastoral Service of the Assemblies of God. DiPaz has also international members such as the WCC, ACT Alliance and other member churches and partners of the WCC. This broad ecumenical cooperation is very encouraging. But we also have to acknowledge that among the churches are many voices which rejected the peace accord.

Despite the efforts of DiPaz, part of the population looks with suspicion at churches that are not reconciled among themselves and sometimes argue against each other. We cannot be content with polite ecumenism or nice individual relationships at the expense of the difficult issues that prevent our witness from being relevant. Ours is the ministry of reconciliation. Let mutual love continue also when we address the issues that are still separating us so that we come closer and closer to each other because we come closer and closer to Christ among us.

The apostle Paul reminds us in 2 Corinthians 5:17–21:

> *So if anyone is in Christ, there is a new creation; everything old has passed away; see, everything has become new! All this is from God who reconciled us to himself through Christ and has given us the ministry of reconciliation; that is, in Christ God was reconciling the world to himself, not counting their trespasses against them, and entrusting the message of reconciliation to us. So we are ambassadors of Christ, since God is making his appeal through us; we entreat you on behalf of Christ, be reconciled to God. For our sake he made him to be sin who knew no sin, so that in him we might become the righteousness of God.*

Thanks be to God! Amen.

Recognising One Another in Christ and Christ in One Another: Telling Our Faith Stories

Why Do We Tell Each Other Our Faith Stories?

Kathryn Johnson

It is fitting that we will spend a good portion of this first day of the Third Global Gathering telling and listening to the stories of our journeys with Jesus Christ.

This practice is one of the distinctive marks of a Global Christian Forum event; some call it a 'charism' of the Forum. It has such a prominent and memorable place because it invites each of us to make part of our own experience here a central goal of the Forum: 'to recognize one another in Christ and Christ in one another.'

As we saw earlier this morning in the video, the aim and the hope of the Forum are not only to bring to the same table but also to bring into the same conversation people from the widest possible range of Christian families and Christian formations. But how do these conversations begin in ways that make a place for every voice? What could we talk about together?

Clearly, we don't begin by jumping directly into our differences in doctrine. Some of us—like me—participate in focused theological dialogues and hold them in high esteem. I thank God for the steps they have taken toward re-examining divisions in our teaching and allowing us to take important steps forward. But theological dialogue is not for every person, and not for every problem. And it is not the most reliable way to build relationships with those whose traditions are in important ways unknown to us, or even puzzling.

It is part of the lore of the GCF, part of its family narrative, that giving a central place to faith stories was not simply 'the way we have always done things.' The value of the practice emerged as a gift from the experience of trying it out. The first reason why the narratives are so valuable is simple; it is true in this hall today as it has been at every Forum gathering. Every Christian has his or her relationship with Jesus Christ; every Christian life is a journey with Jesus. Telling that story is a way of introducing ourselves to each other, Christian to Christian.

But if the storytelling began, at least in part, as a response to the concrete challenge of welcoming every participant, it soon became clear that the practice offers more substantive gifts. It opens our eyes anew to the presence of Christ, and it invites us to listen for the breath of the Spirit—in the lives of those around the circle with us and then in the communities from which they come.

Let us focus first on *telling* our stories. For some of us in this room, giving a testimony, telling our story, is a familiar practice in our communities. For others—and I am included in this group—it is not our custom, and it is not entirely comfortable. It is one of the little ironies of the Forum experience that I then am the one asked to talk about this practice here. I have learned through obedience to this expectation what treasures it can offer. As I can bear witness, it is a gift to be asked to put our experience into words—even as we struggle to search for the words, the patterns and the images with which to tell it.

For those who do this often, there is a different challenge and invitation: to be open to new words, new selections and perspectives, ones shaped by this distinctive occasion. Our story is always both familiar and new. As we change over our lives in our relation to Jesus, we change also in our relationship to ourselves—including in our perspectives on our pasts, and on the ways that our histories will come with us into our journey's next steps.

Our prayer for each of you today is that you come to deepened understanding of your own relationship with Jesus—precisely in the act of putting it into words for others.

But stories are both told and heard, and the *hearing* part is equally important. To listen to a faith story is an opportunity to hear from the heart of another disciple's life—to have a moment of access to what it feels like, from the inside, to live in Christ, to live with Christ, in ways that are not the ones we know most intimately. We are offered a measure of hospitality in the inner home which Christ has made in another person. We can see the shape of that individual life, and that shows us something of how it has been shaped by relationships with others, particularly by the Christian community from which that person comes.

In groups as diverse as this one, we almost always discover that something we just 'knew' about 'those people' is simply not borne out in the stories we are hearing. We are invited at this Gathering to listen as if we do not already know; to listen generously with open minds, hearts and spirits; to listen with our theological disquiets put for the moment on the side; to listen for the surprising work of the Spirit of God. In the holy moments, as stories are spoken into the space between and among us, the Spirit of God is at work. And that Spirit is the Spirit of unity, the unity Christ desires for those who follow him.

There was a wonderful anecdote in this morning's video which helps us think about what can happen when we listen. Anne-Cathy Graber related a memorable conversation between two Middle Eastern Christians at the Second Global Gathering. One was a charismatic pastor, in whose expectation each person's life with Christ would have a clear 'before' and 'after', as did his own. The other was an Orthodox priest who was asked how long he had been a Christian—and the answer was 'For two thousand years.' As Anne-Cathy said, it was difficult for each person to understand the other's perspective—and yet here at the Forum they were in a position to do exactly that.

But we know, of course, that such mutual understanding does not happen by itself, just from putting two perspectives side by side. These two Christians were indeed in a position with the possibility to understand one another. But their movement towards truly understanding did not occur simply because each heard the other speaking from an unfamiliar perspective. Each had to listen with ears open to the faithfulness which that perspective expressed, listening for Christ's presence where it was not expected to be.

We will close now with another story. This anecdote comes from some conversations which sought to harvest the wisdom from the Forum's experience with faith stories. A testimony was given to the importance of testimonies by someone for whom this was a cherished part of praising God. An Orthodox priest offered a challenge: in his tradition they rather told stories of holy people, in order to provide an example to others and, even more, to bear witness to Christ. The Pentecostal retort was swift: 'What do you think our testimonies are for?' And then there was a remarkable silence of mutual re-assessment. On one side, honouring of the memories of saints could be evaluated anew as a form of testimony to God's transformation of a particular life; on the other, the testimony from a living person could be welcomed with thanksgiving for Christ's work at this very moment. Stories reverently offered and prayerfully heard can provide bridges over which we can move to a new place, where the paths of our journeys with Jesus are not so far apart. We share with each other the companionship of the one Christ.

Now we will hear four short samples of faith stories. They are from old churches and new, from women and men, from those experienced with Forum events and those here for the first time.

Faith Story (#1)

David Sang-Ehil Han

Friends, I have an impossible task that I need to complete in three minutes. The task is to share the story of my journey with Christ. But how does a Pentecostal share his faith journey with Jesus Christ in three minutes? Pentecostals are not exactly known for brevity of words. When Pentecostals pray, we engage in a practice called 'praying through' which can take hours. When we preach, our usual practice is not simply to offer a homily but a narrative sermon that would intertwine biblical stories with personal stories. As I am deeply immersed in this faith culture, sharing the story of my faith journey in three minutes is certainly a challenging thing to do. But I shall try.

I was as a pastor's kid in Korea. Growing up as a Pentecostal in Korea in the 1960s, however, I remember being constantly challenged about my Christian identity. At the time, Pentecostals in Korea were often marked as either heretics or pseudo-Christians because of their spiritual practices such as Spirit baptism, speaking in tongues, and divine healing, all of which are evidenced in the New Testament. So, growing up, I often felt that I wasn't allowed to be a part of the 'inner circle' of the Christian faith community ('mainline' Christianity or Christianity 'properly called'); instead, I felt pushed aside to the periphery.

Yet I also remember attending a Methodist church for about three years during a particular period of my childhood when my family had to move a good distance away from my father's church. Those three years were quite formative in my faith life. Another significant memory of my childhood is being close to a friend whose father was a prominent pastor of a local Baptist church. Naturally, I frequently visited his Baptist church. This also influenced the formation of my Christian faith. If time permitted, I could share several other stories that point to the multifarious ways in which I have experienced the intersection of Christian traditions in my faith journey. My differences marked me as a Pentecostal, but God's hand worked in such a way that my faith journey represented not a single thread but multiple threads intersecting with one another. As staunchly as I am committed to a particular Pentecostal tradition, my journey reflects these multifarious facets and layers of the Christian faith.

During the years of my ministerial preparation, I was naturally immersed in the Pentecostal tradition. I attended two Pentecostal institutions, totaling seven years of theological education firmly rooted in a particular faith tradition. But then, as I went further in education, the journey has also taken me to non-Pentecostal institutions, i.e. Yale University and Emory University, where I spent the next thirteen years. During the combined total of twenty years of my educational journey, I have been exposed to not only a Pentecostal tradition but also the multiplicity of other Christian traditions such as Anglicans, Lutherans, Presbyterians, and Methodists. This circle of formational influence would expand exponentially if I were to include my interactions with fellow students who represented an even greater diversity of Christian traditions. Again, as committed as I was and am to being a Pentecostal, the hand of God led me in such a way that the formation of my theology and spirituality was pushed beyond the boundaries of my own Pentecostal asylum.

All this has now brought me to my journey with the Global Christian Forum for the past sixteen years, as well as my current vocation as the dean of Pentecostal Theological Seminary in Cleveland, Tennessee, USA. I bring to my vocation the incredible gifts of relational knowledge that I accumulated through my participation in the Global Christian Forum gatherings. Our differences mark us as unique and distinct. Precisely for that reason, what marks us as different should encourage us to come together in unity, so that we can learn about and from one another. We can learn of the gifts present in one another. Whenever we come together as a community of God in the name of the Global Christian Forum, we come expecting to see, smell and taste the grace of our Lord Jesus Christ in one another as we listen to each other's faith stories and seek to discern together the whispers of the Holy Spirit.

To God be the glory!

Faith Story (#2)

Rosemarie Wenner

My name is Rosemarie Wenner. I am from Germany and I belong to the United Methodist Church. Currently I am working for the World Methodist Council as a liaison to the World Council of Churches and other ecumenical bodies.

There was probably not one day in my life without prayer. When I was too young to pray by myself, my mother and my grandmother prayed with me. I grew up in a small Methodist congregation. There I learnt to follow Christ and I explored the gifts God has given to me. As a teenager, I was struggling with the question whether I was called to study theology and to serve as a pastor. There were not many female pastors in those days. Although some people warned me, I finally said, 'I can do nothing else.' In 1981 I was ordained in the United Methodist Church and I have served in various tasks ever since.

All of this doesn't sound exciting—no conversion story, no big crunch solved by a certain intervention of the Holy Spirit. I never experienced a radical turnaround in my life. Nevertheless, my faith journey is exciting, because I live with the radical call to follow Christ. Day by day I am called to receive God's love in order to share it with others; I am called to proclaim the Gospel, to make room for the Holy Spirit and to serve as a co-worker in God's vineyard. The Methodist tradition and theology have opened my eyes to the beauty in this world, the horror that mankind is often producing and God's transformative power at work. Shaped by the ecumenical spirit that Wesleyans have inherited, I learned to see myself as a part of God's family that is much bigger than the tradition I grew up in.

Let me give one concrete example of a recent experience in my journey with Christ: My aged father died Tuesday after Easter and God answered my prayers so that I was able to be with him. I spent many hours sitting at my father's bed. I prayed the biblical Psalms and I sang the old German chorales, Wesley's hymns, and Taizé songs. I myself was comforted by those treasures of faith and hope. And I realized that at the beginning and at the end of our life on earth, it is not about us. We do not decide when to be born and when to die. We come with nothing and we go with nothing. It is about the whole; it is about faith, love and hope. All the big theological terms became meaningful to me, most of all the term forgiveness. My father was a wonderful dad. And yet, he was a human. I wanted to be a caring daughter, and yet my own interests were often more important than my father. Here we were, waiting for a peaceful death. By God's grace I was convinced that we are forgiven. We are surrounded by love. And we come from God and we go to God. That's more than enough. And it is not only exciting, it is promising!

Faith Story (#3)

Ioan Sauca

If it is difficult for a Pentecostal to keep a message short, as David Han said a few moments ago, I don't know about an Orthodox with an experience of two thousand years! I promised Larry to limit myself to three minutes. I don't know if my message is still three minutes, but he also asked me to be more personal, which is against everything we have in Orthodox tradition. We never speak about ourselves publicly; we share about Christ but not about our personal lives. So I'll try to be different from what I am supposed to be.

I will give a short summary of my experience, with some lessons.

In my youth, the spirit of the Global Christian Forum was always in my heart and with me. First, if you ask me 'Who converted you?' my answer would be not the Sunday School, not the church, not my priest, but my grandmother at home. We had a Christian life at home. And I learned that today it is easy to convert but it is very difficult to help people grow if they don't have a community in which to grow. When I'm asked by my evangelical friends, 'Were you born again?' I say 'Yes, I'm being born again every day. And I will be born again in eternity because if you are born again once for life it would be very boring if you remain the same.' We believe in continuous growth in relationship with God, which makes even eternity appealing.

The second important aspect of my experience is that I remember from my youth, and also in my family life as Christians, that we had many evangelicals, Pentecostals and others who visited us. They prayed together, they shared together. It was a very good life of community and cooperation. But I discovered much later why this was the case; it was because I grew up in a context of persecution. It was a challenge to be a Christian, and I discovered even in our day that Christianity can grow in times of persecution and that in those times believers know how to behave and cooperate. But when there is freedom and prosperity, they start fighting with one another. This was my second lesson: ecumenism of common witness in times of hardship and persecution.

As for how these experiences impacted my life, all my life I have worked in the ecumenical movement except for a few years when I was a professor of theology in Romania. And I retained my love for the traditional historical churches but also for the evangelicals, Pentecostals and other Christians, who are very sincerely witnessing to Christ as Lord and Saviour as I do. And then I participated in a series of encounters between Orthodox, evangelicals and Pentecostals on analysing together what are the elements which bring us together. I came to this discussion from a very concrete reality. In Eastern Europe where I come from, many Orthodox have become evangelicals and Pentecostals, whereas in Western Europe, the Orthodox Church is growing. If we look at the statistics, most of those converting to the Orthodox Church are former evangelicals and Pentecostals. So I brought them together for four seminars and tried to help them understand what made them become what they are now. It means that there is a complementarity between the two traditions. And I discovered many things. On most of the issues raised, we could speak with a common voice. There is a lot of misunderstanding, a lot of difference in how we use expressions, but when we come to terms with what we have in common, we can advance very far forward.

Now I am also director of the Bossey Ecumenical Institute. You may know that historically, those who could apply to come and study in Bossey were from WCC member churches. When I became director, I negotiated with the board to make a new policy and also to intentionally equip and give scholarships to students who come from churches that are not WCC members. From 2001 to the present, about one-third of our students every year are evangelicals and Pentecostals. The spirit of the Global Christian Forum is alive within the WCC.

Now to conclude. I don't want to contradict my sister who said that I was here as an important pillar of the WCC. I did not come as a pillar or important person. But I did come as the head of the delegation of the World Council of Churches. So when I speak to you, it is not my personal conviction but it is the conviction of the WCC which is very much behind and supportive of the idea of the Global Christian Forum. We need a platform where Christians of all confessions and faiths come together to discuss their common challenges and find a common witness for the world today. Thank you.

Glimpse of My Faith Story (#4)
Richard Howell

My journey with Christ started when, at the age of twelve in 1965, I repented of my sins and accepted Christ as my personal saviour and Lord. In fact, the whole family did—my parents and four brothers and a sister, due to the healing of my mother. The preacher stayed in our home for three months and discipled us in faith in Christ with Evangelical and Pentecostal fervour.

My journey with Christ in the Global Christian Forum started in the year 2000 when the Continuation Committee formed at the Bossey Institute met at Fuller Theological Seminary in Pasadena, USA.

What appealed to me was that the GCF is an open space where all Christians can meet to nurture unity by fostering mutual respect and understanding as well as by addressing common challenges together. I do not have to change my vocabulary to make it appealing to the other. I can narrate the story of my faith journey without being judged.

It was in 2002, again at Fuller, when the GCF had its first gathering of church leaders, that I was exposed to the leadership of the Orthodox Church and the Catholic Church in a big way.

We had sharing of faith journeys, and during that time I was in a group where His Eminence Metropolitan Serapion was present. I heard his faith journey, as a person who gave up his medical profession to become a monk and serve Christ and his church. Until then, ignorance fed my prejudice towards understanding the Orthodox and Catholic churches. I had to repent as I saw the beautiful work of the Holy Spirit in his life. When we were writing the purpose statement of the GCF, he gave the wording concerning Christ, perfect in his divinity and humanity. I had read the book *The Myth of God Incarnate* and had known theologians who denied the incarnation and bodily resurrection of Christ. I heard his enriching sermon in Delhi, where he preached in our local church.

Second, I came to know leaders of the Catholic Church. To mention a few: Cardinal Oswald Gracia, Archbishop Concessao, Archbishop Anil Couto, and Archbishop Machado, whom I first heard at Toulouse.

I will close with a youth meeting which we called in Delhi under the National United Christian Forum, where young people shared their faith journeys. One young lady shared of her faith in Christ and how she gave up her job at a television company to obey God. She speaks in tongues and witnesses. She used the vocabulary familiar to charismatics and Pentecostals. The beautiful thing was that she happened to be a Catholic charismatic. That day was a day of enlightenment, where the young people saw the grace of God at work.

Sharing of faith journeys requires vulnerability and the grace of God. It creates bridges of friendship and trust so that we can collaborate in addressing the common issues we face.

The GCF is a God-created facilitating body. God bless us!

Sharing Faith Stories In Global Interchurch Groups

Pirjo-Liisa Penttinen and *Andrzej Choromanski*

Pirjo-Liisa Penttinen and Andrzej Choromanski introduced participants to the two afternoon sessions reserved for sharing faith stories in global interchurch groups of approximately 15 persons each. They presented the 'Sharing of Faith Stories in Groups' guides. (See the appendix of this book for the 'Guide for All Participants' and the 'Guide for Facilitators.')

During the presentation, these words appeared on the large screen behind them:

> **In my journey with you,**
>
> **may I never lose my direction,**
>
> **never lose sight of the landmark**
>
> **toward which I travel.**
>
> **And should anything obscure my vision,**
>
> **may I draw closer to you**
>
> **so that my feet may walk**
>
> **in your footsteps,**
>
> **your words be my encouragement,**
>
> **and your love my protection.**

Revd Adriana Gastellu Camp (Uruguay/Sweden), Dr Janet Scott (UK)

DAY ONE: TUESDAY 24 APRIL
LET MUTUAL LOVE CONTINUE!

AFTERNOON AND EVENING GROUPS

Meetings in global interchurch groups
    Sharing the Stories of Our Journeys with Jesus Christ
    Evening Prayer

Evening meetings in optional confessional groups

Evening Prayer

The Gathering of the Community

The Leader welcomes the community and begins with a prayer

Silence

A song of praise

The Proclamation of the Word

The reading and rereading (multiple languages) of Luke 24:1–12

Silence

A sharing of a word or image that comes to heart and mind of participants

Prayer

Thanksgiving

Intercession

Lord's Prayer (each in our own languages)

Conclusion

L: Let us go in peace. Alleluia!

Sign of peace.

Evening Meetings

Evening meetings in optional confessional groups

- Anglican
- Catholic
- Evangelical
- Lutheran
- Methodist
- Orthodox
- Pentecostal
- Reformed

Revd Dr Odair Pedroso Mateus

DAY TWO: WEDNESDAY 25 APRIL
LET MUTUAL LOVE CONTINUE!
RELATIONSHIPS OLD AND NEW

MORNING PRAYER

Prepared by the World Council of Churches

Leader:

> **Odair Pedroso Mateus** (Brazil/Switzerland), Director, Faith and Order Commission, World Council of Churches

Music:

> **Lutheran Church of Columbia**

Relationships Old and New on the Journey

In the Ecumenical Prayer Cycle, this week we pray with and for the peoples and churches in Armenia, Azerbaijan, Georgia.

(You may stand.)

Opening

L: In the name of the Father and of the Son and of the Holy Spirit.

C: **Amen.**

L: From the East to the West,
from the North and the South,
all nations and peoples
bless the creator of creatures with a new blessing.
For he made the light of the sun rise today over the world.
O congregations of the righteous,
who glorify the Holy Trinity in the morning of light,
praise the Christ, the morning of peace,
together with the Father and the Spirit;
for he has made the light of his knowledge shine over us.

(Matins hymn, Armenian Sunrise Office)

C: **Glory to the Father, and to the Son, and to the Holy Spirit: as it was in the beginning, is now, and will be for ever Amen. Alleluia.**

L: We give you thanks, O Lord our God,
who by your visible light
have given joy to all our creatures,
and by the divine light of your commandments
have enlightened all who believe in you.
Strengthen us also, O Lord,
to keep your commandments in this day and at all times,
that having been enlightened in mind,
we may do your will

and receive your heavenly gifts with all your saints,
through the grace and mercy
of our Lord and Saviour Jesus Christ,
to whom be glory, dominion and honour,
now and forever and unto ages of ages.

C: **Amen.**

(Morning prayer, ancient Armenian prayer book)

Song: Miren qué bueno (sing 2x)

Miren qué bueno, qué bueno es
Miren qué bueno, qué bueno es
Behold, how pleasant, how good it is!
Behold, how pleasant, how good it is!
Seht doch, wie gut und herrlich es ist!
Seht doch, wie gut und herrlich es ist!
Voyez, c'est si beau et c'est si bon
Voyez, c'est si beau et c'est si bon

Psalm 133

L: How very good and pleasant it is
when kindred live together in unity!

C: **It is like the precious oil on the head,
running down upon the beard
on the beard of Aaron,
running down over the collar of his robes.**

L: It is like the dew of Hermon
which falls on the mountains of Zion.

C: **For there the Lord ordained the blessing
of life forevermore.**

Miren qué bueno

(sing several times)

(Please be seated.)

Prayer of confession

L: Loving God,
 our faithful companion on the way,
 we thank you for your love and grace.
 We relish the joy which burns within our hearts when you are with us.
 Yet, sometimes when our burdens are so heavy;
 sadness and anger are so overwhelming,
 we cannot see you walking with us,
 we recognize you as a stranger.

C: **Forgive us, O Merciful One.**

L: We delight in your presence and goodness in our lives.
 Yet, sometimes we hoard your blessings
 and do not share your love with others,
 turning neighbour into stranger,
 and stranger into fearful threat.

C: **Forgive us, O Merciful One.**

L: Remind us that your love is to be carried throughout the world.
 Empower us to walk together with friends and strangers,
 sharing with each other the hope and joy of your love on the life journey,
 so that, being united in Christ and enlightened by the Spirit,
 we may show your way to those who long for peace,
 revive those in whom hope has died,
 and bring new life where the power of death seems so strong.
 We pray in Jesus Christ, our risen Lord and Redeemer.

C: **Amen.**

Song: Ya Rab urham (sing 3x)
 Ya Rab urham
 Ya Rab urham
 Ya Rab urham

Palestine

Words of assurance

L: Listen to the good news:
    God, who is rich in mercy,
    out of the great love with which he loved us
    even when we were dead through our trespasses,
    made us alive together with Christ—
        by grace we have been saved—
    and raised us up with him and seated us with him
    in the heavenly places in Christ Jesus,
    so that in the ages to come he might show
    the immeasurable riches of his grace
    in kindness toward us in Christ Jesus.

(Ephesians 2:4-7)

C: **Thanks be to God.**

(You may stand.)

Song: Gloria a Dios

Gloria a Dios, Gloria a Dios	Glory to God, Glory to God
Gloria en los cielos!	Glory to God in the highest!
A Dios la gloria por siempre!	To God be glory forever!
Alleluya, Amen! (x3)	Alleluia, Amen! (x3)
Gloria a Dios, Gloria a Dios	Glory to God, Glory to God
Gloria a Jesucristo ...	Glory to Christ Jesus ...
Gloria a Dios, Gloris a Dios	Glory to God, Glory to God
Gloria as Espíritu Santo ...	Glory to the Spirit ...

Text and music: Gilmer Torres

Prayer for illumination

L: Open our eyes and soften our hearts, O God,
    through the work of your Holy Spirit,
    that in the hearing of your Word
    we may receive new life.

C: **Amen.**

Song: Alleluia (sing 3x)
Alleluia!
Alleluia!
Alleluia!

Orthodox, Russia

Luke 24:13-35

[13] Now on that same day two of them were going to a village called Emmaus, about seven miles from Jerusalem, [14] and talking with each other about all these things that had happened. [15] While they were talking and discussing, Jesus himself came near and went with them, [16] but their eyes were kept from recognizing him. [17] And he said to them, 'What are you discussing with each other while you walk along?' They stood still, looking sad. [18] Then one of them, whose name was Cleopas, answered him, 'Are you the only stranger in Jerusalem who does not know the things that have taken place there in these days?' [19] He asked them, 'What things?' They replied, 'The things about Jesus of Nazareth, who was a prophet mighty in deed and word before God and all the people, [20] and how our chief priests and leaders handed him over to be condemned to death and crucified him. [21] But we had hoped that he was the one to redeem Israel. Yes, and besides all this, it is now the third day since these things took place. [22] Moreover, some women of our group astounded us. They were at the tomb early this morning, [23] and when they did not find his body there, they came back and told us that they had indeed seen a vision of angels who said that he was alive. [24] Some of those who were with us went to the tomb and found it just as the women had said; but they did not see him.' [25] Then he said to them, 'Oh, how foolish you are, and how slow of heart to believe all that the prophets have declared! [26] Was it not necessary that the Messiah should suffer these things and then enter into his glory?' [27] Then beginning with Moses and all the prophets, he interpreted to them the things about himself in all the scriptures.

[28] As they came near the village to which they were going, he walked ahead as if he were going on. [29] But they urged him strongly, saying, 'Stay with us, because it is almost evening and the day is now

nearly over.' So he went in to stay with them. ³⁰When he was at the table with them, he took bread, blessed and broke it, and gave it to them. ³¹Then their eyes were opened, and they recognized him; and he vanished from their sight. ³²They said to each other, 'Were not our hearts burning within us while he was talking to us on the road, while he was opening the scriptures to us?' ³³That same hour they got up and returned to Jerusalem; and they found the eleven and their companions gathered together. ³⁴They were saying, 'The Lord has risen indeed, and he has appeared to Simon!' ³⁵Then they told what had happened on the road, and how he had been made known to them in the breaking of the bread.

Song: Alleluia (sing 3x)

(Please be seated.)

Silent reflection

(You may stand.)

Song: On the journey to Emmaus

On the journey to Emmaus with our hearts cold as stone
The one who would save us had left us alone
Then a stranger walks with us and to our surprise
He opens our stories and he opens our eyes.

And our hearts burned within us as we talked on the way
How all that was promised was ours on that day
So we begged him, 'Stay with us and grant us your word.'
We welcomed the stranger and we welcomed the Lord.

And that evening at the table as he blessed and broke bread
We knew it was Jesus aris'n from the dead;
Though he vanished before us we knew he was near,
The life in our dying and the hope in our fear.

On our journey to Emmaus, in our stories and feast,
With Jesus we claim that the greatest is least:
And his words burn within us – let none be ignored
Who welcomes the stranger shall welcome the Lord.

Marty Haugen

(Please be seated.)

Prayers of the people

L: Let us pray to Jesus, our Lord, teacher and brother,
that we may be more aware how much he walks with us on the road of life,
and let us say:

C: **Lord Jesus, journey with us.**

L: Lord Jesus, journey with your Church on the roads of peace and love
that leads us to one another and to our destiny of lasting joy,
we pray:

C: **Lord Jesus, journey with us.**

L: Lord Jesus, journey with the churches that claim you as their Lord.
Lead them to one another that you may be their one Lord and shepherd,
we pray:

C: **Lord Jesus, journey with us.**

L: Lord Jesus, journey with our countries. Inspire our leaders with your Spirit
that they may be people of integrity who care about their people and their needs,
we pray:

C: **Lord Jesus, journey with us.**

L: Lord Jesus, journey with all who suffer. Lighten their burdens and pains,
for you experienced how heavy a cross can be, and help us to lift up people from their miseries,
we pray:

C: **Lord Jesus, journey with us.**

L: Lord Jesus, journey with our communities that we may accept and love one another

> so that it becomes evident to all that you live among us,
>> we pray:

C: **Lord Jesus, journey with us.**

L: Lord Jesus, journey with the peoples and churches in Armenia, Azerbaijan, and Georgia.
Bless them with abundant resources, unity among differences, and just peace,
>> we pray:

C: **Lord Jesus, journey with us.**

L: Thank you, Lord, for staying with us. Warm the hearts of all of us with your kind words and your lasting friendship, for you are our Lord for ever.

C: **Amen.**

(Week of Prayer for Christian Unity 2009)

(You may stand.)

Song: *El mensaje que hoy proclamamos*

El mensaje que
hoy proclamamos,
es justicia,
es paz para el mundo
La fe, el amor
La esperanza de un mundo
mejor

Hear the message we are now
proclaiming
about justice and peace for
creation
With faith and with love
and with hope we shall fight
for the world

El mensaje que hoy proclamamos es dar nuevas de vida a los pobres

Hear the gospel we are now proclaiming, it gives new life to those who are poorest.

El mensaje que hoy proclamamos: anunciar libertad a los cautivos

For the gospel we are now proclaiming, it brings liberty for all the captives.

El mensaje que hoy proclamamos: aliviar del quebranto al que sufre.

Yes, the message we are now proclaiming gives relief to the suffering people.

Sending and blessing

L: Let mutual love continue,
and let us walk with hope for this gift of being together,
with joy in God's loving care,
with courage to bring God's peace for every one in every place.

C: **May the God of peace,
who raised to life the great shepherd of the sheep,
make us ready to do his will in every good thing,
through Jesus Christ and in the fellowship of the Holy Spirit,
to whom be glory forever and ever.
Alleluia! Amen.**

Song: Siyahamb' ekukhanye' kwenkhos'

*Siyahamb' ekukhanyan' kwenkhos',
Siyahamb' ekukhanyan' kwenkhos'
Siyahamb' ekukhanyan' kwenkhos',
Siyahamb' ekukhanyan' kwenkhos'
Siyahamba, siyahamba, siyahamb' ekukhanyan' kwenkhos'
Siyahamba, siyahamba, siyahamb' ekukhanyan' kwenkhos'*

*We are marching in the light of God,
We are marching in the light of God
We are marching in the light of God,
We are marching in the light of God
We are marching, we are marching,
We are marching in the light of God
We are marching, we are marching,
We are marching in the light of God*

Dr Ruth Padilla DeBorst

DAY TWO: WEDNESDAY 25 APRIL
LET MUTUAL LOVE CONTINUE!
RELATIONSHIPS OLD AND NEW

9.30AM PLENARY SESSION

Relationships Old and New

Introduction

Christine MacMillan (Canada), Session Moderator, Associate Secretary General for Public Engagement, World Evangelical Alliance

Greetings from the World Evangelical Alliance

Efraim Tendero (Philippines), Secretary General World Evangelical Alliance

Let Mutual Love Continue: Relationships Old and New on the Journey

Biblical Perspective 1 — **Ruth Padilla DeBorst** (Costa Rica), Coordinator, Networking Team, International Fellowship of Mission as Transformation

Biblical Perspective 2 — ***Thomas Schirrmacher*** (Germany), Associate General Secretary for Theological Concerns, WEA, and GCF Committee Member for the WEA

Testimony — From Conflict to Communion: A Bilateral Journey of Reconciliation That Became a Multilateral One

- ***Kaisamari Hintikka*** (Finland/Switzerland), Assistant General Secretary for Ecumenical Relations, Lutheran World Federation
- ***Ivan Abrahams*** (South Africa), General Secretary, World Methodist Council
- ***Alyson Barnett-Cowan*** (Canada), Anglican Communion and President, Canadian Council of Churches
- ***Chris Ferguson*** (Canada/Germany), General Secretary, World Communion of Reformed Churches
- ***Brian Farrell*** (Ireland/Vatican City), Secretary, Pontifical Council for Promoting Christian Unity

Introduction and Greetings

Relationships Old and New: Introduction to the Plenary

Christine MacMillan

Finding ourselves this morning in Bogotá was and is based on a host of relationships. In particular, when stepping out from the airport to see a sign and logo reading 'Global Christian Forum' and then to hear another say, 'You must be Christine', had me break out in a smile. That smile was reciprocated by our great volunteer hosts from the churches in Bogotá, who met us as if we were their relatives. I needed a ride to the hotel and the Global Christian Forum hosts had a ride for me. I could say to myself that relationship is no longer a part of who I am—it is complete. And yet, as I think of the warmth of spirit in which I was met, that relationship is not old. It lives with me as a form of gratitude—a mutual love where an act of kindness can still refresh.

The World Evangelical Alliance, now well over 150 years old, can be viewed as over 150 years young. For all of us coming from our Christian expressions of both new and old, history and history in the making, we ask the question: do relationships get old or stay new for a reason? Now I fully realize that relationships over time build solid recognition that we are known and appreciated (or sometimes unappreciated).

The early beginnings of the World Evangelical Alliance found returned missionaries from various denominations looking for acknowledgement of their experiences. Coming off boats after long journeys, did they have a sense that anyone was interested in their stories of new lands beyond the sea? They had shared in new foods, languages and cultures. They understood that sharing the gospel entailed growing mutual relationships, through their conviction that being an evangelical meant believing that the good news could open up new perspectives and potentials. Relationships had become their new identity through mutual respect, and their missions uncovered the opportunity to form a new, global family of faith. But also included in these experiences was the potential to destroy newly discovered ethnicities and cultures by communicating the gospel in a way that compromised those cultures. In the shadow of the frequent desire for our own cultures to dominate, mutual love became wrapped in power relationships, affecting the openness of heart that believers displayed in recognizing Christ in one another.

I suppose that these returned missionaries did not all get the welcome I received this week at the airport. Their experiences did not generate much interest until others who were also living their faith by going into all the world found one another and returned missionaries began to share in mutual circles of acceptance and accountability. They discovered in themselves a desire for mutual love to continue, and thus the World Evangelical Alliance was birthed. The word 'Alliance' in our title could thus be interpreted as world evangelical relationships, expressed in regional and national relationships in a host of connections for contextual purposes.

When we consider the old and the new in our day, the rapidity of communication in circles of media outlets leaves our brains, let alone our spirits, struggling to understand in depth. The question of how we relate to a flood of information and issues with the intention of building a relational Kingdom of God creates tension for us. I noticed that on the program outline for this session, in brackets after my name, was '(USA)'. I am a Canadian, but who knows—perhaps Canada while I was in flight became the new northern state of the US and the Global Christian Forum, being ahead of their time, picked up on it. Yes, this is a fanciful example, but the mobility of our world has us waking up daily to new constructs while we engage in constructing God's Kingdom.

This morning, our two presenters reflect differences of old and new worlds—differences in gender, language, culture and age—but with a desire to live a message of God who is unchanging and seeking to stabilize our past, present and future in ways of truth and life. We see on the program as well a presentation of testimony—a witness that relationships make a difference. Our uniforms of external expressions, where some look more obvious than others—including our name badges—are not the signposts we want to leave with on Friday. Let us ask ourselves what in the nature of our relationship formation will let mutual love continue, whether the connections of this week involve meeting old friends or developing new friends.

God only knows that the momentum of sixty-five million refugees and displaced persons finding or losing their way, as persons looking for an open space to call home, has this Global Christian Forum wanting our broad base of churches to explore and address together such common challenges. These challenges will be taken up because our mutual love for God's loved and so unloved world calls us with a love that goes beyond the comfort zone of our structures into the imagination that only unity in Christ can create.

World Evangelical Alliance Greeting to the Global Christian Forum

Efraim Tendero

Editor's note: Bishop Efraim was unable to attend in person; this message was read on his behalf by Thomas Schirrmacher.

Greetings! On behalf of the World Evangelical Alliance, I wish to thank all of you for attending the Global Christian Forum's Third Global Gathering and to assure you of my prayers for the great success of this event.

We are grateful to the churches of Bogotá, Colombia for extending a warm welcome and excellent hospitality to everyone. I hope that this Global Gathering will build stronger connections between the Latin American church and the worldwide family of believers.

I have been looking forward to this great event for many months. Unfortunately, some personal matters that arose just last week have forced me to change my plans. However, you will be in my daily prayers this week and I know that Bishop Thomas Schirrmacher, the WEA's Associate General Secretary for Theological Concerns, will represent us superbly. The WEA also has several International Council members,

Senior Leadership Team members, and other leaders participating in this Global Gathering.

The Global Christian Forum has been a precious gift from God to all of us at the WEA. We take seriously Jesus' call to mutual love and unity among all who recognize him as Saviour, but we also know that we must avoid compromises that would undermine our faith. The GCF is a place where we can go with confidence, knowing that our collaboration with brothers and sisters from church bodies around the world will uphold the historic truths of the Christian faith and will strengthen God's kingdom on earth. May the sharing of your respective faith journeys mutually encourage and edify each other and enrich our appreciation and respect for one another.

When we participated last year in the discussion at Bossey, Switzerland on the GCF's future, we strongly supported its continuation. We saw the GCF's unique effectiveness in bringing together believers of many traditions at the powerful 2015 Tirana conference on the persecution of Christians. The GCF has helped us raise worldwide awareness of this crucial concern. It has enabled us to achieve consensus and collaboration on key issues while providing a platform for us to openly discuss sensitive matters, such as the current GCF process on proselytism.

We are deeply grateful for the service that Larry Miller has provided as GCF Secretary for the last six years. With grace, respectfulness, and responsiveness, he has achieved amazing things and made enormous contributions to the GCF's effectiveness. Larry, the WEA will miss you very much! We wish Larry Godspeed in his next steps and look forward to being equally blessed by the service of incoming Secretary Casely Essamuah.

Thank you again and may you be deeply blessed by the powerful expressions of mutual love that I know you will experience this week.

Biblical Perspectives on the themes of the day

Biblical Perspective 1 — The Story of Paul, Onesimus, and Philemon

Ruth Padilla DeBorst

'He belongs with you; you belong to each other.' Paul's words were shocking. They blatantly contravened all logic. They made no economic sense. There was no room for them in the Roman imperial system. After all, Onesimus, the slave, had escaped, taking with him some of his master's property. Natural and legally enforceable expectations included public discredit, severe discipline, and even execution. Onesimus, a slave of Philemon in Colossae, was a nobody—sheer property to be disposed of as the owner saw fit, and subject to tough legal dispositions.

Our topic today is 'Let Mutual Love Continue: Relationships Old and New on the Journey'. The biblical story of Onesimus and Philemon invites us to consider the difficulties, barriers, prejudices and stereotypes that must be overcome if mutual love is to be nurtured among the Christian traditions represented here. Before diving into the narrative, however, I must bring you greetings from my communities.

Greetings from my local community, Casa Adobe, composed of several families and several single people from different countries and Christian traditions who share life and a common pot, accompany our neighbours in urban and community gardening and seek to relocate a few refugee families. Greetings also from INFEMIT, the International Fellowship for Mission as Transformation, and from the Community of Interdisciplinary Theological Studies (CETI), both communities that seek to nourish committed theologizing and an integral living out of the Gospel in Latin America and the world.

Let's go back to the letter, in which Paul boldly and lovingly addresses Philemon, celebrating the love that joins them in Christ and making this subversive call to a new form of belonging. 'Receive Onesimus back. But not now as a slave, much less as a fugitive thief, but as a worthy brother.' The call is not a private matter kept between Paul and Philemon. It is first made public when Paul writes the letter in prison, in the presence of his companions, Epaphras, Mark, Aristarchus, Demas and Luke. It is then made known to yet a broader audience when it is read by Philemon's wife, Apphia, and son Archippus, as well as by the entire church that meets in their house.

How dare Paul expect such out-of-the-norm behaviour from Philemon? What grounds does he have to set the bar so high? Paul rests his entire case on the demands of Jesus' way: the way of love, of human dignity, of reconciled relationships, of belonging in the new community generated by Jesus' life and ministry.

Let's review in further detail. Who are the characters in this story? Paul, a Christian leader of a prominent Jewish family. Philemon, a gentile Christian convert. Onesimus, a young man who belonged to the lowest rung of the social scale. There was no one lower than an escaped slave, who probably could not even read and would now be catalogued as a criminal.

Although Paul has the credentials to demand obedience from Philemon, he does not impose his will but rather begs Philemon 'in the name of love' on behalf of Onesimus (verses 8–9). Paul rests his request precisely on the *koinonía* that joins Onesimus with Paul and, as in a chain, Onesimus with Philemon. He begins by expounding on the intimate relationship he has with Onesimus. He identifies Onesimus lovingly as his 'son', as one who 'came to be my son while I was in prison', with whom 'goes my very heart' and as someone 'very special to me'. Implicit in the letter is the fact that, instead of losing himself in the multitudes of the large city, Onesimus had sought Paul out even though he was in prison. Onesimus had then been discipled by him, and the new fraternal bond between them had inspired in the slave enough trust that he had determined not to continue running away but rather to confront the consequences of his action and return to his owner in spite of the risk of punishment.

Note Paul's literary skill and his touch of humour when he employs a double play of words (11). *Onesimus* means useful. It is pretty obvious that a slave who steals and runs away is anything but useful, and that actually his return could be beneficial to his owner. But Paul uses a synonym of useful, *euchrēstos*, a word whose pronunciation sounds a lot like the title *Christos*. In some way, this points to the fact that, given his new bond with Jesus Christ, the Christian Onesimus is doubly useful, not only for Paul but also for Philemon. He had been no more than socially rejected property; he now is a full person. He had been a useless slave; he is now a 'dear brother in the Lord' (16).

The new bond established 'in Christ' between Onesimus and Paul extends naturally to the relationship between Onesimus and Philemon and should be made visible in very practical ways: renewed value, economic freedom and comforting reconciliation. Paul exhorts Philemon, 'Receive him as you would receive me.' The call is not for Philemon to receive Onesimus and then treat him as his understandable anger or the Greco-Roman social code would dictate. Nor is it a matter of forgiving, forgetting and assimilating Onesimus into the household as if nothing had happened. Love requires an even more radical step: Philemon must value Onesimus as he values Paul, his brother and companion, and treat him according to that renewed vision of his value. Between the lines, the exhortation points to the freedom of the slave and his integration into the family and the faith community as an equal.

At the same time, Paul is also very realistic and concrete. He encourages Philemon, 'Charge [his debts] to my account.' The days or months of a slave's absence meant financial loss for his or her owner. That loss would accumulate as a personal debt that the slave would later have to pay back. In the case of Onesimus, the debt would have increased because of what he had stolen. Paul seeks to dispel any hindrance to the reconciliation between Philemon and Onesimus and commits personally to freeing Philemon of his loss and Onesimus of his debt. This he does 'of his own hand', which formalized his promise into a legal contract. These funds could be considered payment for the freedom of Onesimus, who would then become a freed slave and could even access Roman citizenship.

Paul reminds Philemon indirectly that he owes him even more: since Paul had led Philemon to Christ, he owes Paul his very life. Implicit in this comment is the natural connection between Philemon and Onesimus: they are both debtors. They can both be liberated from their debt by the love of God, which is made tangible by the love of their sisters and brothers.

Having set aside any economic impediment, Paul concludes his persuasive advocacy with the words, 'Refresh my heart.' He insists that the steps Philemon takes in relation to Onesimus will directly impact Paul's well-being. As an ambassador of Christ, the Reconciler, and following his example, Paul stretches as a bridge between the conflicting parties, over and above every ethnic and social difference, to open up a path for mutual encounter and forgiveness. He expresses the hope that, out of love for Christ and for Paul, Philemon will do 'even more' on behalf of Onesimus than Paul has requested.

Some questions naturally arise here. What might Paul have meant when he said, 'You'll do even more than I have asked'? And why might Paul not have attacked slavery more ostensively? A possible response is that, given the social and political conditions of the day and the fragility of the Jesus movement, it would have been fruitless to publicly demand the abolition of slavery. For that reason, instead of launching an openly revolutionary declaration that could have awakened intense persecution and left thousands unprotected, Paul promotes a change from inside the new community, a revolution from the bottom up, which alters the relationships between owners and slaves and acts as an inevitable seed of more systemic changes. Paul is not advocating simply for the freedom of Onesimus, the slave; he is demanding an entire shift in social relations, a total subversion of the honour code, and a radical change in the slave-owner relationship. The stereotypical cultural expectations regarding slaves and freed slaves had to be broken. The call was not primarily to a political revolution that might someday, in the long run, affect Roman law, but rather an appeal to a more transcendent and present reality: the freedom, equality and mutuality of the Good News. Actually, the demands of the Gospel would so alter relations in the new community that they would necessarily impact social patterns and even the institution of slavery itself.

As we know, the first communities of Jesus-followers met in family homes and, breaking all social protocol, their gatherings included people of diverse social conditions: free people, freed slaves, current slaves (Romans 16). In addition, instead of investing their offerings in the construction and maintenance of buildings, they directed them towards the support of missionaries, the freedom of slaves, and the care of widows and orphans. Both biblical and other historical accounts portray this as a community that laughed at humanly constructed borders and imperially imposed exclusions and constructed subversive belonging from the bottom up. It was a community that far transcended its local expressions, subverted the worldly logics of power and dependency, lived out an alternate economic morality, and repositioned all its members as equals at the foot of the cross. Imagine, for example, what it meant for the 'mother church' in Jerusalem to step down from her stand to receive monetary support from the 'mission church' in Asia Minor, and to release precedence when the followers of Jesus in Antioch were granted the privileged name of 'Christian' even before they were! Or for the council in Jerusalem to heed the counsel of the newer Christians spread out across the Greco-Roman world regarding what the way of Jesus really consisted of. Taking such steps demanded (and it demands of us) releasing privilege and recognizing the contributions of other people—even those who look at the world differently than I do, and especially the people whom the world considers useless.

We arrive at the final words (23–25). But before formulating the greetings expected in any epistle, Paul makes a request that demonstrates his daring hope. Although he is writing from prison, he asks Philemon to prepare lodging for him because he is counting on visiting that faith community in the near future. The announcement of his imminent visit would also put some pressure on Philemon, who would have to account for his actions in relation to Onesimus to his mentor. Philemon and Paul were old friends, but Christ's love demanded that their circle expand constantly. Contradicting all economic barriers and cultural stereotypes, the love of the supreme community of love demanded the embrace of a new friend.

Paul is aware that the call he has placed before Philemon and his community is not a simple one. He knows well the debates of a spirit tempted to live according to the expectations of the social and political context—and according to greedy, selfish and personal impulses and ambitions for personal benefit, which would imply the exclusion of others. For that reason, he pleads that the grace of the Lord Jesus Christ—who gave himself to make peace, to establish right relations, to free and give full life to all people—may take root in the heart of that faith community: 'May the grace of the Lord Jesus Christ be with your spirit.'

Now, frequently and erroneously, we think of slavery as a matter of the past that has been overcome. However, today there are more slaves in the world than in any other era; 27 million people are held against their will. In our Latin America, under the veneer of progress, girls and boys, women and men are exploited in forced labour, internal and international trafficking, involuntary recruitment for military forces, child labour in dangerous places like mines, or manipulating chemicals or heavy machinery. Millions more work in infrahuman conditions, with no benefits or security. And scores upon scores of women work double or triple shifts at home and beyond and receive far less pay than their male counterparts. The challenge for God's people today is the same as the one Paul voiced to Philemon and the community of Jesus' followers in Colossae.

We too need to plead that God may shed his grace upon us, so that we may open our eyes and unearth the slavery hidden in our homes, neighbourhoods, cities, and countries. So that we may engage in radical commitment to eradicate the causes of slavery: poverty, exclusion, and discrimination. So that with courage we may confront people, institutions and systems that oppress, even if that demands economic investment and risks to our personal security. So that we may live with integrity as alternative communities, guided by the law of love, acceptance and restorative reconciliation far beyond any doctrinal prejudices, cultural traditions, or privileged or excluded positions. Only by grace will mutual love remain in our pilgrimage of following Jesus in the power of the Spirit for the glory of God, creator and sustainer of all.

Biblical Perspective 2 — Peter's Second Pentecost
Thomas Schirrmacher

We have heard from Ruth Padilla DeBorst how the relationships between Paul, Philemon and Onesimus shaped a new category of personal relations. I want to extend this idea a step further and suggest that this story shows that encounters and relationships also improve our theology and our worldview.

The five years during which I was involved with the development of the document 'Christian Witness in a Multi-religious World', released in 2011 by the Vatican, the World Council of Churches, and the World Evangelical Alliance, powerfully changed my life. This was not because I read a lot of books and papers around the topic, which I did, but because of long-term personal encounters with the other people involved in the project.

When I was introduced as a new member of the committee of the Global Christian Forum, the newsletter of the Forum wrote:

> *In terms of his personal journey Dr Schirrmacher says that, coming from a very conservative evangelical background, 'I would not even enter Catholic or Pentecostal churches. (...) I never expected that one day I would attend two Vatican synods, help to work on close contacts between the World Council of Churches and the WEA, and speak at the General Assembly of the WCC. (...) My change of heart came for several reasons, including my activities on behalf of persecuted churches. In 2005 we started the International Institute for Religious Freedom and I found myself defending people of (...) all churches and confessions. Here I was sitting and praying for the protection for Christians, whom I still thought to be unbelievers. I was also changed though the joining of 'spiritual experience and friendship'. Theology followed later and had the final decision: strange for a professor of Systematic*

> Theology. But still it's the truth. The years of diligent work around the globe changed my perception of the Catholic Church and the World Council of Churches and made me a champion of the goals that are now central to the GCF.

Some Evangelicals have taken issue with my statement that experience came first and theology followed. If I held such a position, they said, I no longer could be the head of the theological concerns department of the WEA. They also said the statement proves that the Global Christian Forum waters down biblical convictions and the strong endorsement of the Global Christian Forum by the WEA is wrong.

But in response I would ask: Is evangelical or even Pentecostal theology with no experience possible, just as a pure academic exercise in comparing and judging theologies? Can we have a correct understanding of the Trinity without the life-changing experience of being loved by, and loving, the triune God? Is not our evangelical and Pentecostal theology always a narrative theology?

The global gathering of the Global Christian Forum and the theme of the day give me the chance to prove from Scripture that experience of how God acts in this world in the lives of other people and churches, and of growing mutual relations with other Christians, is a good road to a sound theology.

By all means, Holy Scripture is God's revelation and our highest authority. This is true for the Orthodox Church as much as for the Catholic Church. What we discuss is only who may be the authoritative interpreter of Scripture, but not the nature of Scripture as such.

But the God who gave Scripture to us used experience to shape the theology of the authors of Scripture. This is why large parts of Scripture are in narrative form. And he shapes our theology to the good by experiences and encounters. In other words, if you are firmly committed to the authority of Scripture, experience of how God acts through other people and churches is indeed a good road to a sound theology.

Job's theology did not become upgraded through the endless theoretical discussions with his friends. Only through his life's experience—ugly and painful as it was—did he reach this conclusion about God:

'So far my ears had heard of you, but now my eyes have seen you' (Job 42:5).

Many prophets and leaders in the Old Testament testify to the fact that only real-life experience of and encounters with God—directly and through other people—enabled them to understand God and his will.

This is still true today. I know more people who started to think more favourably about Pentecostals because they experienced healing or other wonders for themselves or others than I know people who were swayed by heated discussions of Pentecostal systematic theology.

We know that pure, uninterpreted experience does not teach us anything by itself, and we surely do not accept experience as such as the highest authority in the church. By experience I also do not mean that we constantly adapt to cultural circumstances or to the *Zeitgeist*, the spirit of the age. If you marry the *Zeitgeist*, you will be a widow or a widower soon anyway.

But often, personal experience and relationships with others can remove the haze in front of our eyes. Experience opens our minds to things that we perhaps could have known through intellectual research and discussion but do not realize because we have biases that cause us not to see what we do not want to see.

Often in the gospels, Jesus said something and it obviously was true, yet his disciples listening to him understood only much later what he meant, and always after some major event had happened or some experience occurred. The most famous example is that Jesus promised to rebuild the Temple in three days. Only after his resurrection did his followers understand that he was not referring to the Temple made of stone, but to himself (John 2:21–22).

The Apostolic Council of Acts 15:1–33 was about a very serious theological matter. The whole church met—the Apostles, elders, delegates from the churches and apostolic teams. The end result was summarised by the person presiding, James, who claimed that their conclusion must be true because it was in line with Scripture. But even though the interpretation and declaration of Scripture by the authorities was the council's final step, the theological discussion actually centred on reports of experiences. Peter, Paul and Barnabas won the day, so to speak, because of the many moving stories they told, arguing that God had decided the matter already by sending his Holy Spirit to the Gentiles, as they had witnessed it.

Acts tells us that Peter addressed those gathered as follows: 'Brothers and sisters, you know that some time ago God made a choice among you that the Gentiles might hear from my lips the message of the gospel and believe. God, who knows the heart, showed that he accepted them by giving the Holy Spirit to them, just as he did to us' (Acts 15:7–8). And Acts adds, 'The whole assembly became silent as they listened to Barnabas and Paul telling about the miraculous signs and wonders God had done among the Gentiles through them' (15:12).

Telling those stories was Christian and biblical theology at its best, not some inferior method of theological argument!

In Galatians 2:11, Paul wrote, 'When Peter came to Antioch, I opposed him to his face, because he was clearly in the wrong.' Paul added a lengthy explanation of why Peter was wrong, indicating that God accepts people from all nations simply by faith (Gal. 2:11–19).

Was this the same Peter who heard the original oral version of the Great Commission out of Jesus' mouth? Was this the Peter who preached in Jerusalem on the first Pentecost? Was this the Peter in whom Jesus invested so much time in personal encounters and extra lessons, last but not least calling him to shepherd his sheep (John 21:15–21)?

Like all the disciples, Peter learned from the living Word of God himself that the Great Commission is to all nations (Mt. 28:18–20) and that the power of the Holy Spirit would come upon them so that they would be witnesses 'to the end of the earth' (Acts 1:9). God used the emerging leader of the church, Peter, more than anybody else when Pentecost occurred, as he had the privilege of preaching that day and being the first herald of the new age that had come.

Yet despite all his learning and all his correct words, Peter did not believe this deep in his heart. He still believed in the separation of Jews and Gentiles.

How did God convince Peter? By presenting him with a new volume of systematic theology written by Paul? By compiling all statements from Jesus as well as from the Old Testament prophets that are relevant to the topic so as to prove overwhelmingly that people from all nations and languages will enter the kingdom of God? Or even better, did God give him a well-prepared, systematic lecture with nine convincing arguments directly from heaven?

Well, as you all know, God did reveal himself directly to Peter, but not in the way we theologians would have chosen. He used a dream that contained a shocking example and applied it to the upcoming encounter with Cornelius. He had Cornelius wait for Peter so that Peter could see with his own eyes and have a firsthand experience of true theology.

Read carefully the whole story of Cornelius in Acts 10 tonight. How much effort God put into shaping Peter's theology through this experience! He corrected Peter's wrong views, but in a way that changed his life forever and to which he would witness for the rest of his life.

Only after what I like to call 'Peter's second Pentecost' did Peter grasp the theology of the first Pentecost. After the conversion of Cornelius, he declared, 'I now realize how true it is that God does not show favouritism but accepts men from every nation who fear him and do what is right' (Acts 10:34–35) and: 'Can anyone keep these people from being baptized with water? They have received the Holy Spirit just as we have' (Acts 10:47).

Of course, those examples relate directly to what we are doing here in Bogotá. Listening to the faith stories of other Christian leaders, young and old, male and female, is one of the marks of the Global Christian Forum. These sharing times are not just to give more people a chance to say something. They are as much and deep a theological encounter as the superb messages delivered by people like Ruth Padilla DeBorst, who spoke before me.

I hope that those from older churches seize the opportunity here to listen to people from newer churches. I hope those coming from newer churches open their ears wide for the faith stories of people from older churches, as their churches may be long established but their stories are not old! Take as an example my friend His Holiness Patriarch Mor Ignatius Aphrem II, who represents a church that originated where Christianity originated and goes back to the first century. Yet his message and words are up to date and speak spiritually to our churches today.

Let me address my evangelical and Pentecostal friends more directly. In Scripture, Jesus speaks two judgements that I pray will not be spoken over us. While on earth, he described a Pharisee (the closest thing to an evangelical in the Jewish world—ask me about it if you question this!) who came to the Temple and prayed about himself: 'God, I thank you that I am not like the others' (Luke 18:11). This statement was opposed to the 'evangel' (after which 'evangelical' is named), the gospel, which was captured in the other man's prayer: 'God, have mercy on me, a sinner' (Luke 18:13).

The second judgement comes from the risen Lord in his letter to the church at Laodicea: 'You say, "I am rich (...) and do not need anything." But you do not realize that you are wretched, pitiful, poor, blind and naked' (Rev. 3:17).

Our high view of Scripture should not keep us from being always willing to learn more (Rom. 12:1–2). The Holy Spirit has many ways to teach us sound theology, not just the classroom. If we listen, we will often hear profound truths spoken and lived in places where we did not expect it.

If Scripture is God's Word, then we should follow Scripture when it teaches us that we often understand God's deepest thoughts not just by quoting them, but through life-changing encounters and experiences.

Thanks be to the triune God that he did not just leave us a holy book inspired by the Holy Spirit and revealing Jesus as Saviour to us, but that he sent the Holy Spirit himself into us, to understand this book and its divine author. Thank God that he uses multiple means to help us more deeply understand His revelation, put it into practice in our lives, and grow all the more in love for our Father in Heaven, our Saviour Jesus Christ and the Holy Spirit.

Testimonies

From Conflict to Communion: A Bilateral Journey of Reconciliation That Became a Multilateral One

Kaisamari Hintikka

'The things that unite us are greater than the those that divide us.' These words of Pope John XXIII describe in a beautiful way the journey between Lutherans and Catholics during the last fifty years.

After four and a half centuries of theological disputes that turned into animosities and violence and shaped the map of Europe, greatly affected the world, and tore apart the body of Christ, the church, it took courage to hear these words of the pope, stated in the context of the Second Vatican Council.

But we do belong to the one body of Christ through baptism. This awareness was the basis of the beginning of the Lutheran-Catholic dialogue in 1967 when we first gathered around the same dialogue table.

But we were also growing in other kind of awareness of the times of change. New thoughts had begun to move in theological research: it had become more open to other disciplines, other areas of academic research. And we understood that even if the traditionally disputed theological issues between Catholics and Lutherans were still of importance, they had begun to appear 'in a different light because of new insights in the natural, social and historical sciences and biblical theology'.[1]

At the time of the beginning of the dialogue, our understanding was that ultimately we were 'separated over the issue of the right understanding of the gospel'.[2] And as the unity of the church could be unity only in the truth of the gospel, we needed to ask ourselves, 'How can we understand and actualize the gospel today?'[3] Together.

---

1 *Report of the Joint Lutheran-Roman Catholic Study Commission (The Malta Report)*, PCPCU and LWF, Rome and Geneva, 1972, §2 (http://www.christianunity.va/content/unitacristiani/en/dialoghi/sezione-occidentale/luterani/dialogo/documenti-di-dialogo/en4.html).
2 *Ibidem*, §14.
3 *Ibidem*

And indeed, this has been our guiding question throughout the fifty years of continuous dialogue. During these years we have shared many gifts, learned to see one another with new eyes, and learned through our own experience that indeed the things that unite us are greater—and not just greater but far more numerous than we thought at the beginning of this journey. We have grown to understand what it means that we are the branches of the same true vine, Jesus Christ. This understanding has deepened our mutual commitment to this shared journey where we have been and continue to be led by the Holy Spirit. The same spirit has also inspired our local communities to both receive the gifts of the global dialogue.

The Joint Declaration

Along this journey we became increasingly aware that the question we needed to pay special attention to was the question of justification, which 'is the measure or touchstone for the Christian faith' that 'serves to orient all the teaching and practice of our churches to Christ'.[4] Thanks to many Catholic theologians, inspired by our dialogue, who were looking for new approaches to Martin Luther's theology and particularly his understanding of justification, a small group of Lutheran and Catholic theologians entered into a process that led in 1999 to the signing of the Joint Declaration of the Doctrine of Justification.

At that time, we knew that we had taken a step of invaluable importance in our journey. We encouraged our local communities, theological seminaries and individual Christians to careful study of the Joint Declaration. But it had also become clear to us that because of the centrality of justification in our theology and Christian faith, we needed to invite the others to join us.

As it often happens with reception of an ecumenical document, the fruits will grow in ways that sometimes remain unseen by our human eyes and become visible only over the course of time. Time has shown

---

4 *Joint Declaration of the Doctrine of Justificatio*, The Lutheran World Federation and the Catholic Church, Geneva and Rome, 1999, §18 (https://www.lutheranworld.org/sites/default/files/Joint%20Declaration%20on%20the%20Doctrine%20of%20Justification.pdf).

that the Holy Spirit has moved all of us in ways that have deepened our mutual understanding and that of our teachings on the doctrine of justification—and not just between Lutherans and Catholics but also among our sisters and brothers in other Christian world communions. We are immensely grateful for the openness and endeavours of the World Methodist Council, the World Communion of Reformed Churches, and the Anglican Communion that allowed them, through internal consultations and discussions with the signatories of the JDDJ, finally to confirm the Joint Declaration. This is the time to let the others continue the story.

Testimony: Methodists and the Joint Declaration on the Doctrine of Justification

Ivan Abraham

Methodists, joined together by the World Methodist Council, are a young world communion compared to the Catholics and Lutherans. Although we were not part of the 16th-century controversy regarding the doctrine of justification, we felt compelled to associate with and affirm the Joint Declaration on the Doctrine of Justification. Allow me to share why Methodists pursued this action, how the process unfolded, and what is the significance of the Methodist statement for broader ecumenism.

Methodists place a special emphasis on the doctrine of justification and sanctification. In Methodist parlance, we speak of moving towards Christian perfection and holiness. After an exploratory meeting between Catholic, Lutheran, Reformed and Methodist representatives in November 2001, we pursued the idea of affirming the agreement reached in the Joint Declaration. Methodist theologians, led by Professor Geoffrey Wainwright and Bishop Walter Klaiber, prepared a statement of Methodist understanding of justification as it related to the consensus reached in the Joint Declaration. This was sent for study, debate, and comment to all the members of the World Methodist Council. Needless to say, it is our joy that on the 23rd of July 2006, we affirmed our fundamental doctrinal agreement with the teaching expressed in the Joint Declaration. Together with Catholics and Lutherans, we committed to deepening our common understanding of justification in studying, teaching and preaching in order to pursue full communion and common witness to the world.

I believe that the process was significant because it opened a new chapter in ecumenical relationships where a third party joined an agreement established by two churches. One of the fruits of our collaboration and affirmation is an ecumenical study on the biblical teaching of the doctrine of justification, published in 2012. The Joint Declaration has a multilateral character that I believe has not been fully explored. I want to invite other global communions to engage and to affirm the Joint Declaration on the Doctrine of Justification, because it helps us to restate our own self-understanding, provides an opportunity for conversation, repentance and renewal, and will begin our journey to unity.

Anglicans and the Joint Declaration on the Doctrine of Justification

Alyson Barnett-Cowan

The Anglican Communion rather slid up alongside the Joint Declaration on the Doctrine of Justification. During the 1980s, many of the themes that the JDDJ addressed were studied by ARCIC, the Anglican–Roman Catholic International Commission. In 1986 ARCIC issued a statement called 'Salvation and the Church' which did indeed address how we are set free by God's grace. We followed with great interest the development of the Joint Declaration. And with the 500th anniversary of the Reformation approaching, Anglicans were challenged in our conversations with the Lutheran World Federation to consider signing the Joint Declaration as the Methodists had done.

The Anglican Communion Office undertook a survey of theologians and of Anglican member churches and found huge agreement that what we had said previously both amongst ourselves and with Roman

Catholics and Lutherans was consistent with the substance of the JDDJ.

However, Anglicans have this small problem. The churches of the Anglican Communion have not yet come to a common mind as to how we can make binding doctrinal decisions at the global level. It often comes down to whichever body is meeting next that will take some action. So in 2016, the Anglican Consultative Council (ACC; note the adjective 'consultative') passed a resolution welcoming and affirming the substance of the Joint Declaration, noting its profound convergences with our own dialogues with Lutherans and with Roman Catholics.

And because Anglicans put a great deal of stress on liturgy, even if we can't get global authorization to sign a doctrinal statement, we can hold celebrations. A celebration was held in Westminster Abbey on Reformation Day, 2017. In the presence of representatives of the Vatican, of the Lutheran World Federation, of the Methodist World Council, and of the World Communion of Reformed Churches, the Archbishop of Canterbury presented the ACC resolution.

I should note that this celebration was hosted and planned by local churches: the Church of England and the Lutheran Council of Great Britain. And of course we sang 'A Mighty Fortress is Our God', we held a scholarly symposium about the Reformation, and we had a lovely dinner at Lambeth Palace.

But I don't want to leave you with the impression that we Anglicans are not deeply committed to this common agreement. It is truly an awesome thing that the central doctrinal disagreement that gave rise to a major schism in Christianity has to all intents and purposes been resolved. If so many Christian families have now agreed that we are no longer in disagreement about how Christ's saving sacrifice brings salvation to humanity, what is preventing us from being Christ's together in the world?

Testimony: Reformed and the Joint Declaration on the Doctrine of Justification

Chris Ferguson

When one of the most significant points of division in the Christian Church has somehow been overcome, how can we start with anything except celebration, gratitude and thanksgiving? This grace was illustrated where the hard theological work of two communions not only led the way for others, but actually, in the case of the World Communion of Reformed Churches, changed fundamentally the way they understood what was at stake in theological dialogues.

As Ivan Abraham has mentioned, in 2001 there was a consultation. We left the consultation as a world communion convinced that despite the importance of the agreement between the Lutherans and the Catholics—and it was indeed very important—it wasn't the way we would have framed the question. It led, for us, to the question of if one communion can add on to the dialogue of another by simply saying 'yes and amen'. And there is the matter of looking at a particular theological issue from a very different perspective—that is the question that Ivan raised with sanctification; for us it was around justice and justification.

There was a long fallow period: 'Thank you very much, we appreciate the work, but it's not our work.' There's a farmer's joke in Canada about a man who was lost in the field. And he saw someone and said, 'Excuse me, can you tell me how to get to this city far away?' And the farmer replied, 'If I were going there, I wouldn't start from here.' That was pretty much our approach. Instead, we had two excellent ongoing international dialogues, one with the Lutherans and the other with the Roman Catholics.

As 2017 approached, we were invited again to be part of this process and take part, learning from the witness of the Methodists and from the affirmation of the Anglicans. What we learned fundamentally was that our questions about the approach, how the question was framed, and our own theological understanding of the particularly Reformed traditional witness we want to bring to the issue remained. But we also looked deeply and the experience transformed our understanding. The method employed in this dialogue between the Lutherans and the Catholics was the method of differentiating consensus. The point was not whether we see this differently; of course we do. The point was whether this difference overpowers the notion that the power of Christ is indivisible. Should these differences continue to divide us? To this we said no. So we embraced a method and a possibility. We're thankful to the Methodists who had shown us a way. This wasn't signing on to somebody else's document; this was actually advanced math that grew exponentially. It wasn't one plus one plus two, but two all of a sudden became five. We were in a different kind of theological moment of affirming that what was happening today was more important than simply putting to rest what happened in the sixteenth century. We said that in the case of our communion, when we celebrated in 2017 both our repentance for problems of the Reformation that led to divisions and our joy in the recentring of the gospel and the way forward, we're doing it in a different way because the power to divide has been wrong and the power to work together has been reaffirmed.

Testimony: Catholic-Lutheran Relationship

Brian Farrell

As everyone knows, for centuries relations between Catholics and Lutherans were beyond bad. With the word 'Reformation', Protestants associate terms like 'rediscovery of the Gospel', the certainty of faith, and freedom of conscience; Catholics immediately think of division in the Church. That long history includes religious wars with hundreds of thousands of victims.

In 1521, Pope Leo X publicly excommunicated Luther as a heretic. Four hundred ninety-five years later, the successor of Leo, Pope Francis, together with the Lutheran World Federation, went to Lund in Sweden and solemnly commemorated the fifth centenary of the Reformation in the place where the Commission for Catholic-Lutheran dialogue first gathered in 1967.

How was this possible? It involved years of preparation which led to the drafting of three important texts: the fundamental document entitled 'From Conflict to Communion', the 'Ecumenical Worship Service' jointly prepared especially for the occasion (now called the 'Lund Liturgy'), and the 'Joint Statement' signed by Pope Francis on behalf of the Catholic Church and by President Bishop Younan, on behalf of the Lutheran World Federation. All three documents highlight the sentiments that inspired the joint commemoration: gratitude to God for the positive outcomes of the Reformation; regret for the division of the Church; and commitment to a new era of collaboration in service and mission.

You might say that the Catholic journey to the Lund event began almost sixty years ago when the Second Vatican Council acknowledged that in the history of the Church, 'people of both sides were to blame' for the divisions, and that those 'who are now born into these Communities and who grow up believing in Christ cannot be accused of the sin involved in the separation' (*Unitatis redintegratio*, 3). This acknowledgement meant that Catholics admitted that blame for the separation in the sixteenth century was not all on the other side, but on our side too. It opened the road to a deep and transforming *purification of memory*, going beyond the unilateral and self-centred way in which, for centuries, Catholics and Protestants had presented the Reformation.

A brief word about the underlying dynamic of this change is in order. Social memory operates by stereotyping the adversary and by selecting those parts of history that support a partisan view of ourselves as 'the good ones', the ones who were unjustly treated and hurt. Listening carefully to the other led us to correct our partial and self-serving perceptions and to recognize that, behind the confrontation, there remained a substantial *unity in diversity*. Fifty years of ecumenical dialogue between Lutherans and Catholics aimed at seeing things as the other side sees them and gathering the good which is present in each tradition, learning from each other.

This is not about being nice or naive. The purification of memory can take place only by starting from a deeper understanding of the truth of things, overcoming the deformed truths—nowadays called 'fake news'—handed down from generation to generation in defence of each confession's identity and self-affirmation.

So, based on sound historical research, Catholics have come to recognize the legitimate right that Luther had to be indignant about the idea that the eternal salvation of the soul, and first of all his own, was subordinated to a 'system' similar to a barter—a kind of *quid pro quo*—implemented by clerics who were not always examples of good conduct and of theological competence. That is what Luther saw in the practice of indulgences. Not surprisingly, his criticisms, which went to the heart of that 'system', provoked a vigorous reaction.

Lutherans have come to recognize that Luther's particular understanding of the Gospel and his temperament, and the religious, social and political upheaval triggered by his protest, did not lead to the reform of the Church as he first intended, but to its division.

Perhaps the phrase that best describes how a joint commemoration of the Reformation between Catholics and Lutherans became possible is found in the Joint Declaration signed by Pope Francis and Bishop Younan during the common prayer at Lund: 'While the past cannot be changed, its influence upon us today can be transformed.' In ecumenical dialogue, this is the principle behind the purification of memory: the search for a more truthful and balanced understanding and judgement of the deep differences that gave rise to our separation.

Five centuries of conflict, rivalry and prejudice between Catholics and Protestants are being overcome, slowly but surely, through a profound conversion—a journey in the opposite direction—that allows the churches *together* to distance themselves from the mistakes and exaggerations that led to their separation and to discern and take up the gifts that God is giving to each.

The Lund Commemoration

The Joint Commemoration of the Reformation at Lund was not just about Christians of different confessions getting together to pray and remember events of the past. It was a profound spiritual meeting of our corporate, ecclesial communities, recognizing each other as fellow travellers on a path of reconciliation we have chosen together, in response to Jesus' prayer and the urging of the Holy Spirit. This journey is meant to lead us in the end to full and visible communion in the body of Christ.

So Lund was a grace-filled spiritual meeting of communities that refuse to be resigned to division, but instead keep alive the hope of reconciliation. Today, the churches are committed not to continue, as in the past, to use their differences to remain separated.

At Lund we reflected on the Father as the 'vinedresser' who is constantly concerned for our relationship with Jesus (Jn 15:4). The one thing he desires is for us to abide like living branches in his Son Jesus. But Jesus says, 'Apart from me, you can do nothing' (v. 5). The Reformation principle 'by grace alone' means that God always takes the initiative, prior to any human response, even as he seeks to awaken that response. That is why at Lund we gave thanks that the Reformation helped to give greater centrality to sacred Scripture in the life of all our churches. And we Catholics recognized that the spiritual experience of Martin Luther challenges us to remember that apart from God we can do nothing. 'How can I find a propitious God?' was the question that haunted Luther. It is also the decisive question of all our lives.

Lund was a prayerful plea for unity from the very heart of our churches 'so that the world may believe'. Catholics and Lutherans committed themselves to being credible witnesses of forgiveness, renewal and reconciliation in a world that seems ever more divided and empty of meaning. Lund was a point of arrival after many years of growing closeness between Lutherans and Catholics. It was also a point of departure for all the signatories of the Joint Declaration on the Doctrine of Justification towards intermediate goals of greater mutual recognition and more effective, practical cooperation in mission and service. This was exemplified in the signing of an agreement of cooperation between Caritas and Lutheran Service.

The immediate significance of the Lund event is this: clear awareness that Christians, even if still divided, can no longer live in isolation, let alone in conflict, when it comes to witnessing to the Gospel before the world.

Now that Lutherans, Catholics, Methodists, Reformed and Anglicans agree with its substance, practically the whole of Western historical Christianity has overcome one of the fundamental controversies of the sixteenth century. But what does the multilateral JDDJ mean in the life of our churches? I think the question can be posed on two levels: spiritual and ecclesial.

Spiritually, a major source of mutual misunderstanding and apprehension has been taken away. Therefore, the members of the five signatory confessions should expect to feel a deeper sense of fellowship in the grace of Jesus Christ; a fuller recognition of each other as Christians travelling the same path of justification through the grace of Jesus Christ; and a shared commitment to showing that justification in works of goodness and service. In other words, there is no reason for these Christians to hesitate to pray together, to work together and to support each other in every form of solidarity.

The ecclesial question is more difficult. What should the JDDJ mean in institutional relations between the churches? So far, the churches themselves have said little about this hugely hopeful aspect of the agreement. But many of us are convinced that the JDDJ and the Lund event contain something new that the churches have to uncover and assimilate. The Holy Spirit has worked something new that now needs to be understood and acted upon.

As we all know, the churches and their leadership are overwhelmed by enormous demands on their attention and capacity to respond. So it is up to us to help them. The five signatories have agreed to hold a high-level consultation on the ecclesial implications of the Joint Declaration in spring 2019. This is one of the initiatives aimed at 'hearing what the Spirit is saying to the churches' (Rev. 2:29) in this particular area, the importance of which for the future of Christianity is immeasurable.

From this session on 'Relationships Old and New', I hope that we will be convinced that God is guiding his church in new ways. Allow me to repeat some words of Pope Francis:

God is the God of surprises. God is always new. (…) He always surprises us. They did not understand the many signs which Jesus did, (…) they forgot that they were a people on a journey. On a journey! And when we set out on a journey, when we are on a path, we always discover new things, things which we did not know.

Mr Huibert van Beek giving thanks for His Eminence Metropolitan Mor Gregorius Yohanna Ibrahim, who appears on the screen.

DAY TWO: WEDNESDAY 25 APRIL
LET MUTUAL LOVE CONTINUE!
RELATIONSHIPS OLD AND NEW

11.15 PLENARY SESSION

Facing Common Challenges Together in Mutual Love

Introduction

> **Larry Miller,** Session Moderator, Secretary, Global Christian Forum

Presentation of the Report of the Global Consultation on Discrimination, Persecution, and Martyrdom

- *Huibert van Beek* (Netherlands/Switzerland), Secretary (1998-2011), Global Christian Forum
- *Thomas Schirrmacher* (Germany), Associate General Secretary for Theological Concerns, WEA, and GCF Committee Member for the WEA

Giving Thanks for His Eminence Metropolitan Mor Gregorius Yohanna Ibrahim on the Fifth Anniversary of His Abduction

- *Huibert van Beek*
- *Dimitra Koukoura* (Greece), Professor of Homiletics, Aristotle University of Thessaloniki; GCF Committee Member for the World Council of Churches and the Ecumenical Patriarchate
- *Ganoune Diop* (Senegal/USA), Director, Public Affairs and Religious Liberty, Seventh-day Adventist Church; GCF Committee Member for the SDA Church worldwide

Following Christ Together in Discrimination, Persecution, Martyrdom: What Does This Mean for the Global Church Today?

Introduction by *Mor Chrysostomos Mikhael Chamoun* (Syria), Patriarchal Vicar and Director of the Patriarchal Benevolent Institutions in Atchaneh, Syrian Orthodox Church, and GCF Committee Member for the Syrian Orthodox Church

Mor Ignatius Aphrem II (Syria), Patriarch of Antioch and All the East and Supreme Head of the Universal Syrian Orthodox Church

Litany of Prayer for the Persecuted Church

Led by *Munib Younan* (Israel/Palestine), Bishop, Evangelical Lutheran Church in Jordan and the Holy Land

Call to Mission, Perceptions of Proselytism: A Global Conversation – Report to the Third Global Gathering

Rosalee Velloso Ewell (Brazil/United Kingdom), Executive Director, Theological Commission, World Evangelical Alliance (WEA)

Andrzej Choromanski (Poland/Vatican City), Ecumenical Officer, Pontifical Council for Promoting Christian Unity, GCF Committee Member for the PCPCU

Discrimination, Persecution, Martyrdom: Following Christ Together

Presentation of the Book *Discrimination, Persecution, Martyrdom: Following Christ Together: Report of the Global Conversation* (Tirana, Albania, 2-4 November 2015)

Huibert Van Beek

It is already two and a half years ago that the consultation on '*Discrimination, Persecution and Martyrdom: Following Christ Together*' took place in Tirana, Albania. At the time of the consultation, concern about the persecution of Christians was high on the agenda of the churches and specialized organisations, in particular because of the events in Northern Iraq. Daech had taken the cities of Qaraqosh and Mosul and the villages in the plain of Nineveh. The Christians (and other minorities) were targeted and threatened.

Today the situation in that part of Iraq has changed; Daech has been largely defeated. But meanwhile many Christians have left the area, and others are still waiting to return to the places where they used to live.

The issues of discrimination, persecution and martyrdom are as topical and urgent today as they were at the time of the consultation. The Christian presence in the Middle East continues to dwindle because many see no future in the land where their communities lived for centuries. Reports about Iraq predict that the Christian population will decrease to an insignificant percentage in that country. Nobody can say for sure what will happen to the Christian presence in Syria. In India, discrimination and persecution of Christians is on the rise and martyrdom is a reality.

It is therefore timely that the book with the proceedings of the 'Discrimination, Persecution, Martyrdom' consultation has come out. We had hoped to produce it earlier. All the plenary presentations and discussions in Tirana were recorded and a group started within a few months after the event to transcribe the recordings. The reports of the discussion groups were collected and analysed, and a method was developed to synthesize their content as carefully and faithfully as possible, in a style that would invite the reading of this part of the report as a reflection of the concerns of the participants. The message does that too, stating in a brief and powerful way what they, the participants, wanted to say. This is as relevant today as it was when it was made public two and a half years ago.

The target was to have the manuscript ready for editing in mid-2016. For reasons that I will not go into, the tedious work took much longer than we had thought. In consultation with Larry Miller, the deadline was shifted to November 2016, a year after the consultation. By then the manuscript was indeed ready, basically. However, unexpected problems of editing and printing caused further delay.

Yet this book is not just the record of an event that happened two and a half years ago. If that were the case, it would be enough to give it its place on the shelves of our libraries and documentation centres. No, this book is a very timely resource for the ongoing involvement of the churches and the four pillar bodies (the WEA, PWF, WCC and PCP-CU), and indeed all of us, in the issues of discrimination, persecution and martyrdom that continue to impact the life and witness of many of our Christian brothers and sisters, and of people of other faiths, in today's world and in the world of tomorrow. I would like to invite all of you to begin by reading it in that spirit—to read the stories, testimonies, descriptions and analysis, and to dive back into the reality of those three exceptional days in Tirana—as a resource to renew our commitment to prayer and action.[1]

---

1   See the 'Discrimination, Persecution, Martyrdom: Following Christ Together' Consultation Message in the appendices of this book.

The Tirana Consultation Book: a Gift to the Churches

Thomas Schirrmacher

There were two moments during the 'Discrimination, Persecution, Martyrdom' consultation at which I decided for myself that we needed this to become a book that could be distributed free to all churches. One was the presentation given by Archbishop Anastasios on a biblical theology of suffering. It was the best evangelical Bible study I have ever heard. And I thought that it needed to be documented that we really are getting closer together.

And then, very late in the consultation, we were talking about producing a message, as we always do within the Global Christian Forum. And the message we had so far was 'Don't persecute us.' I had the feeling that this was not very innovative. But then Cardinal Koch intervened and said, 'How can we call others not to persecute us if we do not apologize first that in history we have persecuted them and then that we have persecuted each other? The churches have persecuted other churches.' And if you think about the Syrian Orthodox Church, of which we have been speaking, well, it's not only your history of being persecuted by Muslims. This is what we now have in our minds, but there is a long history of Christians persecuting you.

At that moment, I knew that what we were saying was innovative, and that it had to get into the hands of everybody. This message has to be distributed as the evidence that it was in 2015, in Tirana, that we started to apologize to each other, and that on this credible base we now ask others not to persecute and discriminate against our brothers and sisters. And I'm glad this is a gift to the churches now, because Tirana was a gift to us.

Giving thanks for His Eminence Mor Gregorius

Larry Miller

The 'discrimination, persecution, and martyrdom' initiative first landed on the Global Christian Forum committee's agenda in January 2012, in Rome. It was the last meeting which His Eminence Mor Gregorius Youhanna Ibrahim of the Syriac Orthodox Church—a 'founding member' of the Global Christian Forum committee—attended. A year later he was abducted, along with Archbishop Boulos Yaziji of the Greek Orthodox Church. So we now wish to give thanks for our brother Mor Gregorius and what he has meant for the Global Christian Forum from the beginning. Huibert van Beek will offer a few words about Mor Gregorius in the GCF, Dimitra a few more words about his wider ministry, and then we will have a flute tribute for him by one of the members of the Global Christian Forum committee, Ganoune Diop.

Huibert van Beek

His Excellency Mor Gregorios became a member of the Committee of the GCF almost by accident, if I may say so. For the very first meeting on the idea of creating a Forum, in August 1998, the General Secretary of the Middle East Council of Churches, the Revd Riad Jarjour, had been invited. He had a schedule conflict and asked His Excellency Mor Gregorios, who was then a member of the Executive Committee of the MECC, to replace him.

At the end of that consultation, it was decided to set up a Continuation Committee of seven persons. As usual, an effort was made to respect representation of the various ecclesial traditions and regions. His Excellency was the only Oriental Orthodox and the only participant from the Middle East region, more than enough reasons to nominate him, not to speak of his experience and competences in the area of inter-church relationships and Christian unity.

The Continuation Committee became the GCF Committee in 2008 and His Excellency continued to serve as the Oriental Orthodox and

Middle East member of the Committee. In other words, he had been with the GCF from its very inception until the tragic event of April 2013. We all loved him for his accessibility as hierarch of his Church, his ability to speak a liberating word in moments of tension, his insights, and his good humour. His greatest wish was to host a meeting of the Committee, or even better a meeting of the Forum, in Syria. He also kept encouraging us to hold a consultation on the Forum in the Middle East region.

For various reasons, no committee meeting or Forum consultation took place in Syria. But the GCF team that visited the Middle East in 2009 came to Aleppo and was hosted by His Excellency, who arranged for a meeting with the Aleppo church leaders.

Fr Gabriel Hachem of the Greek Catholic Church and I were back in Aleppo in March 2010. His Excellency arranged for us to visit all the church leaders in the city. I remember vividly the visit with His Excellency Boulos Yaziji of the Greek Orthodox Church.

At that time, we were preparing for the very first Forum consultation in the Middle East, which was scheduled for November 2010 in Beirut. The Aleppo church leaders had accepted the invitation. Two weeks before the meeting I got a message from His Excellency that several had decided not to attend, and that therefore he himself would not come either. We had to cancel the meeting. His Excellency was very disappointed.

It was only in April 2013, two weeks before his abduction, that we were able to hold the first Forum consultation in the Middle East, in Amman. By then Syria was in turmoil. His Excellency decided that the situation obliged him to stay in Aleppo, to be with his people. On behalf of Larry Miller and myself I sent him a message with these concluding words:

> *We can only hope and pray that this message will reach you, knowing that the Internet is not always functioning. In any case, Metropolitan, be assured that we are in thoughts and prayers very much with you and with the Christians in Syria, and indeed with all*

who suffer the consequences of the war. May God keep and bless you.

I wish to conclude with a personal word. At the end of the team visit, my wife and I stayed in Aleppo and in Syria for another week. My wife had fallen ill and needed a few days to recover. We were accommodated in His Excellency's guesthouse. He did everything he could to make us feel comfortable, especially my wife. He made sure that a doctor looked after her. I was privileged to be invited to his table for the meals. On our last day in Aleppo, he arranged a trip for us to the northwest, with his car and driver. We drove up almost to the border with Turkey. The scenery of the olive trees on the hills was beautiful and peaceful. We were on the same road, with the same car and the same driver, as he and His Excellency Yaziji were four years later …

Dimitra Koukoura

I confess to you that this is a very, very difficult moment for me. I would like to forget my capacity as a professor of homiletics and I would prefer to follow the golden rule that silence is much more eloquent at special times. I am very touched by the fact that now we mention the name of Mor Gregorius because, as a professor at the University of Thessaloniki, I know students from all Christian churches in the Middle East and especially from Syria quite well. I have visited Syria twice and I am very familiar with all the places that now are in ruins.

At this moment, we recognize His Eminence Metropolitan Mor Gregorius Youhanna Ibrahim, an active member of the GCF committee. But allow me to mention also the name of the Greek Orthodox Archbishop of Aleppo, Boulos Yaziji, who has been sharing the same suffering with Mor Gregorius.

Now let me say a few words about the personality of Mor Gregorius. He was a spiritual leader and politically minded, daring to address the global community regarding the injustice and hypocrisy of the powerful in the Middle East. He was a selfless, devoted pastor and at the same time an ecumenical personality, ready to participate in interfaith and inter-Christian dialogue for the sake of the peaceful coexistence of all people on the earth, especially in the suffering, wounded Middle East, the cradle of Christianity.

And I will add: "Christ is risen."

Ganoune Diop

The early Christians faced persecution and martyrdom from both political and religious leaders of their day. To them, as to His Eminence Metropolitan Mor Gregorius Youhanna Ibrahim, Jesus gave actual words of hope. In the letter to the Christians in Smyrna (Revelation 2:8–11), Jesus says the following: 'To the angel of the church in Smyrna write the words of the first and of the last, who died and came to life. I know your tribulation and your poverty, but you are rich. Do not fear what you are about to suffer. Behold, the devil is about to throw some of you into prison that you may be tested. And for 10 days you will have tribulation. Be faithful unto death and I will give you the crown of life. He who has an ear, let him hear what the Spirit says to the churches. The one who conquers will not be hurt by the second death.'

(Editor's note: After speaking Ganoune Diop offered a moving flute solo as a tribute to His Eminence.)

Introduction of His Holiness

Larry Miller

Several years ago I visited Mor Ignatius Aphrem II, Patriarch of Antioch and All the East, and Supreme Head of the Universal Syriac Orthodox Church. The primary purpose was to ask His Holiness what we should do about the seat in the Global Christian Forum Committee that belongs to His Eminence Mor Gregorius. We agreed that His Holiness would appoint a substitute, since we do not yet know what has happened to His Eminence Mor Gregorius. The representative His Holiness chose to sit in this seat is His Eminence Mikhael Chamoun. I would like to ask you now, Your Eminence, to come and introduce his Holiness.

Mikhael Chamoun

The Middle East is boiling with wars. Christians are experiencing persecution and a new genocide. Syria, Iraq, Lebanon, Egypt, Palestine—Christians in all of these countries are suffering and are witnessing with blood to their faith in our Lord Jesus Christ. From Aleppo, His Holiness comes to Bogotá carrying the thoughts, prayers and hopes of Christians. He comes from the midst of mosques where he lives among his community, shepherding them and strengthening them in the faith. From Iraq, where he visited immediately after the attacks by ISIS, he brings the tears, pain and aspirations of his flock. His Holiness Mor Ignatius Aphrem II, Patriarch of Antioch and All the East, and Supreme Head of the Universal Syriac Orthodox Church, is a true shepherd to his people, a strong leader to the faithful through the most difficult times, a friend of Mor Gregorius Youhanna Ibrahim and his disciple. Your Holiness, welcome to the Third Global Gathering. We are all eager to listen to your speech.

Following Christ Together in Discrimination, Persecution, Martyrdom: What Does This Mean for the Global Church Today?

Mor Ignatius Aphrem II

Dear sisters and brothers in Christ, I wish to start by greeting you all with the paschal season's greetings: Christ is risen.

After giving thanks to our heavenly Father for having brought me safely here to Colombia to participate in this third Global Gathering of the Global Christian Forum, I would like to thank the Forum Committee and its secretary Rev. Larry Miller. I am extremely happy to be with you all and I truly appreciate the opportunity I am given to share a few words with you, trying to highlight two sacred issues which are really inter-connected, namely the abduction of the two Orthodox Archbishops of Aleppo and the suffering of the church in the Middle East, especially in Syria.

I am indeed very happy to be in Colombia, a country that has just recently come out of civil war. We pray for peace in Colombia and for the prosperity of the Colombian people. I also wish to express my gratitude for the witness and ministry of the churches in Colombia. Yesterday, we were given a beautiful introduction to the life of all the churches here, and I wish to bring to the attention of the participants that several jurisdictions of the Orthodox churches are also present and active in Colombia, such as the Greek Orthodox, Russian Orthodox, Serbian Orthodox and our own Syrian Orthodox Church of Antioch. As part of our Archdiocese of Central America with its headquarters in Guatemala, here in Bogotá we have three congregations and nine more in different parts of Colombia. It is our hope that these Orthodox churches will be embraced by the local faith communities and ecumenical councils in Colombia.

Dear friends, on Sunday afternoon I started my journey to Bogotá from Aleppo. Some of you know that last Sunday, April 22, marked the fifth anniversary of the abduction of the Greek Orthodox Archbishop of

Aleppo, Boulos Yaziji, and the Syrian Orthodox Archbishop of Aleppo, Mor Gregorios Youhanna Ibrahim. We went to Aleppo to commemorate the anniversary. In Aleppo, we prayed with the clergy and faithful of both churches. We wept with them but also shared in their hope for an immediate return of their two shepherds.

These two men of God presented no threat to anyone. As disciples of Christ, called by Him to tend His sheep, they were fully dedicated to their mission. Their care and compassion went beyond their immediate flock. It was extended to the community at large regardless of their religious affiliation, which earned them the love and respect of the entire society in Aleppo.

Their abduction, we believe, was a clear message targeting the Christian population of Aleppo in particular and of Syria in general. Unfortunately, the perpetrators of this heinous act of terrorism and barbarism, which amounts to a crime against humanity, have succeeded in their mission. Thousands of Christians have left Aleppo following the abduction of the two Archbishops, and hundreds of thousands have left Syria since the beginning of this global war against Syria.

The abduction of Mor Gregorius Youhanna Ibrahim and Boulos Yaziji had a huge impact on the Christian community in Aleppo, in Syria and even in the entire Middle East. It constituted a threat to the Christians rooted in their homeland in the countries of the Middle East. Their kidnapping reinforced the position of the terrorists whose not-so-hidden message to Christians was 'This land is not yours, leave or you will be killed.'

However, even five years after their abduction, the Christian community in Aleppo, although greatly reduced by numbers, remains steadfast in its faith in Christ.

Dear friends, I wish to express, on behalf of the entire Syrian Orthodox Church of Antioch, our appreciation and gratitude to the leadership of GCF for remembering Mor Gregorios Youhanna Ibrahim and for giving thanks to the Lord for the participation and dedication of Metropolitan Ibrahim in the work of the GCF since its creation.

He was a firm believer in the Forum and its mission. After relinquishing many of his ecumenical commitments, Mor Gregorios remained involved in only two ecumenical initiatives, one of which is the Forum. He saw in the Forum a real possibility to bring together Christians from all traditions of the Christian faith, something which could not be achieved through the WCC or other ecumenical bodies. He therefore held it very dear and near to his heart. I personally learnt a lot about the Forum from Mor Gregorios.

I was at the Harare General Assembly of the WCC when that body agreed to participate in the Forum. At that assembly, I was elected to both the Central and the Executive Committees of the WCC, which meant that I was able to actively join in the discussion concerning GCF involvement. However, my knowledge concerning the GCF and its work was enriched and deepened through my frequent discussions with Mor Gregorios.

(At this point, Mor Aphrem presented a five-minute video about the two abducted Archbishops.)

The Persecuted Church

In the gospel of St. John, we read the following words of the Lord: 'Remember the word that I said to you, "A servant is not greater than his master." If they persecuted Me, they will also persecute you. If they kept My word, they will keep yours also' (John 15:20). These words show the great cost of following Christ. With witnessing to the Lord both in word and in deed comes persecution and martyrdom.

Christianity is not welcomed in the world because it puts people out of their comfort zone. It challenges their worldly philosophical convictions with the simplicity of faith 'For the wisdom of this world is foolishness in God's sight' (1 Corinthians 3:19). During the early era of martyrdom, the pagan world was astonished by the joy of Christians being led to their death. The non-Christian will never understand the power of the Cross.

Christians throughout the world and throughout the centuries are victims of persecution. I come from a church, the Syriac Orthodox Church of Antioch, which faced many tribulations and genocides throughout the centuries. About a hundred years ago, a massive genocide took place in the Ottoman Empire, aiming at eliminating Christianity from the land of its birthplace. More than half a million Syriac-speaking people were massacred in the most horrible ways, together with the Armenians, Greeks and other religious minorities. Today, we continue to suffer persecution at the hands of terrorist groups such as ISIS, Al-Nusra and others, who are targeting Christian congregations and have completely destroyed many of our churches and other institutions. Because of our history of persecution and martyrdom, whenever I think of the marks of the church as being one, holy, catholic and apostolic, I immediately add to it 'persecuted'. The true church that is faithful to her Lord and Saviour has to be a persecuted one. This is also how I understand John 15:20, just quoted above.

For the last several decades, our area in the Middle East has witnessed horrible conflicts and wars which resulted in the exodus of a great number of Christians from Turkey, the Holy Land, Iraq, Lebanon, Egypt and Syria. For example, Iraq has lost more than 80 percent of its Christian population in the last fifteen years.

For the last seven years, Syria has been going through a devastating war, which destroyed most of the country and led to the killing of hundreds of thousands of its people and the exodus of millions of them. The Christian population of Syria has decreased according to our estimation by more than 40 percent since the so-called Arab Spring blossomed in our land.

I was installed, by the grace of God, as the Patriarch of Antioch in May 2014. In June of that year, I travelled to the Nineveh Plain in Iraq to visit the people of Mosul, who were forced out of their homes by ISIS—only to go back some two months later to Arbil, in the Kurdish region of Iraq, to try to comfort this time the people of Mosul together with their hosts, the Christians of the towns and villages of the Nineveh Plain, some 120,000 Christians, mainly Syriac Orthodox, Syriac Catholics and Chaldeans, who in one day became refugees. I saw some of them sleeping on the bare concrete sidewalks in Ankawa, Arbil during the burning heat of August. Others were gathered in public parks, and others were hosted inside churches and church facilities.

During that same year of 2014, I made a visit to the Syriac town of Saddad, on the outskirts of the Syrian desert, to commemorate the one-year anniversary of the martyrdom of 45 Syriac Christians at the hands of the Al-Nusra group, an offshoot of Al-Qaeda which committed the 9/11 terrorist acts. Among the martyrs of Saddad were seven members of the same family, including grandparents and grandchildren, who were killed and their bodies thrown into a well.

In 2015, I was about to depart for Albania for the Tirana consultation of the Global Christian Forum, but I had to cancel and go instead to the northeastern part of Syria, to Al-Kamishli, to try to comfort the Christians of Hassake because ISIS and other Muslim extremist groups started invading the city.

In 2016, as I was inaugurating a monument commemorating the centennial anniversary of the Syriac genocide, or Sayfo, a terrorist blew himself up some forty meters from where we were gathered. Two young people providing security for the event were killed.

Over the last years, the civilian population of Damascus has been under constant threat because of the mortars and missiles thrown at us, especially at the Christian areas of old Damascus, by groups classified by the superpowers as 'moderate opposition'. This threat ended just before Easter, earlier this month.

However, the vicious circle of violence seems to go on in our country. It is very clear that political and economic goals are to be achieved through military means at the expense of the innocent civilian people.

We were hopeful that the reclaiming of most of the Syrian geography by the Syrian army would give a chance for political settlement of the crisis in Syria. However, the attack carried out by the USA, UK and France has once again set our hope back. This unjust act of aggression based on unconfirmed reports of chemical attack carried out in Duma, a suburb of Damascus, is an indication of the low state of affairs our world has reached. While we condemn all kinds of violence committed by all sides, we expect the international community, especially the 'big guys', to respect the UN Charter and to abide by international law.

In this regard, please allow me to share with you parts of the statement issued by the three patriarchs residing in Damascus, Syria in the aftermath of this attack:

> *While we truly appreciate the concerns and prayers of millions of Christians throughout the world, we have high expectations from our sisters and brothers in the faith. We ask you to be our voice in your communities, as the unbalanced media is suffocating our voices. We need your help in lifting the economic sanctions imposed on us unilaterally. These sanctions have a devastating impact on ordinary people, not on governments.*

As a member of the family of Christ, which encompasses all Christians, kindly allow me to bring to your attention a very sensitive matter which is affecting us. Some of our sister churches are making use of this painful situation in Syria and Iraq by practising proselytism. They use food parcels and other humanitarian needs to make followers from among members of our churches, which have followed our Lord and suffered for their faith since the beginning of Christianity. I know that proselytism is not the policy nor the practice of many churches represented here; however, it is being practised nowadays in Syria and elsewhere in the Middle East.

Dear friends, the suffering of our people at the hands of terrorist groups in the name of God and religion is unbearable. Of course, Muslims and Christians are suffering; however, what Christians and other minorities are subjected to is nothing less than religious and ethnic cleansing. The UN and some countries have rightly classified it as genocide. We are hoping to see justice served by bringing to accountability members of these terrorist organizations and those who support them in different ways.

This suffering by our people and many Christians throughout the world is a reminder to all of us that following Christ has led us with Him to Golgotha and eventually to the cross. In other words, it is through the path of suffering that Christians will continue to embrace the cross of Christ, because we know that our salvation and resurrection are through the cross. For Christ has given us victory over death and sin through His death on the cross and His glorious resurrection. We therefore say with St. Paul, 'But God forbid that I should boast except in the cross of our Lord Jesus Christ, by whom the world has been crucified to me, and I to the world' (Galatians 6:14). We take pride in carrying the cross of Christ and witnessing to His resurrection to the whole world.

We continue to be the light of the world, spreading knowledge where there is ignorance and love where there is hatred. This is our mission; this is what we are called for.

Thank you for your patience. May God bless you all.

Introduction to the Litany of Prayer

Munib Younan

Sisters and brothers in Christ, in this serene and difficult moment before we start the prayers, let us remind ourselves that Christ is risen. As we celebrate today the day of Mark the Evangelist, we want to pray together for all our sisters and brothers who are persecuted for their faith in Christ. We remember all those in the Middle East, Pakistan, Iran, Nigeria, Sudan and other countries. Especially, we want to remember in this service our two brothers in Christ, Metropolitan Gregorius Ibrahim and Archbishop Boulos Yaziji, and other priests and Christians who have been abducted. Please pray for them and for all who are persecuted in the world for one reason—they stand firm in their faith in Our Lord and Saviour Jesus Christ.

I will be praying in Arabic, my mother tongue, and I hope you will answer in the language you find suitable for you.

Litany of Prayer for the Persecuted Church

By *Jay Blankespoor*, revised by *Jim Payton*, adapted by *Kim Cain*

Munib Younan: Our Lord Jesus, in describing the work of those who would follow him, said, 'They will deliver you to synagogues and prisons, and you will be brought before kings and governors for my sake. (…) You will be betrayed even by parents, siblings, relatives, and friends (…) some of you will be put to death. You will be hated because of me. But not a hair of your head will perish. By standing firm you will gain life' (Luke 21:12–14).

All: Give us the strength, Lord, to endure any persecution in your name. Help us, and all believers, to stand firm in our faith.

Munib Younan: The letter to the Hebrews tells us, 'Some faced jeers and flogging, while still others were chained and put in prison. They were stoned; they were sawed in two; they were put to death by the sword. They went about in sheepskins and goatskins, destitute, persecuted and mistreated (…) the world was not worthy of them' (Hebrews 11:36–38).

All: Thank you, Lord, for the faithful witness of those who have gone before us over the centuries, risking suffering and persecution to the point of death, in your name. They are the faithful servants whose light endures in our darkened world.

Munib Younan: Jesus said, 'If anyone is ashamed of me and my words in this adulterous and sinful generation, the Son of Man will be ashamed of him when he comes in his Father's glory with the holy angels' (Mark 8:38).

All: Give courage, Lord, to those who face persecution, discrimination, martyrdom in our age, in our time. Today and yesterday; tomorrow and the day after—and in long days and fearful nights to come.

Munib Younan: In speaking of the body of Christ, Paul reminds us that 'if one part suffers, every part suffers with it' (1 Corinthians

12:26). And elsewhere we are instructed, 'Remember those in prison, and those who are mistreated as if you yourselves were suffering' (Hebrews 13:3).

All: Lord, forgive us when we forget those who suffer for His name's sake. Give us courage to always stand in solidarity and hope.

Munib Younan: Lord, you told us, 'Blessed are those who are persecuted because of righteousness, for theirs is the kingdom of heaven. Blessed are you when people insult you and falsely say all kinds of evil against you because of me. Rejoice and be glad, because great is your reward in heaven, for in the same way they persecuted the prophets who were before you' (Matthew 5:10–12).

All: Lord, the proclamation of your Good News has come at great cost. It is precious to us. We are in the debt of the great company of heaven who have endured insult and injury so that your Gospel is alive to us.

Munib Younan: 'Bless those who persecute you; bless and do not curse' (Romans 12:14).

All: And Lord, we pray for those who persecute. Your love is not diminished or divisible, and we plead that their eyes and hearts be opened, and their lives healed. Turn them to your peace.

Munib Younan: In the midst of a desolate world, our Lord gives us this vision of a future reality: 'And I heard a loud voice from the throne saying, "Now the dwelling of God is with humanity, and he will live with them. They will be his people, and God himself will be with them and will be their God. He will wipe every tear from their eyes. There will be no more death or mourning or crying or pain, for the old order of things has passed away"' (Revelation 21:3–4).

All: Come, Lord Jesus. Come quickly; bring your fulness of life to this earth.

Together:

>Who shall separate us from the love of Christ?
>Shall trouble or hardship or persecution

or famine or nakedness or danger or sword?
No, in all these things we are more than conquerors
through him who loved us.

For I am convinced
that neither death nor life,
neither angels nor demons,
neither the present nor the future,
nor any powers, neither height nor depth,
nor anything else in all creation,
will be able to separate us from the love of God
that is in Christ Jesus our Lord. (Romans 8:35–38)

Amen.

'Call to Mission and Perceptions of Proselytism – A Global Conversation'

Report to the Third Global Gathering of the Global Christian Forum

Andrzej Choromanski and *Rosalee Velloso Ewell*

A brief history of the 'Mission and Proselytism' initiative within the GCF

According to its Guiding Purpose Statement, one of the primary aims of the Global Christian Forum is to provide an 'open space' where the representatives of various Christian traditions can address common challenges together in an atmosphere of frankness and mutual trust, especially in regard to the themes where churches are still not in agreement with one another. Following a recommendation from the Second Global Gathering in Manado, Indonesia, in 2011, broad consultation was held among the GCF participants to identify and prioritize common challenges for consideration. Two themes emerged from this conversation as of highest priority: (1) persecution and martyrdom and (2) mission and perceptions of proselytism. Two working groups were set up to dialogue, convene meetings, and prepare texts for discussion and debate so as to offer a way forward for the different Christian traditions. The conversations and discussions about persecution and martyrdom culminated with the international conference held in Tirana, Albania in 2015, about which we have already heard in this gathering.

Regarding the second major challenge, mission and perceptions of proselytism, a separate working group was formed with representatives of the four 'pillars', key leaders from other Christian traditions, and members of the GCF international committee. This working group met various times and convened a major conference in Accra, Ghana, with the original goal of reviewing a draft text for presentation at the Third Global Gathering in Bogotá. However, over the course of the dialogues and in the spirit of mutual respect and growing trust between all participants, it became clear that a 'final' text would not be the most useful or most positive way forward. Rather, the process itself was crucial and needed to continue in the different contexts where mission and proselytism create disunity and divisions within Christ's body. To agree on a final text or statement might suggest that the issues were resolved, yet we know this is not the case. Christians around the globe, in all places and all ages, need to work and to reflect continually on the character of our witness to Christ and the ways in which we heed the apostle Paul's prayer to 'love one another warmly as Christians, and be eager to show respect for one another' (Romans 10:12).

Why the theme 'mission and proselytism'?

God's mission cannot be disassociated from God's character, and it is marked by humility, grace, hope and love (Micah 6:8). Therefore, mission cannot include unethical methods, motivations, coercion, injustice or disrespect. Proselytism is characterized by a series of behaviours that by themselves or in combination undermine the dignity of the human person, humiliate other communities and betray the gospel. Proselytism is a painful, lived experience within the Christian community, one that by its very nature undermines the call of God upon people's lives. It is divisive and creates a significant obstacle to Christian unity and witness.

As mentioned earlier, these themes emerged as significant challenges to the unity of the church during the discussions and conversations of the Second Global Gathering; indeed, the matter of 'mission and proselytism' has been lifted up by GCF participants from the beginning of the Forum as a major challenge to our unity. Although all agree that the church is called to mission and evangelism following Christ's great commission (Matt 28:18–20), there is little agreement on what mission means and implies.

Powerful emotions emerge when the topic is brought up for discussion, especially when one considers the different ways in which various traditions understand and practise rites such as baptism or marriage. There has been hurt and pain on all sides, and recognizing how Christians have been a source of hurt for other Christians is one initial step in the process towards reconciliation and unity. Accusations and uses of terms such as 'sheep stealing' or 'nominal Christians' have popped up throughout the history of the church. Some churches consider themselves to be victims of 'sheep stealing', while others believe themselves to be falsely accused of proselytism. At the same time, due to prejudices and wounded feelings there is often little or no communication at all between these different streams. Therefore, the suggestion was made that through the GCF platform churches could engage in an honest and constructive conversation on this matter.

The process

We rejoice that around the world there is increasing collaboration among Christians of many different traditions on various themes and projects. The GCF working group that gathered around the theme of mission and perceptions of proselytism is just one example of such collaboration. The work of this group itself was only possible because of previous work exercised through bilateral dialogues, scholarly research and pastoral letters over many decades. Such previous dialogues were fundamental for the process of the working group, which gathered for discussion and debate and to learn from the many resources already produced on the concerns caused by proselytism.

This process included bringing together representatives from all the major Christian traditions worldwide for gatherings in Strasbourg, Geneva, Accra, and Rome, during which the working group compiled documents, letters and stories related to mission and proselytism. During subsequent meetings, key themes began to emerge, which would serve as a suggested way forward for ongoing conversations.

A larger conference with approximately 80 representatives from all the major Christian traditions worldwide took place at the headquarters of the Church of Pentecost outside Accra, Ghana in June 2017. At this conference, big topics such as the definition of proselytism, mission in contexts of persecution, and ethics of mission methods were raised as pivotal areas for further learning, debate and dialogue.

In October 2017, a smaller working group gathered in Rome and agreed that the following areas needed to be part of an ongoing process:

(1) God's love excludes no one and is the context for how we should talk about mission.

(2) God calls all Christians to love and respect one another.

(3) There is an increasing diversity of the Christian population in each local context. Such diversity brings with it challenges and opportunities.

(4) Mission belongs to the very essence of the church.

(5) Mission in our times is marked by globalization, by an unprecedented migration of peoples, and by ethnic and religious persecution.

(6) Our ongoing participation in God's mission must reflect God's character and love for all creation.

An attempt was made to draft a text that could be presented to the Third Global Gathering as a way to promote further reflection on these themes. However, due to time constraints and scheduling issues, it has not been possible to complete such a draft. It was also decided that the process was not a closed one and that it required further reflection by all churches in their different contexts.

It is the hope of all who participated in the working group and in this process that these conversations and spaces for discussion will continue both inside and outside the GCF. These are conversations for all Christians everywhere, but the shape and ways in which these will happen will differ from place to place and from tradition to tradition. It also remains the working group's hope that such dialogues will result in better and increased cooperation and Christian unity for the sake of the gospel of Jesus Christ.

Prospects for the future of the mission/proselytism initiative

The Third Global Gathering marks a culminating point of the conversation on mission and proselytism within the GCF context and is meant to be an important part of the process. As has already been stated, we now encourage the churches to continue common reflection on these issues in either bilateral or multilateral dialogues. Such reflections could also include recommendations for ethical witness and a renewed commitment to witnessing together in unity and respect.

As a final suggestion, the working group prepared some questions aimed at facilitating discussions both during the Third Global Gathering and in future group conversations. It is fitting for a report on an open process to end with these.

Questions for discussion in groups

- In your local context, do you experience tensions between your church and other churches related to mission activities of your own church or other churches? If so, can you identify the exact reasons for these tensions? Are they due to contrasting understandings of the missionary mandate?

- How would you define the difference between 'legitimate' mission on one hand and 'illegitimate' proselytism on the other hand?

- Is it admissible to address individual Christians from other churches in order to share with them the good news of salvation in Christ? If so, what are the necessary conditions for such activity? In what circumstances should addressing a Christian from a church other than one's own be considered as inadmissible proselytism?

- What are our common challenges related to mission and evangelism in the context of the modern world?

- What 'good practices' could you propose to be adopted and promoted by the churches in order to overcome competition and promote cooperation and mutual support in evangelizing the world today?

- What signs of hope can you share from your local context with regard to evangelism?

Members of the working group

ADELEYE Femi (Evangelical, Nigeria/Ghana)
Director, Institute for Christian Impact (Africa); Associate Director (Africa); Langham Preaching; Board member, Lausanne Movement; GCF international committee member

BAXTER BROWN John (Evangelical, United Kingdom)
Secretary of Ecumenical Affairs and Senior Advisor on Evangelism, World Evangelical Alliance

CHOROMANSKI Andrzej (Catholic, Vatican City/Poland)
Ecumenical Officer, Catholic Church, Pontifical Council for Promoting Christian Unity; GCF international committee member representing the PCPCU

COORILOS Geevarghese (Oriental Orthodox, India)
Metroplitan, Syrian Orthodox Patriarchate of Antioch and All the East; Moderator, Commission on World Mission and Evangelism, World Council of Churches

GOUNDIAEV Mikhail (Russian Orthodox, Switzerland/Russia)
Archpriest, Russian Orthodox Church; Permanent Representative, Russian Orthodox Church in Geneva; GCF international committee member representing the Moscow Patriarchate

HÄMÄLÄINEN Arto (Pentecostal, Finland)
Chairman, Missions Commission, Pentecostal World Fellowship; Member of the Advisory Committee, Pentecostal World Fellowship

JOHNSON Kathryn (Lutheran, USA)
Director, Ecumenical and Inter-Religious Relations, Evangelical Lutheran Church in America; GCF international committee member for the Lutheran World Federation

KEUM Jooseop (Presbyterian, Republic of Korea)
Director, Commission on World Mission and Evangelism, World Council of Churches

LUBAALE Nicta (African Instituted, Kenya/Uganda) —
General Secretary, Organization of African Instituted Churches; GCF international committee member for the Organization of African Instituted Churches

MILLER Larry (Mennonite, France/USA)
Secretary, Global Christian Forum

ROBECK, Cecil M. (Pentecostal, USA)
Professor of Church History and Ecumenics, Director of the David J. DuPlessis Center for Christian Spirituality, Fuller Theological Seminary; GCF international committee member

SCHIRRMACHER Thomas (Evangelical, Germany)
Chair, World Evangelical Alliance Theological Commission; WEA Ambassador for Human Rights; Executive Director, International Institute for Religious Freedom, WEA

VAN HOUTEN Richard (Reformed, USA)
Consultation Task Group Coordinator and Working Group Staff

VELLOSO EWELL Rosalee (Evangelical, United Kingdom/Brazil)
Executive Director, World Evangelical Alliance Theological Commission

Together in song and prayer

DAY TWO: WEDNESDAY 25 APRIL
LET MUTUAL LOVE CONTINUE!
RELATIONSHIPS OLD AND NEW

AFTERNOON INTERCHURCH GROUPS

14.30 Meetings in global interchurch groups

Conversations on Subjects from Previous Sessions and Other Group Agenda in Global Perspective

16.30 Meetings in regional interchurch groups

Conversations on Subjects from Previous Sessions and Other Group Agenda in Regional Perspective

18.30 Evening Prayer in regional interchurch groups

Evening Prayer

The Gathering of the Community

The Leader welcomes the community and begins with a prayer

Silence

A song of praise

The Proclamation of the Word

The reading and rereading (multiple languages) of Luke 24:13–27

Silence

A sharing of a word or image that comes to heart and mind of participants

Prayer

Thanksgiving

Intercession

Lord's Prayer (each in own languages)

Conclusion

L: Let us go in peace. Alleluia!

Sign of peace.

Dr Gina Zurlo

DAY TWO: WEDNESDAY 25 APRIL
LET MUTUAL LOVE CONTINUE!
RELATIONSHIPS OLD AND NEW

20.30 PLENARY SESSION

Together in the Global Church

Moderator: **Hana Kim** (Republic of Korea), Lead Pastor, Myungsung Presbyterian Church, Seoul

Prayer

Cecil M. (Mel) Robeck, Jr. (USA), Pentecostal, Global Christian Forum Committee Member

Global Christianity: Continuity and Change

Gina A. Zurlo (USA), Co-Director, Center for the Study of Global Christianity; Co-Author, *The World Christian Encyclopedia*

The Global Bible Landscape

Michael Perreau (United Kingdom), Director General, United Bible Societies

Receptive Learning Between Churches

Gabrielle Thomas (United Kingdom), Research Fellow, Transformation through Receptive Learning Between Churches, Durham University

Prayer

Cecil M. (Mel) Robeck, Jr.

Your Church is broken, O Lord, and all of us participate in that brokenness.

You gave us but one Church. Today, we exist in over 42,000 denominations and countless independent congregations.

We were all born into this ecclesial brokenness, and far too many of us take this reality as normal. But it is not.

All too often, our actions towards one another suggest, 'We have no need of you.' We have confused division with the diversity with which you gifted your Body. We have been content to live with stereotypes. We have distanced ourselves from one another. We have borne false witness against one another.

And all too often, we have worked against one another, hoping that they would fail.

You told us to go and make disciples of all nations, baptizing them and teaching them all that you have commanded us. 'A new commandment I give to you. Love one another. As I have loved you, so you must love one another.' 'If you love me, keep my commandments.'

In many ways, we have failed you. Some of us have failed to take seriously the expressions of faith that others hold dearly. Some of us have stolen sheep from the flocks rightly belonging to others. Some of us have failed to speak directly to those who have offended them or stolen from them.

We have not loved one another as we should, and now we have the issue of proselytism before us.

Grant us, O Lord, the wisdom to speak boldly to this issue. Grant us the patience to demonstrate your love one to another by resolving this issue between us.

We need your forgiveness—all of us—so that the world will see a new standard of love among us, and unity will prevail.

We have gathered here under the banner, 'Let mutual love continue', but our love is small. Help this love to grow as we seek to do what you have commanded us to do: 'Love one another as I have loved you.'

Amen.

Together in the Global Church

Global Christianity: Continuity and Change

Gina A. Zurlo

My presentation tonight tells the story of Christianity through the dual lenses of continuity and change. I am the assistant director of the Center for the Study of Global Christianity at Gordon-Conwell Theological Seminary in South Hamilton, Massachusetts, USA. We are an academic research centre that monitors worldwide demographic trends in Christianity, including outreach and mission. We provide a comprehensive collection of information on the past, present, and future of Christianity in every country of the world. Our data and publications help churches, mission agencies, and non-governmental organizations to be strategic, thoughtful and sensitive to local contexts. Some of you might already follow our research, or perhaps you knew our founder, David Barrett, or our current director, Todd Johnson.

One of our two main projects right now is the *Edinburgh Companions to Global Christianity* (Figure 1), a ten-volume series highlighting regional trends and issues in Christianity throughout the world, featuring articles written by local Christians everywhere. The first volume, on sub-Saharan Africa, came out last year, and this year's volume on North Africa and West Asia will be out next month. Our second big project is the third edition of the *World Christian Encyclopedia* (Figure 2), which will feature all new data, updated articles on the history of Christianity in every country of the world, and a full-colour online version.

The purpose of my talk tonight is to provide a broad picture of the makeup of global Christianity as it stands today and to point out some prominent trends as we think about the global church in the twenty-first century. Some questions for us to consider as we take this demographic journey include: Where has Christianity moved over time? Who makes up global Christianity? What diversity exists within global Christianity? What does global Christianity look like today?

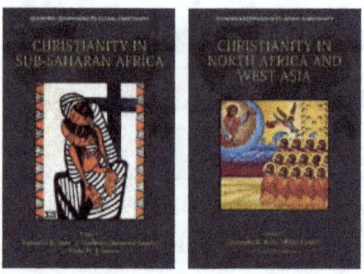 

Figure 1 (left): *Edinburgh Companions to Global Christianity*
Figure 2 (right): *World Christian Encyclopedia*, November 2019

I'd like to highlight three important findings as we explore these questions. The first is Africa's new place in global Christianity as of 2018. Second is the rise of independent Christianity—that is, Christians who self-identify separately from Catholics, Orthodox, and Protestants. The third is a new feature of our research, a level of denominational affiliation that we're calling ecclesiastical 'families'.

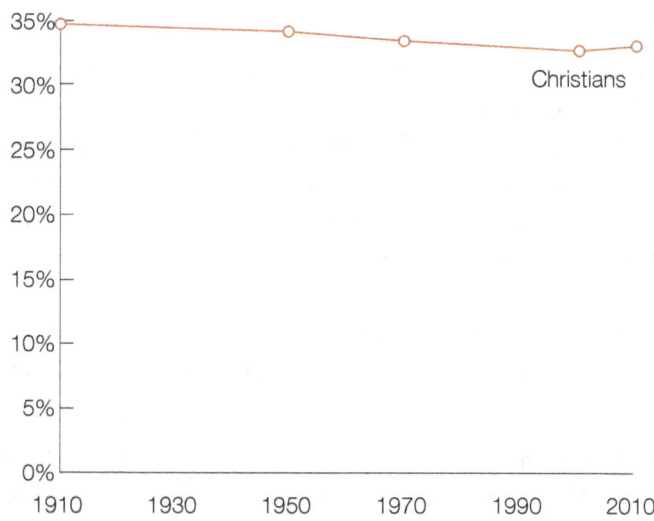

Figure 3: Christianity over time, 1910-2010

This boring line graph in Figure 3 doesn't appear to tell a very exciting story of Christianity in the twentieth century. Our 2009 Atlas of Global Christianity reported that 35 percent of the world was Christian in

1910, and roughly 32 percent was Christian in 2010. This flat line hides the massive changes in global Christianity over the century, often described as the shift of Christianity to the Global South.

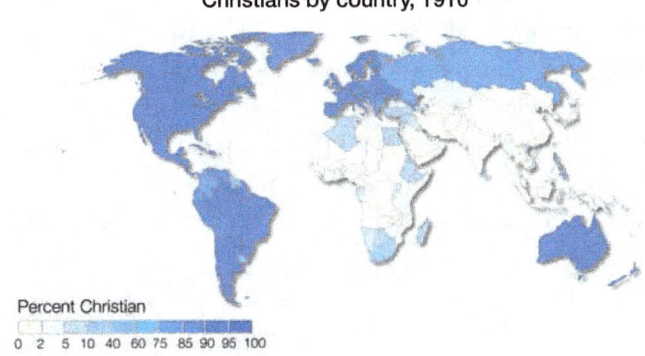

Figure 4: Christianity by country, 1910

Figure 4 is a map of Christian affiliation in the year 1910, where the darker blue represents a higher percentage of Christians. Unsurprisingly, Christianity was concentrated in the historic areas of 'Christendom' in Europe and North America. However, over the hundred-year period, Christian affiliation has decreased slightly in the north and increased substantially in the south. Take, for example, sub-Saharan Africa, which is now very dark blue. In 2010 (Figure 5), you could also see large concentrations of Christians in East Asia, Southeast Asia, and India.

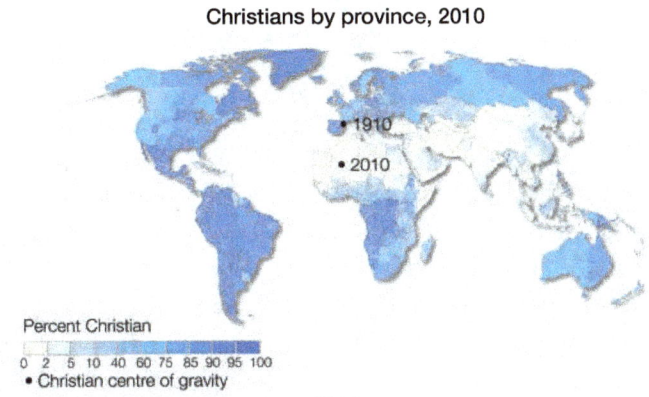

Figure 5: Christianity by province, 2010

Let's take a closer look at sub-Saharan Africa and changes between 1970 and today. Sub-Saharan Africa was home to 134 million Christians in 1970 and grew to an astounding 621 million Christians by 2018. You can see a gradual lightening of the blue as you move further up the region toward Muslim-majority North Africa in Figure 6. The line graph shows change over time—that is, a rapid growth of Christianity in the region from 1970 to 2000 and an easing of growth since the turn of the twenty-first century. In a sense, we can conceptualize Christianity in sub-Saharan Africa as 'continuity' over the 48-year period. Christianity continues to grow, although now at a slower rate.

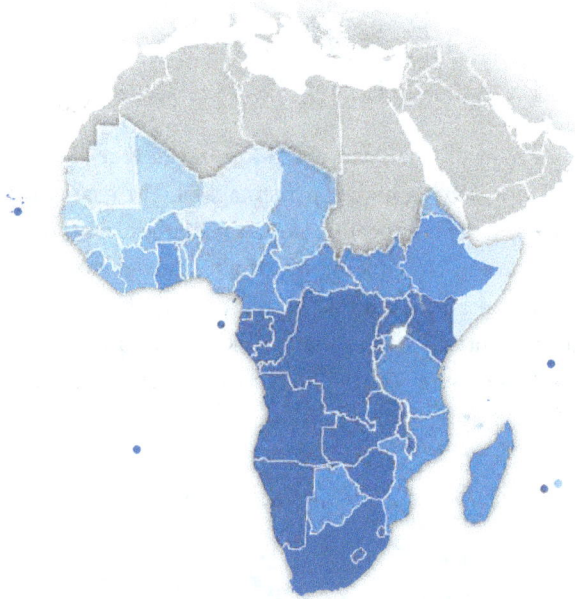

Figure 6: Christians in Africa, 2015

In contrast to the continuity narrative in sub-Saharan Africa is the narrative of change in North Africa and West Asia (or the Middle East; Figure 7). This region was home to twelve million Christians in 1970 and twenty-five million in 2018, but these figures hide the tragic exodus of historic Christian communities in the region, despite roughly four hundred years of Christian stability in the region before the twentieth century. Looking at the two dates comparatively reveals a downward trend of Christian affiliation due to war, strife and persecution. It is critical to keep the story of Christianity in the Middle East at the front and centre of discussions of world Christianity to prevent the narrative of growth from overcoming the narrative of struggle and survival.

Christians in North Africa and West Asia, 2015

Figure 7: Christians in North Africa and West Asia, 2015

Figure 8 shows the layout of all Christians today by continent, as 2.5 billion people and 33% of the world's population. Latin America is home to the highest percentage of Christian affiliation at 92 percent, followed by Europe (77%) and North America (76%). However, what this map doesn't show is that 2018 marks the first year that Africa has the most Christians—thirty million more than Latin America. This year marks a milestone for African Christianity and raises several important theological issues related to Christianity's shift to the south. Are Christian resources also shifting? Is theological writing shifting? Is Africa the new centre of global Christianity and if so, what does that mean for the gradual decline of Christianity in the West?

Christians by continent, 2018
2.5 billion total, 33% of global population

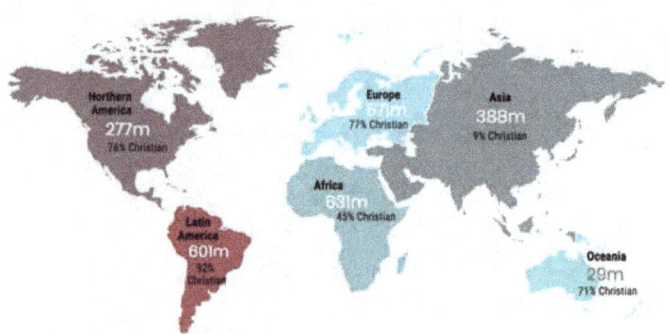

Figure 8: Christians by continent, 2018. 2020 marks the first year that Africa has the most Christians – 30 million more than Latin America. (Source: Todd M. Johnson & Gina A. Zurlo, eds. *World Christian Database.* Leiden/Boston: Brill, accessed April 2018. Not equal to total Christians because unaffiliated and double-counted are excluded.

Looking more closely at the shift to the south, we can see that this is a trend that we expect to continue. The bar chart in Figure 9 gives us a longer perspective on Christianity's shift to the south. It shows the steady decline and then more recent growth in the percentage of Christians in the Global South from the time of Christ to the present. Note that Christians in the Global South represented at least 50 percent of all Christians from the beginning of Christianity until the year 923. For over a thousand years after that, Christians in the Global North dominated Christian demographics. By the time of the Reformation, 92 percent of all Christians were Europeans. But in the twentieth century a dramatic turnaround resulted in the majority of Christians once again living in the Global South. In 1970, 43 percent of Christians lived in the Global South. Christianity became a majority–Global South faith in 1981, and today in 2018, a full two-thirds of Christians live in Asia, Africa, and Latin America (Figure 10).

Looking at the north-south dynamic in all four major Christian traditions—Catholics, Orthodox, Protestants, and independents—reveals an interesting picture of global Christianity. Similar to Christianity as a whole, independent Christianity has shifted to the south with the increase of independent denominations in Asia and Africa since the 1950s, moving the centre of gravity away from North America.

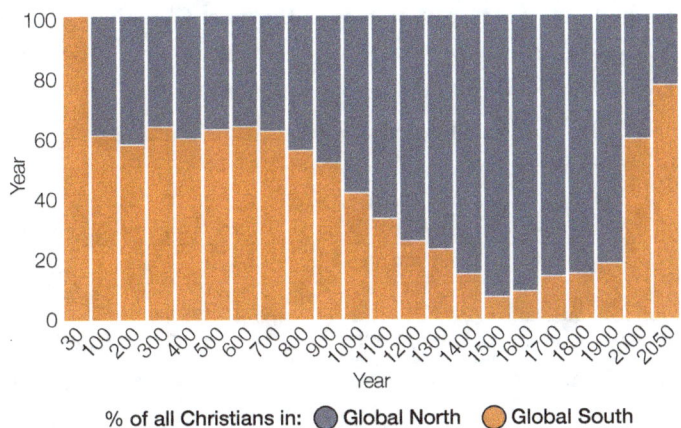

Figure 9: Christianity in the Global North and South, 33–2050 (Source: World Christian Database)

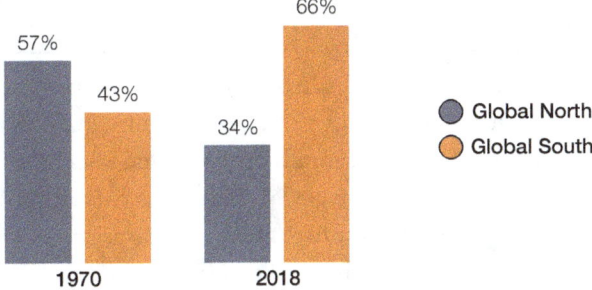

Figure 10: Christians in the Global North and South, 1970 and 2018

Orthodox Christianity is quite different from the other traditions, as it is historically home to the Middle East and Eastern Europe. Protestantism has seen a dramatic shift to the south since the twentieth century, and now Africa is home to more Protestants than Europe. Finally, Catholicism has been centred in the Global North for centuries, but only in the mid- to late twentieth century did we start to see that trend reverse.

Looking at a more local level, the following tables show the countries with the most Christians in 1970. You can see only three in the Global South on the list: Brazil, Mexico, and the Philippines, ranked second, fourth, and ninth. However, as of 2018, the picture is drastically different. Eight of the ten countries with the most Christians are in the Global South: Brazil, Mexico, China, the Philippines, Nigeria, the Democratic Republic of the Congo, India and Ethiopia.

Table 1: Countries with the most Christians, 1970 and 2018

1970			2018		
1.	United States	191,277,000	1.	United States	251,823,000
2.	Brazil	90,739,000	2.	Brazil	191,254,000
3.	Germany	70,516,000	3.	Mexico	125,347,000
4.	Mexico	50,620,000	4.	China	123,005,000
5.	Russia	49,731,000	5.	Russia	118,127,000
6.	United Kingdom	49,297,000	6.	Philippines	96,621,000
7.	Italy	47,360,000	7.	Nigeria	91,122,000
8.	France	42,644,000	8.	DR Congo	80,052,000
9.	Philippines	33,607,000	9.	India	65,156,000
10.	Spain	33,203,000	10.	Ethiopia	64,037,000

We also see change in global Christianity when looking at its make-up by tradition (Figure 11). In 1970, over half of all Christians were Catholics, followed by Protestants, Orthodox, and then independents. However, over this period the global church has experienced the rise of independent Christianity, where independents nearly equal Protestants in number and are likely soon to outnumber them.

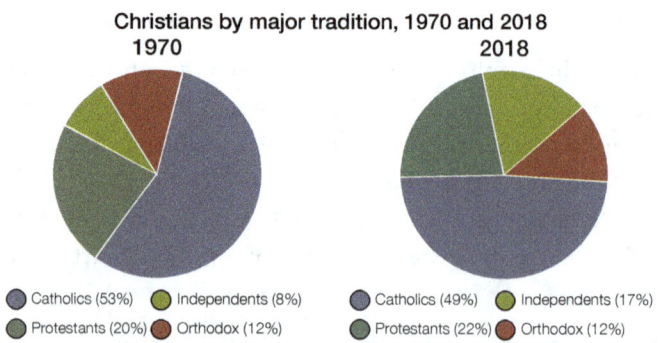

Figure 11: Christians by major tradition, 1970 and 2018. Percentage of all Christians excluding unaffiliated and double-affiliated.

Independent Christians are those who self-identify outside of traditional Catholic, Orthodox, and Protestant Christianity, such as African Independent Churches, house-church movements in China and elsewhere, independent charismatic networks, informal networks, and churches that claim a 'post-denominational' characterization. Independent Christianity represents the latest in a long line of major historical realignments within global Christianity. These leaders and members typically self-identify as 'independent' and are not formally connected to Orthodox, Catholic, and Protestant Christianity.

There are two primary ways for a denomination to be independent. The first is by splintering from an existing, usually mainline denomination. There are numerous historical examples of this, such as the Stone-Campbell Movement. The Disciples of Christ are Protestants, but the Christian Churches and Churches of Christ are independents because they broke from the Disciples of Christ. The Churches of Christ are open in their self-identification as outside of historic, mainstream Protestantism.

Another example is the Methodist Pentecostal Church of Chile, which split from the Methodist church in 1909; the Pentecostal Church of Chile broke from the Methodist Pentecostal Church in 1947 and the Pentecostal Mission Church broke from the Evangelical Pentecostal Church in 1952. There are more contemporary examples as well, such as the splintering of the Anglican Church of North America from the Episcopal Church USA. Despite having 'Anglican' in its name, the ACNA is not a part of the Anglican Communion because it split from the Episcopal Church, which is a part of the Communion. The creation of independent churches from Protestants is quite common both in the past and present.

The second kind of independents is those that began independently of Catholic, Orthodox, and Protestant Christianity. Often these movements began with revivals or around charismatic leadership and grew into legitimate denominations in their own right. The Church of Jesus Christ of Latter-day Saints is an example, as are numerous African Independent Churches that sprouted in the second half of the twentieth century. A highly visible example is the Universal Church of the Reign of God, founded by Edir Macedo in 1977. Macedo was a part of a mission-founded Pentecostal church but was not accepted by its leadership and eventually founded a separate denomination. Another example is the Zion Christian Church, found throughout Southern Africa, which was founded by Engenas Lekganyane in 1925. Lekganyane was originally part of an Anglican mission but founded his own movement after receiving a vision from God in 1924. Independent churches have been growing by leaps and bounds and represent a new era of world Christianity.

The two bar charts in Figure 12 illustrate the makeup of Christianity by a new way of demographically conceptualizing the word *church*—by what we're calling 'families'. These are families of autonomous churches or denominations around the world that are linked by similar ecclesiastical tradition, history and name, and usually by some informal or formal organizations. These terms probably sound familiar to you: Baptist, Lutheran, Methodist, Anglican, etc. Although these sound like traditional Protestant denominations, these families are made up of both Protestants and independents. For example, there are Protestant Baptist denominations like the Southern Baptist Convention and the Baptist General Conference, but there are also independent Baptist denominations like the National Baptist Convention and Baptist Bible Fellowship International. Likewise, there are Protestant Methodists like the United Methodist Church, but also independent Methodists like the African Methodist Episcopal Church and the Jesus Korean Methodist Church. These families are different from global councils of churches, such as the Lutheran Federation, which typically don't consider independents as part of the family. In creating this level in the taxonomy, we're making a statement that, first, independent denominations exist and are important in world Christianity, and second, that they are still related ecclesiastically with their Protestant counterparts.

These bar charts (and accompanying table) reveal another set of continuity and change in global Christianity. Historic 'mainline' churches have remained somewhat static as a portion of the world's Christians between 1970 and today, but we've seen a significant rise in Pentecostal/charismatic churches, many of which are independents. In 1970, only 5 percent of the world's Christians were Pentecostal/charismatic, but as of

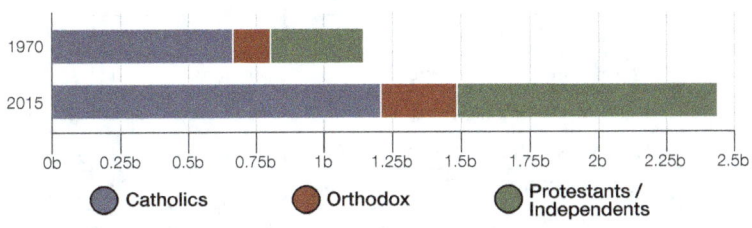

Catholics	Orthodox
Latin-rite Catholic (49%)	Eastern Orthodox (8.9%)
Eastern-rite Catholic (0.8%)	Oriental and other Orthodox (2.6%)
Old Catholic Church (0.2%)	

Protestants / Independents	
Pentecostal / Charismatic (13.5%)	Jehovah's Witnesses (0.8%)
Anglican (3.8%)	Latter-day Saints (Mormons) (0.7%)
Nondenominational (3.5%)	Holiness (0.6%)
Baptist (3.4%)	Restorationist, Disciple (0.3%)
United Church or joint mission (2.8%)	Congregational (0.2%)
Lutheran (2.6%)	Hidden believers in Christ (0.2%)
Reformed, Presbyterian (2.6%)	Christian Bretheren (0.2%)
Methodist (1.3%)	Mennonite (0.1%)
Adventist (1.1%)	Other Protestant/Independent (1.3%)

Figure 12: Christianity by 'family', 1970 and 2015.
(Source: Todd M. Johnson & Gina A. Zurlo, eds. *World Christian Database.* Leiden/Boston: Brill, accessed April 2018. Not equal to total Christians because unaffiliated and double-counted are excluded.)

2018, over 27 percent are. Asia is home to the largest proportion of Pentecostals/charismatics (40%), followed by Africa (34%), Latin America (33%), and Northern America (28%). Europe has the smallest concentration of Pentecostal/charismatics at only 4 percent in 2018.

Table 2: Largest Denominations by Country, 2015

1.	Igreja Católica no Brasil	Brazil	149,550,000
2.	Iglesia Católica en México	Mexico	111,233,000
3.	Russian Orthodox Church	Russia	109,650,000
4.	Han house Church	China	82,400,000
5.	Catholic Church in the Philippines	Philippines	78,271,000
6.	Catholic Church in the USA	United States	72,798,000
7.	Chiesa Cattolica in Italia	Italy	45,563,000
8.	Eglise Catholique au Congo-Zaire	DR Congo	42,891,000
9.	Iglesia Cathólica en Colombia	Colombia	42,706,000
10.	Iglesia Cathólica en España	Spain	39,967,000

Largest Protestant/Independent Denominations by Country, 2015

1.	Han house churches	China	82,400,000
2.	Three-Self Patriotic Movement	China	26,000,000
3.	Assemblelias de Deus	Brazil	25,000,000
4.	Evangelische Kirche in Deutchland	Germany	24,450,000
5.	Church of England	United Kingdom	23,400,000
6.	Anglican Church of Nigeria	Nigeria	22,000,000
7.	Southern Baptist Convention	United States	20,000,000
8.	Church of Uganda	Uganda	14,185,000
9.	Eglise de Jésus Christ sur la Terre par Son Envoyé Spécial Simon Kambangu	DR Congo	12,000,000
10.	National Baptist Convention	United States	9,195,000

(Source: Todd M. Johnson & Gina A. Zurlo, eds. *World Christian Database.* Leiden/Boston: Brill, accessed April 2018.)

Moving to the denominational level, Table 2 presents the largest denominations by country today. The top table (above) shows that, with the notable exceptions of the Russian Orthodox Church in Russia and house churches in China, the Catholic Church is the largest denomination in many countries with large Christian populations. The bottom table (above) gives a different country-level perspective by looking at only Protestant and independent denominations. Here you can see a greater diversity of world Christianity, with the Assemblies of God,

Evangelical Church, Anglicans, Baptists, and Kimbanguists. These tables also allow for some interesting comparisons and intriguing lines of thought as we look to the future of world Christianity. China is the world's largest country with 1.3 billion people. Even though China is only roughly 8 percent Christian, it is home to two of the largest church networks in the world, one officially sanctioned by the government and the other unsanctioned, or 'underground'.

Reflecting on the dual trends of continuity and change in global Christianity brings us to several important questions. What are the theological implications of Christianity's shift to the south? What are the implications of the continued growth of independent Christianity? How can we help make independent Christianity more visible to the church in the West? What can churches in the West learn from those in the Global South who are now in the majority? How does the new makeup of global Christianity impact mission efforts worldwide?

The Global Bible Landscape

Michael Perreau

We live today in a '**FUTURES**' world. It's **F**ast and **U**rban with more people living in urbanized environments because of economic attractions. The population is increasingly **T**echnologically minded and **U**niversally connected through digital means. Yet despite these trends, our world is becoming more nationalistic and **R**adical and our future generations are becoming more vocal on **E**nvironmental issues. In the midst of all this, people continue to yearn for **S**piritual connection.

The global Bible landscape can best be summarized into four dimensions of challenges:

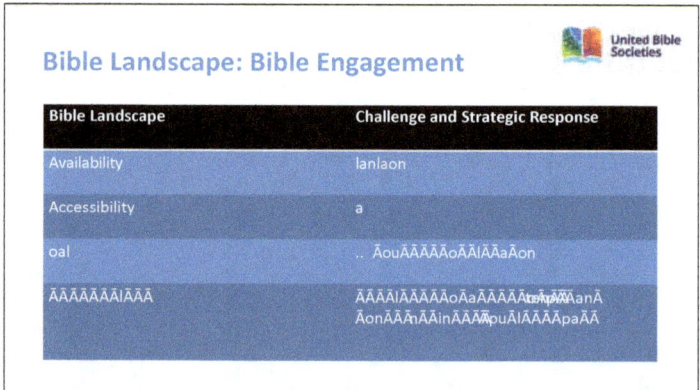

- There are parts of the world where the challenge for the Bible is credibility. Within these environments, we need to become more competent and confident in the public space.

- Where accessibility of the Bible is a challenge, we need to leverage creative resourcefulness and utilize digital opportunities, for example.

- There are still places where both the availability and affordability of the Bible are a challenge. Within these environments, the priority is to provide access to Bibles that are translated into people's heart language.

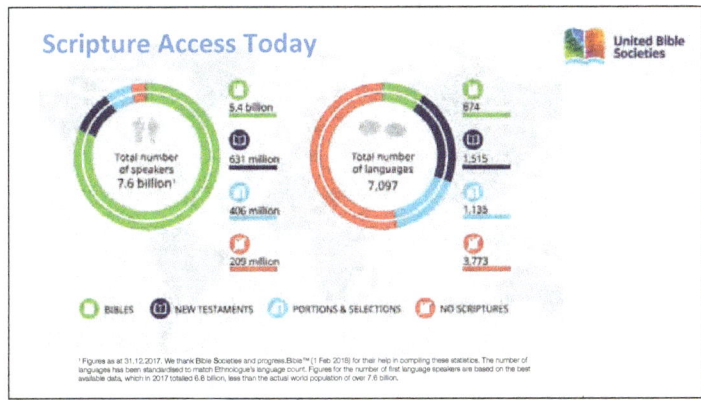

We invite you to join your hands and hearts to help us to address the challenges and to seize the opportunities before us as we live and work to make the Bible available to everyone.

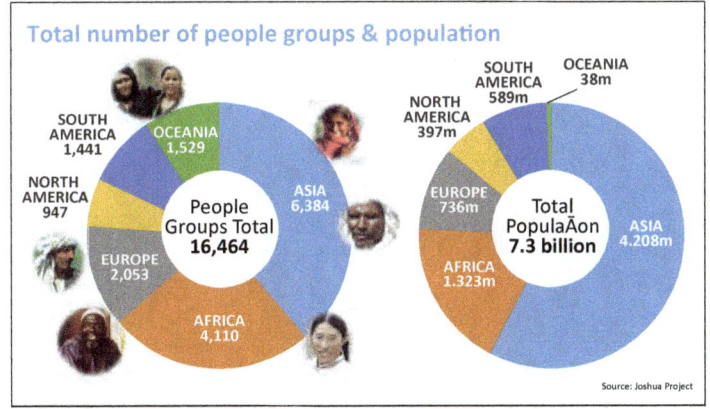

After this I looked, and there before me was a great multitude that no one could count, from every nation, tribe, people and language, standing before the throne and before the Lamb. They were wearing white robes and were holding palm branches in their hands.
—Revelation 7:9 (New International Version)

Receptive Learning Between Churches
Gabrielle Thomas

Thank you for inviting me to share with you all this evening. I value the opportunity to engage with and learn from brothers and sisters in Christ from across the globe. I've been asked to speak about perspectives for learning and transformation across our churches, particularly in the context of Christian traditions which are diverse.

I work as a researcher at Durham University, in the northeast of England, and I am an ordained priest in the Church of England, serving in Durham Cathedral. The research I am leading asks, 'How might diverse churches both learn from and receive gifts from one another?' This question forms the basis of the following presentation, 'Receptive Learning Between Churches'. We shall explore briefly how both learning and receiving gifts from one another's churches can lead to transformation.

My motivation for being involved in the area of research on which I am speaking this evening stems from when I was a young teenager. I grew up in a rural village in England in which there was one small Anglican Church, since other denominations gradually closed due to lack of numbers. I was the only young person who went to church each week. As I grew up, in order to meet with other young Christians, I joined a lively youth group hosted by a Baptist church in a nearby town. They welcomed young people from all kinds of churches, and there were a number of us who came from different denominations. This meant that we were a diverse group, and we enjoyed our diversity. Consequently, during my formative teenage years, I prayed with, worshipped with, and was involved in various aspects of mission with Christians from very diverse churches. As a young Christian, this made a big impact upon me. It has shaped my subsequent passion for engaging with churches and exploring how the Spirit is gifting and equipping churches in different ways, and also how we might learn from one another to better serve Christ.

My presentation this evening will move through three phases. First, I shall highlight important learning from Scripture, which undergirds the churches' motivations for engaging with one another in this way. Second, I shall offer a brief overview of what receptive learning entails and the methodological principles involved. Finally, I shall close by suggesting the potential impact of churches seeking to learn and receive from one another and I will leave you with some resources so that you can follow up on this when you are back home.

Scriptural witness

Learning receptively from other churches takes seriously the way in which Scripture calls believers to live peaceably and in unity with one another. I shall discuss just three of the themes in the Bible which point to why we would want to think about learning and receiving from one another's diverse traditions, although there are many more. One example of why Christians would want to receive from one another is John 17:20–21:

> *I ask not only on behalf of these, but also on behalf of those who will believe in me through their word, that they may all be one. As you, Father, are in me and I in you, may they also be in us, so that the world may believe that you have sent me. The glory you have given me, I have given them, so that they may be one as we are one.*

This is Christ's final prayer for his followers in John's gospel. It is no coincidence that the last prayer that Jesus prays is for believers to love one another and live in unity. This verse is often cited when Christians speak about church unity. It's not simply that Christians need to love one another for Jesus to be glorified, but this also points to the importance of our shared life in Christ. We seek to learn from other churches because we want to draw closer to one another and demonstrate the love of Christ in the world.

Second, we draw from the theme in the book of Revelation, which repeats the phrase, 'Let anyone who has an ear hear what the Spirit is saying to the churches.' In Revelation, each time the Spirit speaks to the churches, they are called to repentance and transformation. In light of this, we ask, 'In what ways is the Spirit calling our churches to repent?' Key to receptive learning is the assumption that none of our churches are perfectly serving the Kingdom of God. Therefore, we lean into the Spirit and ask for guidance regarding our denominational weaknesses. This requires courage and humility, since it can be painful to come face to face with our own weaknesses and failings as churches. But we hope and trust in the Spirit for transformation and renewal. We know that the Spirit longs to lead us into unity and for Christ's prayer to be fulfilled.

The third theme arising in Scripture recognises God as the giver of all good gifts. This is a recurring theme throughout the whole biblical narrative, but we will note one example in Matthew 7:7–11:

> *Ask, and it will be given you; search, and you will find; knock, and the door will be opened for you. For everyone who asks receives, and everyone who searches finds, and for everyone who knocks, the door will be opened. Is there anyone among you who, if your child asks for bread, will give a stone? Or if the child asks for a fish, will give a snake? If you then, who are evil, know how to give good gifts to your children, how much more will your Father in heaven give good things to those who ask him!*

As God's children we are told to 'ask and you will receive, seek and you will find.' In light of this, receptive learning is about acknowledging that the Spirit gives gifts to the churches, equipping believers for mission and ministry. Therefore, through prayer and conversation, we open ourselves to the possibilities of receiving gifts from other churches, particularly in relation to where we are weakest.[1]

Receptive learning

With the backdrop of the biblical witness in place, let us turn to what we mean by receptive learning. Originally developed in the northeast of England just over a decade ago, in the past few years receptive learning has begun to be applied globally. We have experienced enthusiastic attendance at conferences in the UK and USA, and most recently, in November 2017, Christians from over 15 denominations gathered together to learn from one another in Canberra, Australia. One aspect of its appeal is that participation is possible on a number

---

1 For further reading on the Scriptural Witness, see chapter 1 in Gabrielle Thomas, *For the Good of the Church* (London, SCM Press, 2021).

of different levels and in a variety of contexts. It can be applied in any setting from grass-roots groups to formal discussions.

The first point I want to make is that receptive learning is not simply a method which we can follow to achieve certain results. In many ways, receptive learning complements the values embodied in the Global Christian Forum. Rather than taking the form of a dogmatic method, receptive learning resembles more a way of churches engaging with one another in order to learn and receive from each other. It is highly relational, since without hospitable and trusted relationships receptive learning will not flourish. Because of its fluidity, how receptive learning works itself out in the Global North would most likely look different in the Global South. Therefore, what I offer this evening should not be taken as a strict method to be transported word for word. Rather, it is best adapted to suit the context which we inhabit.

Receptive learning is a journey which involves repentance and conversion. Repentance is key to becoming more like Christ. Each church is encouraged to examine itself and ask, 'Where are we broken?' or 'Where do we need healing?' How we approach this can vary. For example, a church might want to examine itself in relation to structure, organisation, practices, worship, leadership, culture, or any practical aspect of church life. Or there might be aspects of our doctrines which we need to interrogate. An important early stage is being able to examine our churches and move on to take the courageous step of recognising where we need to change or develop. This is no easy task and calls for the kind of humility which we find in Philippians 2:

> *If then there is any encouragement in Christ, any consolation from love, any sharing in the Spirit, any compassion and sympathy, make my joy complete: be of the same mind, having the same love, being in full accord and of one mind. Do nothing from selfish ambition or conceit, but in humility regard others as better than yourselves.*

So, before any engagement with other churches occurs, in humility we examine ourselves in a particular area, either one in which we find ourselves struggling or one in which we recognise that we are broken.

We ask, 'What are the challenges we face and how are other churches approaching these challenges?' We must be willing to repent and allow the possibility of the Spirit healing and transforming us through others.

The next move consists of listening and learning. Churches practising receptive learning seek to listen to one another. This cannot be done outside of trusting and hospitable relationships, which is where it reflects the values of GCF gatherings. The theme of our gathering this year is taken from Hebrews 13:1, 'Let mutual love continue.' In the same way that we are meeting with one another here, with a view to forming new relationships and continuing to develop existing friendships, receptive learning cannot occur outside of mutual love and trust. No one wants to learn from someone whom they do not trust. Mutual love and hospitality are key to being able to listen, learn from and receive from the other.

Rather than coming together and expecting to teach a church about our practices, instead we come to listen and to learn from another. This is a little different from how we sometimes approach other churches. When we come together, we might be keen to explain why our church is best. Instead, receptive learning means that we come to another church and listen. Having recognised our own weaknesses, we encounter another church expectantly, trusting that the Spirit has given to the other church gifts and treasures from which we may learn. It is not intended to be a purely cognitive process; it has been described as a 'matter of the heart', which consists of 'falling in love with the experienced presence and action of God in the people, practices, even structures of another tradition'.[2] The idea is not that we learn *about* but that we learn *from*. This means that churches are required to be open and willing to engage with one another. However, it's not about one church turning into another. Each church is called to become more fully itself, more whole, more like Jesus.

---

2   Paul D. Murray, 'Receptive Ecumenism and Catholic Learning: Establishing the Agenda', in *Receptive Ecumenism and the Call to Catholic Learning: Exploring a Way for Contemporary Ecumenism*, ed. Paul D. Murray (Oxford: Oxford University Press, 2008), 14.

After listening and learning, we move to receiving gifts with wounded hands. I offer the image of opening hands out to receive gifts from other churches. As a church holds out its hands, we see that the hands bear wounds. The church does not pretend to be perfect, since each church humbly recognises that it does not image Christ fully. The hands are ready to receive, and they are accompanied by a recognition that there are gifts to be received from other churches—gifts which may heal our brokenness.

Undergirding all these principles is the belief that the unity of the churches is the will of the Spirit. Receptive learning takes seriously the scriptural call to unity. This is not the work of humankind but rather the transforming work of the Spirit, who is calling churches to grow visibly together in structural and sacramental unity. This is not a quick fix or a short-term project, but a commitment to journeying towards union in God and unity with one another.

It is not an easy path. Often, as churches, we are far more comfortable to come together and tell each other about why our church practices or doctrines are correct. Often, we are more comfortable to have others think like us. It takes courage and humility to seek to learn from others, rather than to teach them our way of being church. The following prayer encapsulates the spirit of receptive learning:

> Loving God, Father, Son and Holy Spirit, we ask that you would help us to allow your Holy Spirit to work in us and through us.
>
> Grant us a spirit of generosity to reach out to you and one another in trust.
>
> Give to us, we pray, the humility to accept that our church is broken.
>
> Give to us, we pray, the discernment to recognise where we may learn from others.
>
> Give to us, we pray, the gift of hospitality so that we may receive gifts from others.
>
> Thank you, gracious God, for all your gifts to us. Amen.

Potential Impact

The potential impact of receptive learning on our churches is:

- Repentance and healing
- Learning and receiving
- Transformation and renewal
- Moving towards visible unity across the churches

Over the past eighteen months I have been leading research which draws on receptive learning to explore women's experiences of working across diverse churches in England. Five focus groups have met across the UK in order to explore the gifts and wounds in each other's traditions. Christian women came from Catholic, Anglican, Baptist, Methodist, Orthodox, United Reformed, Assemblies of God, Independent Evangelical and Independent Pentecostal churches. This research has been the first to engage both older and newer churches together and the participants gave positive feedback on the value of learning from others. An Assemblies of God pastor said that she had found receptive learning 'incredibly powerful and a great way of breaking barriers down with those from radically different views'. A Catholic lay-worker said, 'We were brought to a place of recognising brokenness without judgement and were able to receive one another's gifts, even gifts of women which had been rejected elsewhere. It was precious and powerful.' The report from this research is found on the Durham University website:

> *https://www.dur.ac.uk/theology.religion/ccs/constructivetheology/receptiveecumensim/*

The website explains a little more about receptive learning and also describes the different ways that this way of engagement can be put into practice. You will find on the website some project reports which involve the collaboration of Catholic, Baptist, Anglican, United Reformed, Salvation Army and Methodist churches. They explored together issues such as governance and finance, leadership and ministry, learning and formation. The impact and outcomes from this research can be found here:

*https://www.dur.ac.uk/theology.religion/ccs/projects/
receptiveecumenism/projects/localchurch/*

The Australian Council of Churches has been inspired by receptive learning and has produced a helpful booklet for local church use:

*https://www.dur.ac.uk/resources/theology.religion/Healing_
Gifts_for_Wounded_Hands_May_2014.pdf*

The Anglican–Roman Catholic International Commission (ARCIC) held the seventh meeting of its current phase (ARCIC III) in Erfurt, Germany on 14–20 May 2017 (published 2018). They applied receptive learning as their way of engagement. Entitled 'Walking Together on the Way', the document examines the structures by which Catholics and Anglicans order and maintain communion at the local, regional and universal levels. The report can be found here:

*https://iarccum.org/archive/ARCIC3/2018-05-21_arcic-iii_
walking-together-on-the-way_en.pdf*

Whether you explore receptive learning for the purpose of thinking theologically about difficult issues or to learn about how another church approaches evangelism, I pray that God will bless as you continue to journey closer to unity with one another.

Pentecostal Worship Team

DAY THREE: THURSDAY 26 APRIL
LET MUTUAL LOVE CONTINUE!
ENVISIONING THE JOURNEY AHEAD

MORNING PRAYER

Prepared by the Pentecostal World Fellowship with the Assemblies of God Church, Colombia

Morning Reflection

Greeting and Prayer

A.D. Beecham, Jr. (USA), General Superintendent, International Pentecostal Holiness Church; Executive Committee Member, Pentecostal World Fellowship

We have had late nights and now it is early on the third day. Christ is risen! So please join me in prayer. In many Pentecostal circles we hold our hands out or we hold them up when we pray. Let's open our hands, in whichever way you prefer, and let's open our hearts to the presence of the Holy Spirit with us today.

We give you thanks, our Heavenly Father, for your wonderful love that has been poured out to us in Jesus Christ. We thank you for your mercy, your truth, your grace. We thank you for the work of your Spirit that is drawing our hearts together, that is opening our understanding. We thank you that as the Apostle Paul prayed, the spirit of wisdom and revelation is being given to us to understand your glorious purposes for your body, the Church. We come before you with open hands. With open hands we turn loose from our fears, we turn loose from our disappointments, we turn loose from the rancour in our hearts. And with open hands we receive your grace, your love, your care. We cast our cares upon you because you care for us. Come Holy Spirit. Fill our hearts this day, not only in this time of worship, but through the course of this day, and throughout the remainder of this very special gathering of your children from around this globe. Come Holy Spirit, open our hearts. Come Holy Spirit, bind us together. In the name of the Father, the Son, and the Holy Spirit we pray. Amen.

Old Testament Reading

Jonathan Wells (Canada)

2 Chronicles 30:1-5, 23-27:

> *Hezekiah sent word to all Israel and Judah and also wrote letters to Ephraim and Manasseh, inviting them to come to the temple of the Lord in Jerusalem and celebrate the Passover to the Lord, the God of Israel. ²The king and his officials and the whole assembly in Jerusalem decided to celebrate the Passover in the second month. ³They had not been able to celebrate it at the regular time because not enough priests had consecrated themselves and the people had not assembled in Jerusalem. ⁴The plan seemed right both to the king and to the whole assembly. ⁵They decided to send a proclamation throughout Israel, from Beersheba to Dan, calling the people to come to Jerusalem and celebrate the Passover to the Lord, the God of Israel. It had not been celebrated in large numbers according to what was written (...) The whole assembly then agreed to celebrate the festival seven more days; so for another seven days they celebrated joyfully. ²⁴Hezekiah king of Judah provided a thousand bulls and seven thousand sheep and goats for the assembly, and the officials provided them with a thousand bulls and ten thousand sheep and goats. A great number of priests consecrated themselves. ²⁵The entire assembly of Judah rejoiced, along with the priests and Levites and all who had assembled from Israel, including the foreigners who had come from Israel and also those who resided in Judah. ²⁶There was great joy in Jerusalem, for since the days of Solomon son of David king of Israel there had been nothing like this in Jerusalem. ²⁷The priests and the Levites stood to bless the people, and God heard them, for their prayer reached heaven, his holy dwelling place.*

Worship

Colombian Pentecostal Worship Team

New Testament Reading

Tony Suarez (USA), Executive Vice President, National Hispanic Christian Leadership Conference

Philippians 2:1-11:

> *Therefore, if you have any encouragement from being united with Christ, if any comfort from his love, if any common sharing in the Spirit, if any tenderness and compassion, ²then make my joy complete by being like-minded, having the same love, being one in spirit and of one mind. ³Do nothing out of selfish ambition or vain conceit. Rather, in humility value others above yourselves, ⁴not looking to your own interests but each of you to the interests of the others.*
>
> *⁵In your relationships with one another, have the same mindset as Christ Jesus:*
>
> *⁶Who, being in very nature God,*
>   *did not consider equality with God something to be used to his own advantage;*
>
> *⁷rather, he made himself nothing*
>   *by taking the very nature of a servant,*
>   *being made in human likeness.*
>
> *⁸And being found in appearance as a man,*
>   *he humbled himself*
>   *by becoming obedient to death—*
>   *even death on a cross!*
>
> *⁹Therefore God exalted him to the highest place*
>   *and gave him the name that is above every name,*
>
> *¹⁰that at the name of Jesus every knee should bow,*
>   *in heaven and on earth and under the earth,*
>
> *¹¹and every tongue acknowledge that Jesus Christ is Lord,*
>   *to the glory of God the Father.*

Music

Assemblies of God Church, Colombia

Envisioning the Journey Ahead: Unity Is Hard Work!

Revd David Wells, Vice Chair, Pentecostal World Fellowship and General Superintendent, The Pentecostal Assemblies of Canada

Texts: 2 Chronicles 30:1-5, 23-27; Philippians 2:1-11

Unity is hard work!

In my journey of relationship with the broader body of Christ, I have realized both the privileges and costs involved in coming to the family table with other sisters and brothers in Christ.

Within the Christian faith, we all have communities we belong to. With that connectedness come many benefits, which include a shared sense of belonging, our common beliefs, rituals and practices, and a mutual history that links our story with our faith community. Generally, it is a great thing to belong! In my case, that is true of my place within the Pentecostal and evangelical family in Canada and within our global communities.

However, there are limitations to our knowledge, perspective and faith development if we know only the relationships, history and insights found exclusively within our own community. One can have a fixed, set identity where our language, experiences and understanding are the only frame through which we see other communities. This can easily lead to attitudes of arrogance, dismissal and judgement of 'the other'. At the very least, it lends itself to a myopic point of view that is accompanied by an unhealthy naivete and a lack of teachability regarding the history and perspective of other church families. As a result, the development of broader relationships that can provide vibrancy and life to one's faith journey does not occur.

My experience, greatly assisted by involvement with the Global Christian Forum and other platforms of Christian interaction, is that one must be prepared for a seemingly paradoxical journey if one is to come to the table of the broader Christian community. As a starting point, I am convinced with multitudes of brothers and sisters globally regarding the truth resident within the Apostles' Creed. Parallel to that, I have grown to be even more convinced about the core tenets and understandings of Pentecostal and evangelical belief and practice, while not being confined to a fixed, set identity. Those understandings provide a central core identity of who I and many of those I represent are.

One way to consider the central core of my Pentecostal identity is described by Dr James K. Smith in his book *Thinking in Tongues*.[1] Let me succinctly summarize how he speaks of the Pentecostal worldview, along with some of my own observations.

(1) Being open to God doing new things—renewing, reviving, restoring, creative. 'I will do a new thing, says the Lord.' Therefore, 'newer' churches can be frustrating to 'historic' churches regarding their worship, mission and thinking.

(2) Recognizing spiritual realities in every area of the natural world—an 'enchanted' worldview. A continual sense of God's presence, of openness to hearing the Spirit's voice and experiencing the Spirit's leadership and empowerment.

(3) Jesus' work on the cross provides both spiritual and physical restoration; it is all-sufficient for salvation, 'wholeness'. Thus, the complete person (body, soul and spirit) is transformed and being transformed, healed and being healed by the efficacy of Jesus' work. Pentecostals are criticized for being 'heavenly minded', but the reality is that they take the physical world very seriously as well.

(4) High value is placed on the faith stories of salvation and the miraculous; evidences of the ongoing work of the Holy

---

1 James K. A. Smith, *Thinking in Tongues: Pentecostal Contributions to Christian Philosophy* (Grand Rapids: Eerdmans, 2010).

Spirit in His power are expected. We anticipate divine encounters and signs of the Kingdom among us.

(5) Mission is taken very seriously, especially to the poor, the broken and those who have never heard the good news. It is expected that all followers of Jesus will be involved in the mission of God. 'The Spirit of the Lord is upon us…'. I am proud of my son, Jonathan, who is with me at this Gathering, as the Spirit of the Lord is upon him as he works through Habitat for Humanity to care for those in need of affordable housing. It is the expected norm that empowered by the Spirit, we will fulfil God's calling of mission in our lives.

Confident in those convictions, I have found great freedom to come to the table of the broader Christian community and value the life and truth of Christ in many I meet there. It's a veritable feast!

So theologically and spiritually, why is unity such hard work?

There is the human factor—fear, lack of understanding, arrogance, ignorance.

There are the spiritual realities—we wrestle not only with fellow humans (flesh and blood) but with spiritual powers. 'For our struggle is not against flesh and blood, but against the rulers, against the authorities, against the powers of this dark world and against the spiritual forces of evil in the heavenly realms' (Eph. 6:12). Those spiritual powers resist what unity will produce:

(6) The glorification of Jesus. 'I pray also for those who will believe in me through their message, that all of them may be one, Father, just as you are in me and I am in you. May they also be in us so that the world may believe that you have sent me. I have given them the glory that you gave me, that they may be one as we are one: I in them and you in me. May they be brought to complete unity to let the world know that you sent me and have loved them even as you have loved me' (Jn 17:20–23). In the face of spiritual resistance, we do the hard

(7) The blessing of God—life forevermore. 'How good and pleasant it is when brothers live together in unity! It is like precious oil poured on the head, running down on the beard, running down on Aaron's beard, down upon the collar of his robes. It is as if the dew of Hermon were falling on Mount Zion. For there the LORD bestows his blessing, even life forevermore' (Psalm 133). In the face of spiritual resistance, we do the hard work of unity so that the blessing of God will be experienced, life forevermore. Jesus has come to give life, life to the full.

And so, secure in what our spiritual birth families have instilled in us regarding our Lord, His Church and His Word, we are drawn to the table of the full body of Christ, to feast on a full understanding of Father, Son and Spirit. There we will see our Lord glorified and the blessing of God, life forevermore experienced.

Song of Worship

Colombian Pentecostal Worship Team

Closing remarks and prayer

Bob Rodgers (USA), Senior Pastor, Evangel World Prayer Center, and *Jorge Olea* (USA), Pastor, Spanish Church Congregation, Evangel World Prayer Center

Bishop Brian Farrell

DAY THREE: THURSDAY 26 APRIL
LET MUTUAL LOVE CONTINUE!
ENVISIONING THE JOURNEY AHEAD

MORNING MEETINGS

9.30 Plenary Sesion

Moderator: **Juan Usma-Gomez** (Colombia/Vatican City), Head of the Western Section, Pontifical Council for Promoting Christian Unity

Message from His Holiness Pope Francis

Read by **Juan Usma-Gomez**

Envisioning the Journey Ahead: Perspectives from the Regions of the World

- *Middle East* — **Antoine Audo** (Syria), Bishop, Chaldean Catholic Church
- *Africa* — **Richard Kuuia Baawobr** (Ghana), Bishop of Wa
- *Asia* — **Felix Machado** (India), Bishop of Vasai; Chairman, Office of Ecumenical and Interreligious Affairs, Federation of Asian Bishops Conference

- *North America* — **Catherine Clifford** (Canada), Professor of Systematic and Historical Theology, Saint Paul University, Ottawa
- *South America* — **Marcial Maçaneiro** (Brazil), Professor of Theology, University of Paraná, Curitiba

Envisioning the Journey Ahead: Biblical Perspective

Brian Farrell (Ireland/Vatican City), Bishop, Secretary, Pontifical Council for Promoting Christian Unity

Testimony

Lord Elorm Donkor (Ghana/United Kingdom), District Pastor, Church of Pentecost and Principal, Birmingham Christian College; together with *Brother Paolo* (France), Taizé Community

The Future of Global Christianity: Introduction

Jean-Daniel Plüss (Switzerland), Chair, European Pentecostal Charismatic Research Association; Chair, Fondation du Forum Chrétien Mondial

11.15 Regional Interchurch Groups –

The Future of Global Christianity: Identifying Hopes and Challenges

Introduction

Juan Usma-Gomez

In the first two days of this global gathering we have considered the recent past in the life of Global Christian Forum. Today we begin to open new horizons. We want to consider the road we still have to travel and that we want to travel together with God's help.

This morning we are going to have five moments. We will hear a message of greeting from His Holiness Pope Francis, followed by a panel of voices of Christian leaders from five continents, then a biblical reflection on the way forward and two testimonies, and finally a presentation on the future of world Christianity.

Let us begin with the message of Pope Francis, which I will read in the original English.

Greetings

A message of greeting from *Pope Francis*

To the most reverend Brian Farrell, secretary of the Pontifical Council for Promoting Christian Unity

I extend warm greetings to you and to all those participating in the Third Gathering of the Global Christian Forum, as you assemble in Bogotá, Colombia, from 24 to 27 April 2018. I join you in giving thanks to Almighty God on this occasion, as the Forum is a grace-filled opportunity for representatives of many Christian communities to meet as brothers and sisters and journey towards the fulfilment of Jesus' prayer that all may be one so that the world may believe (*cf.* Jn 17:21). l pray that the Forum may be a time to share personal and ecclesial faith experiences, and provide an open and respectful space to address together new contemporary challenges, by promoting Christian solidarity and cooperation in a fresh and innovative way. Humanity is in great need of such solidarity, which fosters respect and esteem, mutual forgiveness and the effective defense of human dignity in every situation. I assure you and all present of my spiritual closeness during these days, and I invoke upon you Almighty God's blessings of wisdom, courage and strength.

FRANCISCUS PP.

From the Vatican, 19 April 2018.

Panel of Perspectives

Reflections *(Middle East)*

Bishop Antoine Audo

I come from Syria, the cradle of Christianity where, near Damascus, the apostle Paul met Christ and was baptized when Ananias laid hands on him.

I come from Syria where, in Antioch and at the dawning of the proclamation of the gospel, the first believers were named 'Christians'.

I come from Syria, where a beautiful mosaic of churches (Orthodox, Catholic, Evangelical), of liturgies (Armenian, Byzantine and Syriac), of multiple theological and ethnic traditions live together and are proud to witness to their faith amidst a Muslim majority and a population dreadfully tried and tested.

I come from Syria where, for over seven years now, war has calculated its numbers of victims by the million. Out of a population of 23 million people, we can account for:

- five million refugees in neighbouring countries (Turkey, Lebanon, Jordan);
- seven million displaced inside Syria;
- two million out-of-school children;
- two million immigrants in Europe;
- over half a million people dead;
- and thousands of persons left physically disabled.

In this Global Gathering in Colombia, I feel privileged to share with you the concerns and hopes of a pastor coming from Aleppo in Syria, a region of the Middle East so tormented and in the throes of suffering.

The war in Syria

To understand the fears and hopes experienced by the Christian communities in Syria, one needs to backtrack to 2011, which is when the war started destroying and destabilizing the country. This conflict is three-dimensional: local, regional and international.

First, the regional conflict is at the heart of this three-dimensional situation, with a key component being the battle between the Sunnis and the Shiites. Each group is vying for hegemony over Islam. Indeed, everyone knows that two antagonistic countries are backing the war in Syria, i.e. pro-Shiite Iran and pro-Sunni Saudi Arabia. This has proven to be a key issue in the history of Islam. We believe the origin stems from the threats Islam is facing from modernity, a modernity of rationalism and one spreading globalization, atheism, and agnosticism. To face up to the challenge, Islam has started escalating further into violence and, it would seem, without the mediation of any dialogue!

A second component explaining the war in Syria is its economic and strategic aspects, defended by major world powers such as the United States and Russia. The oil and gas reserves in the Middle East undeniably represent effective economic and strategic assets for these political powers who, in turn, find themselves caught up in competitive dynamics of rivalry and world domination.

I do not need to point out how many Americans, Russians and their allies are involved in the Syrian war, sending arms plus military forces and the entire specialized arsenal they carry with them.

The third component is a local one: the location of combat and fighting within the country of Syria. Several forces are at work within the country:

- Sunnis, Alawis, Ismailis, Druze, Circassians and Kurds;
- Orthodox, Catholic and Protestant Christians of all traditions: Byzantine, Syriac and Armenian, as I noted at the beginning of this presentation. And we must also mention Maronites, Chaldeans and Latins, but only those Catholic Latins.

What challenges are the Christians facing?

Due to this war, there is a high level of migration amongst families and particularly young Christians, over issues of insecurity, poverty and mandatory military service.

Above: *From left to right: Mr Huibert van Beek (first GCF Secretary); Revd Dr Larry Miller (second GCF Secretary); Revd Dr Casely Essamuah (third GCF Secretary) (Photo: Albin Hillert)*

Below: *Participants in plenary (Photo: Albin Hillert)*

Above: Ms Esther Schirrmacher, Youth delegate, World Evangelical Alliance, Josephine Ntihinyuzwa, GCF Staff, and Dr Rosalee Velloso Ewell, World Evangelical Alliance (Photo: Harri Koskela)

Below: Ms Raimy Ramírez, local GCF staff and her baby Camilo Sarria (Photo: Albin Hillert)

Above: Participants in plenary (Photo: Albin Hillert)

Left: His Eminence Metropolitan Mor Gregorius Yohanna Ibrahim (Photo: Kim Cain)

Left: Commissioner Christine MacMillan, Associate Secretary General for Public Engagement; World Evangelical Alliance (Photo: Albin Hillert)

Right: Bishop Ivan Abrahams, General Secretary, World Methodist Council (Photo: Albin Hillert)

Right: Dr Lorena Ríos, Director of the Office of Religious Affairs, Colombia (Photo: Albin Hillert)

Left: Dr Ganoune Diop, Director of Public Affairs and Religious Liberty, Seventh-day Adventist Church (Photo: Albin Hillert)

Above: Prof. Dr Thomas Schirrmacher, Associate Secretary General, World Evangelical Alliance, Germany (Photo: Albin Hillert)

Below: H.H. Patriarch Mor Ignatius Aphrem II and Archbishop Michael Chamoun, Syriac Orthodox Patriarchate of Antioch and All the East (Photo: Albin Hillert)

Above: Little Maya Sarria Ramírez, daughter of Raimy Ramírez, joins the dance during the Colombian Cultural night (Photo: Albin Hillert)

Below: Left: Bishop Victoria Matthews, Anglican Communion in New Zealand. Right: The Revd Canon Dr Alyson Barnett-Cowan, President of the Canadian Council of Churches (Photo: Albin Hillert)

Left: Monsignor Juan Usma Gómez, Pontifical Council for Promoting Christian Unity (Photo: Albin Hillert)

Right: Bishop Richard Baaworb, Catholic Church in Ghana (Photo: Albin Hillert)

Right: Brother Paolo, Taizé Community (Photo: Albin Hillert)

Left: Father Limin Wang, China (Photo: Albin Hillert)

Left: Dr Robert Baah, The Church of Pentecost in the USA, Coordinator of Latin America churches (Photo: Albin Hillert)

Below: Revd Dr Chris Ferguson, General Secretary, World Communion of Reformed Churches; Revd William Gyekye, Methodist Church Ghana (Photo: Albin Hillert)

Left: *Prof. Dr Catherine Clifford, Catholic Church, Canada (Photo: Albin Hillert)*

Below: *Commissioning Service for Revd Dr Casely Essamuah, with Bishop James E. Swanson, the United Methodist Church, USA, speaking (Photo: Albin Hillert)*

Above: Metropolitan Geevarghese Coorilos, Syriac Orthodox Patriarchate of Antioch and All the East/Commission on World Mission and Evangelism, World Council of Churches; Prof. Dr Souraya Bechealany, General Secretary, Middle East Council of Churches; Prof. Dr Raimundo Barreto, Princeton Theological Seminary, USA; Prof. Dr Wonsuk Ma, Oral Roberts University, USA (Photo: Albin Hillert)

Below: Pedro López, Assemblies of God, Peru (Photo: Albin Hillert)

Above: *Archbishop Joris Vercammen, International Old Catholic Bishops Conference (Photo: Albin Hillert)*

Below: *Revd Dr Aiah Foday-Khabenje, General Secretary, Association of Evangelicals in Africa (Photo: Albin Hillert)*

Left: *Revd Stacey Duensing, Youth Delegate, Reformed Church in America (Photo: Albin Hillert)*

Below: *Revd Dr Casely Baiden Essamuah and Fr Prof. Dr Ioan Sauca, Deputy General Secretary, World Council of Churches (Photo: Albin Hillert)*

Right: Revd Pirjo-Liisa Penttinen, Young Women's Christian Association and Evangelical Lutheran Church Finland (Photo: Albin Hillert)

Left: Revd Richard Howell, World Evangelical Alliance / Asia Evangelical Alliance (Photo: Kim Cain)

Above: Ms Adriana Gastellu Camp, Church of Sweden (Photo: Albin Hillert)

Below: Farewell to Larry and Eleanor Miller, with Prof. Dr Kathryn Johnson (Photo: Albin Hillert)

Above: Revd Dr Casely Essamuah (Photo: Albin Hillert)

Left: Prof. Dr Katherine Shirk Lucas, Institut Catholique de Paris, France (Photo: Albin Hillert)

Above: Third Global Gathering participants Photo (Photo: Albin Hillert)

Below: Happy at the end! Ms Magali Moreno, GCF Event Coordinator and Kim Cain, GCF Communications Assistant (Photo: Peter Kenny)

Violence has led the Christians to experience a loss of confidence, fear and distrust, particularly because of the war 'in the name of Islam'. All the armed groups have Islamist names!

As far as society in general is concerned, the Christians are horrified by the multiplication of armed groups and of mercenaries, and by the general spread of corruption, theft, and moral degradation at all levels.

In a nutshell, war has generated economic as well as moral corruption. And to a certain extent, this corruption is wearing down the Christians' level of resilience, leading to an increase in migration flows.

The hopes of the churches in our region

Among the tasks that have been entrusted to me, as bishop of the Chaldean Catholic Church in Syria, I am seeking above all to develop two ideas that are both dear to me and rooted in the Second Vatican Council's declarations.

Indeed, that Council prompted Christians and all members of the church to consider their presence in the Arab and Muslim world as a *dynamic of communion*. Such a dynamic is to be sought first between Christians, then between Christians and Muslims.

First, the expression 'Together becoming Christians' can guide us in an ecumenical dialogue, seeking unity in our journey as we follow in the footsteps of Jesus, who gathers us together as His disciples and sends us into the world as apostles to proclaim the good news of the Gospel: 'You are loved by God, fear not!'

Second, engaging with the various Muslim groups, I am eager to deepen the understanding of the statement 'Together becoming citizens'. This task is far from easy but is one that the Christians in the Middle East are eager to promote, hoping that it will help them obtain increased religious freedom and deference when differences are considered.

To close regarding these two forms of life together, we could point out that, at the very heart of present-day Syrian society and in the middle of raging violence, all Christians have displayed a remarkable example of solidarity and stewardship towards the poorest without any discrimination whatsoever, thus drawing the attention of the Muslims and stirring up questions on their part as to the Christian faith!

Conclusion

In closing, a few ideas from Benedict XVI could give us pointers for our journey together on the road towards greater communion between churches and towards increased witnessing to the Gospel. These are drawn from the Pope's Apostolic Exhortation of 14 September 2012, *Ecclesia in Medio Oriente: communion and witness*.

The first idea applies to ecumenism. After having invited the Christians of the East to take part in the study of Holy Scripture, Benedict XVI wrote:

> *Particularly fruitful forms of cooperation in the area of charitable activities and the promotion of the values of human life, justice and peace could also be developed or expanded. All this will contribute to greater mutual knowledge and the creation of a climate of esteem; these are indispensable conditions for promoting fraternity.*

The second idea concerns relations with the Muslims, or inter-religious dialogue:

> *As an integral part of the Middle East, Christians have developed over the centuries a type of relationship with their surroundings which can prove instructive. They have let themselves be challenged by Muslim devotion and piety, and have continued, in accordance with their means and to the extent possible, to live by and to promote the values of the Gospel in the surrounding culture. The result has been a particular form of symbiosis.*

Ecumenism and communion of life with the Muslims are therefore to be seen as priority tasks for Middle East Christians as well as for our globalized world, since they form an integral part of human reality for absolutely everyone.

Today's Global Gathering in Bogotá demonstrates that such ideals are far from being just lip service and are experienced by a large number of Christians from all walks of life! May the Lord bless us all, wherever we are, that we may go on journeying together as disciples and apostles of Christ, for the glory of God and the salvation of the world!

Promoting Fraternal Relations between Churches: Lessons from Ghana *(Africa)*

Bishop Richard Kuuia Baawobr

Brothers and sisters in Christ and all people of good will, I bring you greetings from your brothers and sisters in Ghana, and especially in the Upper West region of the country.

Our theme for this third day of our gathering, 'Let Mutual Love Continue: Envisioning the Journey Ahead', certainly offers us the opportunity to see what we are doing together and how we can improve it. I would like to share with you how we, in the Upper West region of northern Ghana, try to promote fraternal relations between Christian churches.

Today, increased mobility, large-scale movement of refugees and economic migrations have resulted in more people of diverse faiths living side by side. These contacts are opportunities to foster greater knowledge, awareness and cooperation among people of different religions. Unfortunately, increased relations between communities have sometimes been marred by tension and fear. For many communities, this tension confirms the need to protect their traditional identities and distinctiveness.

Many African theologians confirm that Africans are notoriously religious. There is a thirst for God and many people go to different places to pray when they are in difficulty. Sometimes they end up going from one church to the other and depleting their meagre resources also. Religion is a major asset among our people, but it can also be a source of divisions and impoverishment if not properly managed. Here lies my greatest fear and at the same time my greatest hope for the future of religions among my people in particular and for Africa in general. This makes it essential that we take seriously Christ's prayer that all

Christians should be one as our first witness to the world. This we can do through fostering fraternal relations among ourselves.

The multiplicity of Christian churches calls us to look out for how we can respond together to the thirst for God among our people rather than confusing them at times because of our theological differences. In this context, a major role of the ecumenical movement is to prevent polarization between religious communities. Religion must never be used to divide communities.

To promote fraternal relations between the churches in our region, we have formed a local council of churches. This is an umbrella that can stimulate the promotion of communion with other churches. Its formation itself is a sign of communion among the local churches. It comprises the leaders or pastors of the different Christian churches and a representative from the Catholic Church. Through our monthly meetings we are promoting fraternal relations in two main areas. Our efforts are based sometimes consciously and at other times unconsciously on what I call the 'theological foundation'.

Common Social Action

Because we live together in the same neighbourhood, our members do not distinguish and discriminate when it comes to putting forth their social concerns to the appropriate authority.

Religious leaders are being called on by government and non-governmental agencies to address public issues of moral concern. However, to speak collectively and with moral authority, religious communities must discern their common values, decide to what extent they can express themselves with one voice and discuss how they can avoid being manipulated by political forces.

When, as religious leaders of the region, we met to prepare a message for the President of the republic, we raised issues that we felt were common for all our members: security on our roads, health, education, unfinished government projects, the politicization of development, etc.

Collaboration with other believers can promote a religious perspective on issues of justice and peace, support for family life, and respect for minority communities. In this collaboration and cooperation Christians can appeal together to their common biblical and theological sources, thereby bringing Christian insights to this broader context in a way that fosters Christian unity as well.

Catholics can also work together with other believers to fight against religious fanaticism and sectarianism.

Times of mourning are another important time when we experience and promote fraternal relations. Neighbours and friends contribute to support the bereaved family, irrespective of the Church in which he or she prays. It would seem that such moments bind people more strongly together than even their faith.

Also, when pastors or priests visit each other's families or presbyteries and come together to celebrate Christmas and Easter with their families and other events, bonds are strengthened.

Praying Together

United interreligious prayer is an occasion where people of different religions plan, prepare and participate together. Some feel that this practice risks reducing prayer to the lowest common denominator and can take away from the unique spirituality of each religion. For others, such prayer is not at all possible. Yet for some, praying together could be a spiritually enriching occasion. All these different responses indicate that serious conversations among Christians on this issue are not a finished job.

Participation in multi-religious prayer is a way of promoting communion with other churches. Concrete situations in everyday life provide opportunities for communion with other believers. These include interreligious marriages, personal friendships, and praying together for a common purpose, such as for peace or in a particular crisis situation. The occasion may also be a national holiday, religious festival, school assembly or other gatherings.

There are also various forms of prayer among people of different religions. Catholics may be invited to other places of worship, where they should be respectful of the practices of that tradition. Catholics may invite guests of another religion to a church service and should ensure a welcoming hospitality. Multi-religious prayer juxtaposes the prayer of different traditions. The advantage is that the variety and integrity of each tradition is honoured and that we are praying in the presence of each other. The disadvantage may be that one remains a bystander.

Participating and celebrating the Week of Prayer for Christian Unity is a concrete way of promoting communion with other churches. Let us all try to take an active part in the celebration of this week.

The Theological Foundation

To promote communion with other churches, the principles of spiritual sharing or practical cooperation should apply. The only basis for such sharing and cooperation is the recognition on all sides of a certain, though imperfect, communion that already exists. Openness and mutual respect are the logical consequences of such recognition.

In promoting communion with other churches, we must recognize that the mystery of God's salvation is not exhausted by our theological affirmations. Promoting communion with other churches will drive all communities to self-criticism and to re-think the ways in which they have interpreted their faith traditions.

Ecumenism can bring about change in the experience of faith, helping people to deepen and grow in their faith in unexpected ways. In ecumenism we affirm hope. In the midst of the many divisions, conflicts and violence, there is hope that it is possible to create a human community that lives in justice and peace.

Ecumenism is a cooperative and collaborative activity. All partners involved need to be included in the planning process from the very beginning. The strength of setting the agenda together lies in the fact that all partners own the agenda and become committed to making it work. For the conduct of ecumenism, clear objectives and commonly agreed criteria for participation and regular assessment are essential.

I thank you all for your attention!

Aggressive and Competitive Christian Mission: A Challenge to Intra-Christian and Interreligious Harmony in Asia

Felix Machado

Introduction

Asia has given an example to the world of peace and interreligious harmony in a multi-religious and multi-cultural society. The Gospel of Jesus Christ needs to be continuously proclaimed with renewed vigour within this context of the Asian ethos. Christians need to see that Jesus Christ is loved and accepted freely and willingly. Thus, the right to freedom of religion must be insisted upon.[1] At the same time, a question must be asked—namely, to what extent our human right of religious freedom, including the constitutional right to public self-expression and our right to propagate religious belief, may and must be limited by other rights.[2] Christian witness is not an ethics-free space. It requires an ethical foundation which is biblically based so that we Christians truly do what Christ has assigned us to do.

What Exactly Does Christianity Teach about Preaching the Gospel of Jesus Christ?

I will answer this question from the Catholic point of view. The Second Vatican Ecumenical Council (1962–1965) gave sound principles which the *Catechism of the Catholic Church (CCC)* summarised in three criteria for interpreting the Scriptures in order to bear witness to Jesus Christ and his Gospel:

(1) Be especially attentive to the content and unity of the whole Scripture. The Scriptures are a unity by reason of the unity of God's plan, of which Jesus Christ is the centre and heart.

---

1 It is indispensable that each person should be able to follow his or her own conscience in all circumstances and that no one may force him or her to act against it. In spite of the widely observed danger of religious fanaticism even on the Asian continent, religions in general, by the content of their essential teaching, do lend themselves to openness and dialogue. That can be considered a good soil to sow seeds of the Gospel.
2 Cf. Heiner Bielefeldt, *Freedom of Religion or Belief: Thematic Reports of the United Nations Special Rapporteur 2010-2016*, ed. by Thomas Schirrmacher (Bonn: Verlag fur Kultur und Wissenschaft, 2017).

(2) Read the Scriptures within the 'living Tradition of the whole Church'. The Church carries in her Tradition the living memorial of God's Word.

(3) Be attentive to the analogy of faith. By 'analogy of faith' is meant the coherence of the truths of faith among themselves and within the whole plan of revelation (*cf. CCC*, 112–14).

The Context in Which the Preaching Takes Place

Christians in Asia should be aware of the challenge to situate this teaching of Jesus in a multi-religious and multi-cultural context.

Witnessing to the Word of God in a multi-religious world, for example, where Christians are surrounded by people of other religions, the Christian must bear in mind three objectives: (1) to develop a deep respect for people of other religions and for their respective religious traditions; (2) to safeguard the integrity of the Christian faith; and (3) to continue the evangelizing mission of the Church, *i.e.* to proclaim the message of Jesus in all its forms (*cf.* John Paul II, *Redemptoris Missio*, n. 55: 'Interreligious dialogue is part of the evangelizing mission of the Church').

One can find reasons for openness and respect within the teachings of Christianity. Respect for people of other religions must not be instrumentalized in order to achieve one's own objectives. People need to be attracted to Christ; they must not be proselytized. Every Christian is a missionary. However, no Christian needs to or should live out his or her faith through an aggressive and competitive mission.

The Second Vatican Ecumenical Council reaffirms the traditional doctrine according to which salvation in Jesus Christ is, in a mysterious way, a reality open to all persons of good will. But the Council has also openly acknowledged the presence of positive values not only in the religious life of individual adherents of other religions but also in the religious traditions to which they belong. It attributed these values to the active presence of God through his Word (*semina Verbi*), pointing out the universal action of the Spirit (*cf.* Second Vatican Ecumenical Council, *Lumen Gentium*, n. 16).[3]

---

3 *Cf.* also the Vatican Congregation for the Evangelization of Peoples and

It should be remembered that 'Christians who lack appreciation and respect for other believers and their religious traditions are ill-prepared to proclaim the Gospel to them' (Pontifical Council for Inter-Religious Dialogue [PCID], *Dialogue and Proclamation*, n. 73c). In proclaiming the Word of God (preaching), every Christian believer needs to have an attitude which bears qualities such as the following (PCID, *Dialogue and Proclamation*, n. 70):

(1) To be respectful of the presence and action of the Spirit of God in the hearts of those who listen to the message, in the recognition that the Spirit is the 'principal agent of evangelization' (Paul VI, *Evangelii Nuntiandi*, n. 75).

(2) To be dialogical, for in proclamation the hearer of the Word is not expected to be a passive receiver. There is a gradual progress from the 'seeds of the Word' already present in the hearer to the full mystery of salvation in Jesus Christ. In other words, the Church must recognize a process of purification and enlightenment in obedience of faith.

Pontifical Council for Interreligious Dialogue, *Dialogue and Proclamation* (DP, 1991), which helps us to clarify the Church's relationship to other religions: 'While proclaiming the message of God in Jesus Christ, the evangelizing Church must always remember that her task is not exercised in a complete void. For the Holy Spirit, the Spirit of Jesus Christ, is present and active among the hearers of the Good News even before the Church's missionary action comes into operation.' Cf. John Paul II, *Redemptor Hominis* (1979) and n. 12; *Dominum Vivificante* (1986), n. 53. They (hearers of the Good News) may in many cases have already responded implicitly to God's offer of salvation in Jesus Christ, a sign of this being the sincere practice of their own religious traditions, insofar as these contain authentic religious values. They may have already been touched by the Spirit and in some way associated unknowingly to the paschal mystery (suffering, dying and rising to new life) of Jesus Christ (cf. *Gaudium et Spes*, n. 22). Cf. also DP, n. 16, which states: 'Making its own the vision and the terminology of some early Church Fathers, *Nostra Aetate* (NA) speaks of the presence in these traditions of a "ray of that Truth which enlightens all" (NA, n. 2). *Ad Gentes* recognizes the presence of "seeds of the word", and points to the riches which a generous God has distributed among the nations (n. 10). Again, *Lumen Gentium* refers to the good which is "found sown" not only "in minds and hearts", but also "in the rites and customs of peoples" (n. 17).' How and why the Church must relate positively to other religions and to their respective adherents is explained succinctly and clearly in the Encyclical Letter *Redemptoris Missio* (John Paul II, 7 December 1990, nn. 55–57).

(3) To be inculturated by being incarnated in the culture and the spiritual tradition of those addressed, so that the message is not only intelligible to them but is also conceived as responding to their deepest aspirations as truly the Good News, which in the depths of their hearts they have been longing for (*cf.* Paul VI, *Evangelii Nuntiandi*, n. 20, 62).

Clarity and Direction in Preaching the Christian Message

What is the basis for Christian witness? The good news of Jesus' Gospel is to be shared with the poor. We are to proclaim release to the captives and recovery of sight for the blind, to set at liberty those who are oppressed, and to proclaim the acceptable year of the Lord (Lk 4:18–19). A Christian proclaims the good news even in a difficult situation. However, no Christians should engage in inappropriate methods of exercising mission by resorting to deception and coercive means; if they do so, they betray the good news of Jesus and cause suffering to others. Conversion of any person to follow Jesus and his good news is ultimately the work of God (Holy Spirit) whom no man or woman can stop or force.

Asia is the continent of the poor; it is characteristically multi-religious and multicultural. Therefore, here are some principles for Christians to follow.

The mission must be done in an appropriate manner. Loving as God loves, imitation of Jesus Christ, and living in Christian virtues, such as conducting oneself with integrity, charity, compassion and humility and overcoming all arrogance, condescension and disparagement, are hallmarks of Christian witness in a multi-religious world. Paul exhorts Christians in Galatians 5:22, 'The fruit of the Spirit is love, joy, peace, patience, kindness, goodness, faithfulness, gentleness, self-control.'

Acts of service and justice are at the heart of the Christian witness. Christians are warned that 'the exploitation of situations of poverty and need has no place in Christian outreach. Christians should denounce and refrain from offering all forms of allurements, including financial incentives and rewards, in their acts of service.'

Full respect for the God-given human dignity of every human person is at the centre of Christian witness. Christians are further exhorted to never engage in any form of violence.

The witness of Christians must also be prophetic. What does that mean? It means denouncing the instrumentalization of religion by political, economic or ideological powers. Christians are encouraged to collaborate by proactively promoting, together with people of other religions, justice, peace and the common good. This contributes to mutual respect and solidarity among people in a pluralistic world.

Christian witness must also take into account respect for all people without any discrimination. Christians are exhorted to denounce any case of false witness which they find, because Christians are to first listen and understand others' beliefs and practices and appreciate what is true and good in them. If anyone is desiring to follow Jesus Christ, a proper discernment process is proposed to the witnessing Christian. This means sufficient time for adequate reflection and preparation, through a process ensuring full personal freedom.

Those who take the name of Jesus Christ must proactively build relationships of respect and trust with people of different religions so as to facilitate deeper mutual understanding, reconciliation and cooperation for the common good.

Conclusion

Some concrete recommendations: Christians are to build bridges of friendship, engaging in ongoing interreligious dialogue, because interreligious dialogue can provide new opportunities for resolving conflicts, restoring justice, healing of memories, reconciliation and peace building. It is also important that Christians deepen and strengthen their own religious identity and faith while deepening their knowledge and understanding of different religions. Christians are exhorted to avoid misrepresenting the beliefs and practices of people of different religions. Christians should cooperate with other religious communities, engaging in interreligious advocacy towards justice and the common good and, wherever possible, standing together in solidarity with people who are in situations of conflict. Christians should also call on their governments to ensure that freedom of religion is properly and comprehensively respected. Finally, Christians should pray for their neighbours and their well-being, recognizing that prayer is integral to who we are and what we do, as well as to Christ's mission.

Reflections (North America)

Catherine E. Clifford

I offer these few reflections based on my experience of ecumenical work in the North American context, and more specifically from my perspective in Canada. It is important to note from the outset that the demographic picture of Christianity in Canada differs greatly from the context of the United States. Historically, there has been a strong presence of 'mainline' Christian churches in Canada (Catholic, Anglican, United, Presbyterian, Lutheran, Reformed). Evangelical and Pentecostal communities represent a relatively small portion of the Christian population.[4]

Over the past twenty years, we have seen a strengthening of relationships between Evangelical and mainline churches. In the period leading up to the millennium celebrations of the year 2000, the leadership of the Evangelical Fellowship of Canada approached the Canadian Council of Churches with a desire to find new ways of giving common witness. Since then, Evangelicals and other Christians have come to know one another better and have grown together in friendship and trust. The establishment of official dialogue between Evangelicals and Catholics in 2010 has led to the discovery that we have often misunderstood or misrepresented one another's practice and belief. Dialogue and sustained friendship are helping us to correct many

---

4   The last accurate census of religion in Canada was taken in the 2011 National Household Census by Statistics Canada. At that time, 67.3% of Canadians identified as 'Christians', 8.1% as belonging to other religions (Muslims, Hindus, Sikhs, Jews), and 24% as having no religious affiliation. Of the Christian population, 39% of Canadians identified as Catholic, 6.1% United Church, 5% Anglican, 1.7% Orthodox, 1.5% Lutheran, 1.4% Presbyterian, and approximately 6% 'other Protestants'. The latter demographic would include Christian Reformed, Evangelical and Pentecostal groups. Less than 1.5% identified as Pentecostals.

misperceptions. Theological conversations have explored the role of Scripture, the understanding of salvation, and understanding the nature and mission of the church.

An important impetus for new relationships between evangelicals and Catholics, or other more conservative churches, has been a desire to find allies on a host of ethical issues. The most important of these pertain to human sexuality and, more recently, medically assisted dying. The inability of the churches to find common ground on new moral issues has given rise to new fears that we may not be able to remain together on the path to unity. It has sometimes overshadowed significant levels of agreement on matters pertaining to the heart of the Christian faith: the common confession of faith, the mutual recognition of baptism, agreement on eucharistic doctrine, and the theology of ordained ministry. This consensus in faith, combined with a growing awareness of the need for common witness and of our shared mission in service of the world, continues to bind us together.

One of the most significant challenges at this juncture of the ecumenical movement is that the achievements of the last century are being eclipsed, lost from view, and risk being forgotten. In Canada, this means not only the achievements of international theological dialogue, but also many of the mutually agreed pastoral guidelines between Canadian churches that address principles for common prayer;[5] the mutual recognition and non-repetition of baptism;[6] the joint preparation and celebration of inter-church marriage;[7] the re-

---

5   See, for example, Anglican-Roman Catholic Bishops' Dialogue of Canada, 'Summary of Pastoral Practice: When Anglicans and Catholics are at Eucharist Together' (2007), at https://www.anglican.ca/wp-content/uploads/2012/06/ARCB_Ang_and_RC_at_Euch-English.pdf.
6   Mainline Canadian churches concluded an agreement on the mutual recognition of baptism by water and in the name of the Father, Son and Spirit in 1975. In 1991, the Canadian Council of Churches undertook a new ecumenical study with suggestions for sound pastoral practice. See 'Initiation into Christ: Common Teaching and Ecumenical Reflections on Preparation for Baptism', https://www.councilofchurches.ca/wp-content/uploads/2013/12/INITIATION-INTO-CHRIST.pdf. See also Matt Gardner, 'Canadian Churches Mark 40 Years of Recognizing One Baptism', *Anglican Journal* (November 19, 2015), https://www.anglican.ca/news/canadian-churches-mark-40-years-of-recognizing-one-baptism/30013405/.
7   Anglican-Catholic Dialogue of Canada, 'Pastoral Guidelines for Interchurch

ception into full communion of baptized Christians who freely choose to change their church of belonging;[8] and the exchange or transfer of clergy between churches.[9] In my own church (Roman Catholic), many young priests approach the question of sacramental sharing with a rigid and fearful attitude, failing to discern those contexts where spiritual need and shared faith invite a more generous practice of hospitality (*e.g.* pastoral care of mixed marriages, persons in hospitals, homes for the elderly, isolated rural communities).[10] In the absence of mutually agreed guidelines for these common pastoral occurrences, uninformed pastors sometimes act in ways that offend and do harm

---

Marriages', in *Common Witness to the Gospel: Documents on Anglican-Roman Catholic Relations*. 1983–1995, ed. by J. Gros, E. R. Elder, and E. K. Wondra (Washington, DC: U.S. Conference of Catholic Bishops, 1997), 221–30. Among the first principles in responsible pastoral practice is full respect for the freedom of conscience and religious freedom of each spouse, including 'the mutual respect of the faith and doctrine of the partner, which must not be forced or manipulated' (article 9). This precludes any proselytizing by the ministers of either church.

8   In Catholic pastoral practice, it is clearly stated that 'no greater burden than necessary' be asked of such persons who ask to be received into the Catholic communion. As well, 'any appearance of triumphalism' is to be avoided in receiving other Christians. This is in marked contrast to the past, when other Christians were required to make a public renunciation of their previous adherence. See 'Reception of Baptized Christians into the Full Communion of the Catholic Church', in *Rite of Christian Initiation of Adults* (Ottawa: Canadian Conference of Catholic Bishops, 1987), 225–27.

9   Anglican Catholic Dialogue of Canada, 'Pastoral Guidelines for Churches in the Case of Clergy Moving from One Communion to the Other', in *Common Witness to the Gospel*, 177–83. Full communion between the Anglican Church of Canada and the Evangelical Lutheran Church in Canada following the 2001 Waterloo Declaration has also led to the establishment of protocols for the exchange of clergy and shared ministries, including 'Anglican-Lutheran Guidelines for Clergy Serving in Each Other's Churches' and 'Anglican-Lutheran Worship Guidelines', at https://www.anglican.ca/faith/eir/full-communion-partnership/. See also the *Ecumenical Shared Ministries Handbook*, prepared in collaboration with the Anglican, Evangelical Lutheran, United, and Presbyterian Churches of Canada, at https://www.anglican.ca/wp-content/uploads/2010/10/Ecumenical-Shared-Ministries-Handbook.pdf.

10 For an exemplary model of guidelines for the application of CIC 844 on the question of sacramental sharing, see Roman Catholic Diocese of Saskatoon, 'Sacramental Sharing', at https://rcdos.ca/sites/default/files/groupfiles/Media%20browser/p.d._brochure_english_revised_sept_22_08.pdf. Similar guidelines were issued in other dioceses across Canada following a study by the Canadian Conference of Catholic Bishops. For a fuller theological and canonical reflection, see John Huels, 'A Policy on Canon 844, Paragraph 4 for Canadian Dioceses', *Studia Canonica* 34, no. 1 (2001): 91–118.

to ecumenical partners. Uninformed and unprincipled actions undermine mutual trust and give rise to the perception of hostility, indifference or unscrupulous proselytism. Existing agreements must be updated and better disseminated, and new ones developed that take account of new ecumenical partnerships.

In light of these challenges, our common future will require a redoubling of efforts in ecumenical formation. This begins with the theological formation of clergy and pastoral workers. In Canada, we have enjoyed a long history of collaboration and sharing resources for theological education, where students from many denominations study together in consortia of denominational schools. Yet this experience of practical ecumenism has not always provided students with a direct knowledge of sound principles for ecumenical collaboration or of the history and achievements of the ecumenical movement. This must be required learning for all those preparing to embark on pastoral ministry, to enable them to develop the habits of ecumenical courtesy, to be agents of dialogue and protagonists of common witness at every opportunity.[11] The need for ecumenical formation must extend to every stage of Christian faith formation.

---

11 The Second Vatican Council's Decree on Priestly Formation, *Optatam Totus* (article 16), recognizes the need for all priests to be instructed concerning other churches and ecclesial communities so that they might contribute to the re-establishment of unity among Christians. See http://www.vatican.va/archive/hist_councils/ii_vatican_council/documents/vat-ii_decree_19651028_optatam-totius_en.html. The 1993 *Directory for the Application of the Principles and Norms of Ecumenism* dedicates an entire chapter to 'Ecumenical Formation', and it stipulates that all candidates for ministry should take at least one 'compulsory' course on ecumenism (nos. 79-80). The 'ecumenical dimension' is to be considered in all aspects of the curriculum (no. 84). Students are also encouraged to take part in opportunities to encounter other Christians as part of their formative experience (no. 82). See http://www.vatican.va/roman_curia/pontifical_councils/chrstuni/documents/rc_pc_chrstuni_doc_25031993_principles-and-norms-on-ecumenism_en.html.

Considerations in Light of Hebrews 13:1 (South America)

Rev P. Marcial Maçaneiro

In many contexts where we live, in the diversity of our churches, communions and ministries, the exhortation of Hebrews 13:1 is both prophetic and necessary. It is so because the hope that brotherly love will continue among us is an imperative of the Gospel. Jesus himself said it: 'As I have loved you, so also you must love one another. By this all will know that you are my disciples, if you have love for one another' (Jn 13:34–35). That means that no division that we still experience—be it institutional or relational—takes precedence over love, which is the measure of all the gifts of the Holy Spirit for the body of Christ (*cf.* 1 Cor. 13).

On the contrary, sincere, manifest and shared love among us is a grace that allows us to heal the wounds of division and to approach the other as a true brother and sister in Jesus Christ, opening paths of reconciliation and joint witness (*cf.* 2 Cor. 5:18). The same letter to the Hebrews, in the following verses of Chapter 13, speaks of hospitality, solidarity, family life, living together in harmony, eschatological hope, intercession in community, joy, and justice (*cf.* Heb. 13:2-18). And the writer encourages us: 'Do not neglect charity and sharing with others; these are the sacrifices that please God' (Heb. 13:16).

Under the light of this word and considering 'the signs of the times' (Mt. 16:3), as we look at the present and the future of our communities in this Global Christian Forum, we propose three steps to follow together:

- In the face of violence, with its manifestations of extremism and aggression, even among Christian groups: insist on the Gospel of peace according to the beatitudes (*cf.* Mt. 5:9), in the community, pastoral and mediating spaces of our churches and institutions, with actions that lead towards peace and eventually to celebrations of mutual forgiveness among us Christians.

- Facing sectarianism and proselytism, especially in the religious setting: educate people to dialogue according to the Gospel of reconciliation (*cf.* 2 Cor 5:18), with attention to formative programs for ministry and mission, equipping more people, especially young people, for the ecumenical task.

- In the face of proposals of religious mercantilism, in which the gifts of God are often offered as a means of achieving success or as a result of financial donations: proclaim together the Gospel of grace (*cf.* Eph. 2), with dialogues, consultations or demonstrations to affirm our nature as communities of sharing and solidarity.

In this way, I believe, the love proposed in the letter to the Hebrews, besides inspiring hearts, will becomes a driving force producing through mission-focused reform in our churches and ministries.

Envisioning the Journey Ahead: Biblical Perspective

Brian Farrell

> *As Jesus walked along, he saw a man blind from birth. His disciples asked him, 'Rabbi, who sinned, this man or his parents, that he was born blind?'*

In the ninth chapter of John's gospel we read the story of someone who journeys from physical blindness, a sign of his social and religious exclusion, to belief in Jesus the light of the world. Who is this blind man? The whole human race? The poor and discriminated of the world? Or the whole Christian community, Christians like us, who claim to believe in Christ, but are living in a situation of division, which is a form of 'unloving'? 'By this everyone will know that you are my disciples, if you love one another' (John 13:35). But we don't love one another, at least not enough. In the past, Christians have persecuted one another and waged wars against each other. Even today in places, there is rivalry and mutual rejection.

Our concern here, though, is not about our sins, or about who is to blame—'this man or his parents', we or our forebears. Here, let us concentrate on the Spirit-filled transformation that turns the blind man into a courageous follower of Christ. 'Neither this man nor his parents sinned; he was born blind so that God's works might be revealed in him.' He went, he washed in the pool of Siloam as Jesus ordered, and he sees.

The neighbours wanted to know: 'How were your eyes opened?' He answered, 'The man called Jesus made mud, spread it on my eyes, and said to me, "Go to Siloam and wash." I went and washed and received my sight.' They said to him, 'Where is he?' He said, 'I do not know.'

How hard it is to recognize and accept God's works! Is there some wonderful work of God happening in the Gatherings of the Global Christian Forum?

The leaders too doubted him; and that created a series of problems for the man. 'How can someone who is a sinner perform such signs? (because Jesus had cured on the Sabbath). And they were divided. So they said again to the blind man, "What do you say about him?" He said, "He is a prophet."' The beginning of the man's faith: a first recognition that someone loves him for his own sake.

Even his parents abandon him, for the leaders had already agreed that anyone who confessed Jesus to be the Messiah would be put out of the synagogue: 'We know (…) that he was born blind; but we do not know how it is that now he sees, nor do we know who opened his eyes. Ask him; he is of age. He will speak for himself.'

Nobody around the man wants to believe that there is something wonderful happening here. But he knows there is! His faith is growing stronger with each rebuff. 'Here is an astonishing thing! (…) Never since the world began has it been heard that anyone opened the eyes of a person born blind. If this man were not from God, he could do nothing.' The leaders insist: 'We know that God has spoken to Moses, but as for this man, we do not know where he comes from.' They expel him. But the man is now a believer. And while he is rejected by those around him, he has found his Saviour.

There is little room in the dominant culture of today for genuine faith in God and for faithful Christian witness. In this twenty-first century, human society is undergoing a revolutionary breakthrough in information and communication technology, combined with another mega-trend in the flow of human history that has enormous effect on religion and the Christian churches: globalization. Social media emphasize horizontal, immediate interests; they almost always ignore the transcendental dimension of life. Globalization subjects everyone and everything to standardization and regulation. Faith and religion are unwelcome intruders.

> *Jesus heard that they had driven him out, and when he found him, he said, 'Do you believe in the Son of Man?' He answered, 'And who is he, sir? Tell me, so that I may believe in him.' Jesus said to him, 'You have seen him, and the one speaking with you is he.' He said, 'Lord, I believe.' And he worshipped him.* (John 9:35)
>
> *Being a Christian is the encounter with an event, a person, who gives life a new horizon and a decisive direction* (Benedict XVI).

Jesus had given him his sight but he had left him in real trouble: separation from his family, expulsion from his community. There is a price to be paid for the gift of faith.

We may be women and men of faith, but we are living in a broken, sinful situation. We are not one as we are supposed to be, as Jesus and the Father are one—in mutual love. We are divided. Still, most of us are conscious that some form of visible unity is what Jesus prayed for. We don't yet know what that one Christian community would look like. Nor do we know how to get there. We are in an interim, transitional time: 'already but not yet'.

If the Global Christian Forum stands for anything worthwhile it is this: to create the conditions for a new era of friendship and solidarity between all Christian communions, emphasizing the grace we share and not harping on the differences that divide. Only in this way can we fulfil the Lord's command to preach the Gospel to the nations, 'so that the world may believe'. Let us not be afraid of one another. If we meet in fraternal love, the Spirit will surely enkindle in our communities an affective and effective love, as the theme of this third Gathering of the Global Christian Forum urges us: 'Let mutual love continue' (Heb 13:1). The love brought by Jesus, and poured into our hearts by the Holy Spirit, is the only energy and force that we Christians have for advancing God's Kingdom on earth.

We need contact and dialogue to really know each other and to trust one another, to learn from one another and to learn to work together, and not to use our differences to stay apart and separated, let alone in conflict with one another. In a world where we are reminded every day of so much human suffering, poverty, hunger and violence, Christians and their churches have an extreme obligation to show clearly before the world that they live by the Gospel message of reconciliation, healing and universal brotherhood. We will succeed only if Christians and their churches stand together, speak with one voice, and work together in mission, evangelism and service.

'Envisioning the Journey Ahead': that is the title given to this presentation. Do I have a wish list for the years ahead? I hope and pray that the Global Christian Forum will help to do the following:

(a) Call the mainline churches to take the new Pentecostal, Evangelical and charismatic communities seriously. These new experiences of faith challenge longstanding positions regarding many of our customs, laws and traditions, and they especially challenge our lack of courage in regard to moral and ethical standards.

(b) Call the new religious bodies to deepen their theological base in order to avoid uncritical understandings of Scripture and its implications for Christian witness and mission. This will facilitate the meeting between historic continuity and 'newness'.

(c) Concretely, that means renunciation of all kinds of open or hidden proselytizing; it implies respect for one another as Christians, including mutual recognition of our baptism wherever this entering into communion with God and into the Christian community is performed in the biblical way, through water and the Trinitarian formula.

(d) Enable Christians who have been suspicious of the ecumenical movement to recognize that it is a movement rooted in the Gospel and inspired by the Holy Spirit, so that the primarily spiritual and theological nature of the ecumenical movement will be reaffirmed, and so that the goal of our ecumenical efforts will be the full unity willed by Jesus at the Last Supper.

(e) Help us move on from sterile discussions on structures and governance to a new appropriation of our shared Gospel faith. 'He asked them, "What were you arguing about on the way?" But they were silent, for on the way they had argued with one another who was the greatest. He sat down, called the twelve, and said to them, "Whoever wants to be first must be last of all and servant of all"' (Mark 9:33–35).

(f) Ensure that our churches do not place obstacles in the way of doing together much more than we actually do: common Bible study, joint prayer, sharing spiritual experiences; co-operation in biblical and theological research; interaction between our candidates studying for ministry; co-operation in mission and social witness, in the area of development and the preservation of the environment, in mass media, etc.

And this brings us to the heart of the question. Nothing of what our churches hope and seek to do will be achieved without a renewal of our personal faith and our commitment to follow Jesus. In other words, Christians and Christianity have no future without holiness of life. God's words in the Book of Leviticus are addressed to every one of us: 'Be holy, for I am holy' (Lev. 11:44; *cf.* 1 Pet. 1:16). In the end, it is Christ who lives and loves and works in us. It is the Spirit who enlivens us: 'The measure of our holiness stems from the stature that Christ achieves in us, to the extent that, by the power of the Holy Spirit, we model our whole life on his' (Pope Francis).

A few weeks ago, at the world meeting on Mission and Evangelism, in Tanzania, I was asked to share a dream. I thought a lot about it. But in the end I thought: there is only one thing that counts. How present is Jesus in our lives? How active and transforming is the grace of the Holy Spirit in us? So my dream was about how clearly I, and we all together, recognize Jesus as he passes through our lives, and how completely we accept him in our hearts.

A poem was written by an Anglican priest about a hundred years ago, against the background of the terrible upheaval of the First World War. The author called it 'Indifference'. It tells what happened when Jesus came to Birmingham, England, or maybe to Bogotá, or to wherever Christians are gathered together:

> When Jesus came to Golgotha, they hanged Him on a tree,
>
> They drove great nails through hands and feet, and made a Calvary;
>
> They crowned Him with a crown of thorns, red were his wounds and deep,
>
> For those were crude and cruel days, and human flesh was cheap.
>
> When Jesus came to Birmingham [or wherever!], they simply passed Him by.
>
> They would not hurt a hair of Him, they only let Him die;
>
> For men had grown more tender, and they would not give Him pain,
>
> They only just passed down the street, and left Him in the rain.
>
> Still Jesus cried, 'Forgive them, for they know not what they do',
>
> And still it rained the winter rain that drenched Him through and through;
>
> The crowds went home and left the streets without a soul to see,

And Jesus crouched against a wall, and cried for Calvary.

(G. Studdert Kennedy, 1883–1929)

Too often, we and our churches have failed to see what Dietrich Bonhoeffer so deeply experienced in the drama of his own imprisonment: God does not come to our help and save us through his omnipotence, but through his weakness. In his weakest moment, on the cross, Jesus redeemed the world. And 'what has cost God much cannot be cheap for us.' Too often, we and our churches want discipleship without the cross, we want to evangelize without the cost of discipleship! We want our churches to preach the Gospel, without renouncing the pride and self-affirmation that keep us apart and scandalize the world.

Our hope and prayer should be that our communities, and all of us personally, have the same transforming experience as the blind man: to hear the voice and feel the touch of Jesus, leading us out of darkness into the Light. Most often the Jesus who comes to heal us is not 'in power and majesty', or with worldly influence. He is likely to be carrying his cross.

And if we see Jesus leaning against a wall and pining for Calvary and the cross, let us never be afraid; let us gather around him and lift him up, and together go forth with him, in the Holy Spirit, to preach the Gospel to every creature. Amen.

Testimony

Lord Elorm-Donkor

Thank you for the opportunity to share a testimony. The privilege I have this morning to share a testimony is in itself a testimony. Apostle Opoku Onyinah, head of my denomination, the Church of Pentecost, was invited to this gathering. Since he couldn't attend, he delegated my colleague Revd Nana Baah and me to represent him. We bring you his greetings and his commendation of the good work the GCF is doing.

Sharing of testimonies is a vital part of Pentecostal liturgy because it reminds us that our triune God is Emmanuel: he is always with us, acting according to his own will in revealing himself more and more to us, in ways and places we had not expected. Our testimony becomes a shared living experience with others and encourages them to keep hoping in the Lord.

The Church of Pentecost, which was started in Ghana by a European missionary in the 1930s, has grown to become one of the major participants in world Christianity today. Apart from Ghana, it now has churches in 90 other countries on every continent in the world. However, one of the challenges that we discuss and pray about constantly is how to nurture the faith of the youth—second- and third-generation members of our church who have been born and educated in the ever-secularising Western environment—to remain in Christ and follow the Lord. We are aware of the general trend of youth leaving the faith in these contexts. But we are also hopeful in the Lord.

In 2015 I was delegated to attend the 75th anniversary of the founding of the Taizé Community in southern France. I was amazed how Brother Roger's vision for reconciliation led him to establish a community that has specialised in bringing youth from all over the world, from every tribe and nation, to stay in the community for a week to experience the love of God together with others.

I was surprised at how over four thousand youth attended prayers three times a day with passion and participated in daily Bible studies. I was encouraged that there is hope. Since then I have kept the relationship with the Taizé Community and participated in their activities. I returned to Taizé for two weeks for silent retreat and cannot forget the experience. I have hosted two young volunteers from the community in Birmingham when they toured the UK, speaking in schools and in churches about the Taizé experience.

I worked closely with Brother Paolo on the Hidden Treasure gathering in Birmingham and have kept constant contact with him. All these experiences give me hope that our God is bigger than our individual talents and gifts. So we need to be open to others and to let mutual love continue. We don't fully know where these collaborations will take us. But we believe that our God, who is Emmanuel, will lead us on in mutual love. Thank you.

Brother Paolo

Brother Alois, the prior of our community, should have been here today. He regrets not being able to make it, and I am replacing him.

In my life at the Taizé Community, the thing that most stimulates my thinking and prayer is when, after daily evening prayer, a number of us stand in the church, available for people to come to speak. You never know what's coming next. Often you realise that you are in front of a young person who has never before found an adult whom they trust and in whom they can confide.

I first met with Lord intending to try to answer any questions he had about Taizé. But I was in for a surprise. As he spoke, I found that my heart resonated with the deep pastoral concern he has for the young people of his community.

This was during the 2015 commemoration of the life of Brother Roger. He would have been so happy that to celebrate his life we were joined not only by the friends we already had, but by pastors of churches and people of organisations with which we had previously had no contact. The Global Christian Forum was the network that made this possible. Thank you!

When I was a young brother in our community, in the early 1980s, Brother Roger only rarely spoke with us about his own vocation. Once, though, he told us how as a child, in the small village in Switzerland where he was brought up, on Sunday mornings he would see two streams of people passing through the village in opposite directions: one towards the Protestant Church, the other to the Catholic one. And how to him, as a child, this was incomprehensible. For turning to God meant discovering the deep source of unity with all people.

His dismay as a child at discovering the division of the Church deserves to be taken seriously. In his case, it led him to seek a life of community which would remain within the Church, but at the same time would also be a space where there are no more denominational tags. I don't know how this is possible. I don't think any of us at Taizé understand how this is possible. It certainly does not come from anything special about the brothers of the community. This space of freedom spills over into the youth meetings at Taizé. And it is also nourished in return by the many visitors we receive.

Our theme today is 'Envisioning the Journey Ahead'. At Taizé we know there is a journey, that we have not yet arrived. Brother Roger wrote in our Rule, 'Make the unity of the body of Christ your passionate concern.' Yet the experience I want to share is not about envisioning the journey, but more like an encouragement, perhaps even a humble confirmation, that our journey really does have a destination.

Often in ecumenical gatherings we say, 'Unity is to be discovered, not made.' I can say that in the stability of our community life we experience the truth of this. It's like when you are in a swimming pool and, needing to rest, you reach down with your feet and find the floor is there. The Church, the one Church, is there.

In Taizé we are quite a large group living together. In the last two or three years, a number of young brothers have entered the community. For several of them, I do not know which churches they come from. Is this carelessness? Probably it will come out in a conversation this year or next. In the meantime, we are entering into a lifelong community life together, and most usually God gives us other things to talk about.

The Future of Global Christianity: Introduction

Jean-Daniel Plüss

Christ is risen! He is risen indeed!

During the past two days, we have been looking back in one way or another. We have been reflecting on our faith journey. We have remembered events of the past and we have had conversations about topics that emerged from the last global gathering in Manado.

This reminds me a bit of the Emmaus story, where Jesus is asking the disciples, 'What are you discussing as you are walking along?' But we know that the Emmaus story does not stop with disappointment and shattered dreams. It continues and will culminate in a big surprise and with a discovery that is full of hope.

In a similar fashion, we have come to a turning point in our gathering today, as we have begun to look forward. We dare you to think about the future of global Christianity. When we will be meeting this afternoon in regional interchurch groups, we will be talking about challenges that we see. But I believe with all my heart that we will also discover developments that will fill us with hope.

What did we sing on the first day? 'Tenemos esperanza!' We have hope!

I am not here to give a long speech, or otherwise I could give you examples of how I was surprised to discover, on more than one occasion, how the Holy Spirit revitalizes the Church of our Lord Jesus Christ to the glory of God.

We invite you therefore to share, in your regional group, your own stories of what is happening, how we as Christians can respond to the divine calling and the needs of a world that God loves so much.

We invite you to listen and receive. And towards the end of your group session, we ask you to write down three challenges and three hopes that have emerged and are most relevant in your context.

In the afternoon, we will then hear a short three-minute report from each region on what has impressed you most.

May your eyes be opened and may you emerge from your meeting with burning hearts because the Spirit of Christ has inspired you.

Revd Dr Martin Junge

DAY THREE: THURSDAY 26 APRIL
LET MUTUAL LOVE CONTINUE!
ENVISIONING THE JOURNEY AHEAD

14.30 PLENARY SESSION

The Future of Global Christianity: Identifying Hopes and Challenges

Moderator: **Martin Junge** (Chile/Switzerland), General Secretary, Lutheran World Federation

Regional Interchurch Group Reports

- *Africa* — **Richard Baawobr** (Ghana), Bishop of Wa
- *Asia* — **Samuel Saxena** (India), Assistant Professor, Department of Advanced Theological Studies, Sam Higginbottom University, Allahabad
- *Europe* — **Amanda Jackson** (United Kingdom), Executive Director, Women's Commission, World Evangelical Alliance

- *Middle East* — **Joy Mallouh** (Lebanon), Church of God in Lebanon and Syria; President, Mediterranean Bible College
- *North America* — **Allyson Barnett-Cowan** (Canada), Anglican Communion, and President, Canadian Council of Churches; **Catherine Clifford** (Canada), Professor of Systematic and Historical Theology, Saint Paul University, Ottawa
- *Latin America and the Caribbean* — **Samuel Murillo** (Mexico), President, Youth and Young Adults, World Methodist Council

Plenary Discussion of Regional Reports

Third Global Gathering Message: Presentation of the Process and the Message Committee Members

Wesley Granberg-Michaelson (USA), Global Christian Forum Committee Member representing the World

Introduction

Martin Junge

I have been encouraged to speak in my native language, Spanish. I believe this is part of the experience that we are having as the Global Christian Forum. In this Global Gathering, we are trying to transcend linguistic barriers so that we can engage in the conversations to which we have been summoned. When I reflected on this fact, I thought about the possibility of special headphones that would allow us to interpret not only our different languages but also the different theological and social places from which we come to this meeting. What if there could be a translation system that would help us to clarify exactly where we are coming from when we say what we are saying? Or what if there were an interpretive device that would help us interpret silences? We have had conversations, but there have also been silences, and those silences speak, saying things that we do not know how to interpret.

Even with all of today's technological advances, with artificial intelligence, I do not believe that these technologies can be developed. However, we are not here as experts in artificial intelligence but as people who place our trust in spiritual intelligence. So when we meet and relate to each other, we allow ourselves to begin to speak, to begin to understand each other, to begin to decipher the worlds beyond our languages—our theological worlds, our stories, our experiences.

As the Lutheran World Federation, we see the great value of this Forum space in which we have come together. It is a space to begin to open the dialogue and to break the silences, not because some technology is helping us but because spiritual intelligence, specifically the call of God, has brought us together. I remain deeply convinced that Christian faith is profoundly relational in nature, and that this is a good thing.

In Christ, God opens a cosmic conversation with humanity. God places the Word of creation into the world to initiate a conversation with his creation, regarding its redemption and salvation. It is in this mission that we continue to walk and to which we continue to be called, a mission of dialogue and relationships. This conversation is impossible, it seems to me, without the dialogue with us that God has opened up in Christ. It is impossible, as Christian communities, to tell him that we cannot commit ourselves to dialogue. It is impossible, to me, for us not to open ourselves to relationships when God is seeking to bridge and overcome the great chasm between himself and us so as to relate to humanity.

This plenary is a key turning point, a moment of transition in the course of this gathering of the Global Christian Forum. Thus far we have been listening in plenary sessions. We have been receiving a lot of information—things to think about, ideas, biblical and theological elements to enhance understanding. We have spoken together in regional and global groups. Some of us have gathered as our different communions. Now comes the time to bring together all that has been talked about and to direct all this conversation towards the future. It is the time to start seeing what are the great themes that will continue to call us forward together as the Global Christian Forum, to see what issues are emerging from our group conversations.

We will receive reports from six regional groups, which I am going to call on in alphabetical order so as not to make any errors of protocol: Africa, Asia, Europe, Latin America and the Caribbean, the Middle East, and North America. These groups will share with us their reflections along two main axes as we look towards the future: what our great hopes are and where we see challenges. Then we will speak to and listen to each other to begin discerning the collective voice of this meeting and to see how we carry it forward. A group of people will be taking notes on both what is presented here and the comments that are shared in response. Tomorrow, that group will summarize the main themes of what has been said.

Regional Interchurch Group Reports: Reflections on Hopes and Challenges

AFRICA

Richard Baawobr

When we considered hopes, we noticed that, given the shift of gravity of Christianity to the Global South with its centre now on the African continent, the youthful church and the population of 630 million offer great potential to the church. And our faith stories unite us because stories are a common feature of our culture. The Ubuntu vision, especially the sense of community, if lived to the full, is a Christian value that we can offer to the global church. For the Global Christian Forum to thrive in Africa, the space that is currently offered for special ministries, especially the active participation of women in our churches, makes us believe that opening spaces to the youth and the differently abled will help the church.

With regard to challenges, we notice that the imbalance in the world economic order and the corruption rampant on the continent hinder what we can offer to the global church. Second, we want to have a space for African theology, brewed in an African pot, and to be able to approach issues such as conflict leading to communion, and the erosion of certain values of community life due to poverty, individualism, insecurity, etc. We need to offer an African theological reflection on such subjects. But we are challenged to do that. And finally, the fragmentation in our churches because of ethnicity, prejudices, stereotyping, politics, criticism of each other, and conflicting theologies is certainly a challenge to us.

ASIA

Samuel Saxena

We found three areas of challenge:

(1) Challenges coming from the multi-religious context of Asia and the minority status of Christianity in most countries. In this context, we discussed religious nationalism, religious intolerance, and the lack of religious freedom due to both religious and social political structures. As a consequence, there is an increase in persecution, marginalization and martyrdom.

(2) Challenges coming from rapid social change that includes secularism, urbanization, migration, family structures under threat, poverty, environmental crisis, and human trafficking.

(3) Challenges coming from divided churches, due to failing to recognize brothers and sisters within the body of Christ. Consequently, we have failed to give and receive gifts of mutual love out of the richness of each tradition. So we do not have a united voice or credible witness to society, nor does the church engage robustly to communicate the gospel in the cultural context.

We identified three areas of hope:

(1) The most important area is the vibrancy of Asian churches. Churches have been increasing in number. For example, there is the rebirth and growth of Chinese Christianity in spite of social and political challenges. There are signs of spiritual renewal and holistic engagement in serving society, reaching out to the younger generation, prayer movements and new music.

(2) There are signs of increasing ecumenical engagement, including the Global Christian Forum's Asia chapter. This

should be revived very strongly. We look forward to the churches being fully reconciled with each other.

(3) Lastly, when churches engage in relating to each other, historic churches can enrich younger churches with longstanding tenets of faith, while the younger churches may share their contemporary spiritual experiences.

EUROPE

Amanda Jackson

I'm speaking on behalf of Europeans and people like me who have been adopted by Europe.

There were four European groups, so to condense all those ideas is a bit tricky but I will try.

Two clear challenges emerged in all four groups. The first one was secularism and increasing nominalism, young people having no faith language or experience and an emphasis on material success, and the fact that Christianity is so often sidelined at best or seen as a dangerous superstition. The second clear challenge was proselytism. It is a challenge only in some countries and contexts, but it can divide churches and we are about unity. It can be the result of a lack of knowledge about a country's Christian tradition. It can neglect the fact that there exist different expressions of vibrant Christian faith.

Other important challenges were identified, and some of them have been mentioned by others: individualism, in that people feel that they don't need a church community; a lack of discipleship; a lack of solid grounding and growth in faith; migration and refugees, who pose a huge challenge; technology and the fact that churches are not adapting to new technology; increasing discrimination against Christians and other faiths; and the breakdown of healthy families, which helps to break the tradition of passing on faith from generation to generation.

But some of those challenges can easily be turned around and seen as causes for opportunity and hope. With increasing secularism, churches old and new have a renewed vision for evangelism. Out of that have come a variety of fresh expressions that are invigorating churches:

new ways of doing prayer and worship; trying different forms of spirituality inside traditional and newer churches. Similarly, the migrant and refugee challenge becomes a hope which offers richness to Europe and opportunities to evangelize. Christian migrants are coming to Europe and are helping to re-enliven local churches. Non-Christian migrants are finding Jesus in large numbers, and there are many stories of small churches being renewed and of new churches springing up in all forms. Similarly, technology, while being a huge challenge, is also obviously a huge opportunity and source of hope. If these things can be used to spread the good news in Europe, that is a new way of bringing hope in Jesus.

Some other things as well caused us to have hope. There was a strong sense that we do not have to be overcome by the statistics of decline in Europe—they tell only a part of the picture. The church can bring hope in situations of challenge, poverty and inequality. After all, we have Jesus and Jesus is the answer. Sometimes we forget that. Also, there was a sense that growing discrimination, and even persecution, can help to unite Christians and make our faith and our perseverance stronger. We can lose some of our complacent flabbiness. And there is a sense that Jesus is our hope in the future and that, as one person said, it gives us the opportunities to show Europeans the beauty of meeting Jesus.

LATIN AMERICAN AND CARIBBEAN
Samuel Murillo

In Latin America, our hope seems to be grounded in our openness to explore together our common faith from the living Word and with a Christological method that unites us. We find that young people seem to have resolved in their daily lives many of the differences like those that we discuss in this forum. Every day there are spaces of active listening, of acceptance, of mutual recognition that build a sense of real community in the daily life of our people.

We are spiritual beings and it is necessary to continue to explore convergences and divergences in our communities and spiritualities. There is a need for us to go out together and discover our common challenges and goals.

There are many ways in which we as churches have supported each other throughout our history and our presence in Latin America. There is great diversity in the region; it is celebrated by many whereas others live in fear or in sectarianism.

With regard to our challenges, we need to engage in serious reflection and reach a conviction that the unity of the church is a gift from God. This must be discovered by all and experienced in different ways in each of our cultures throughout the region. At times it seems that a discourse of absolute truths dominates, often leading to intolerance of one another. We must dare to rediscover our common humanity and then try to explore our common faith.

Education and teaching—academic, theological, and experiential—are fundamental points that lead our communities towards openness, mutual recognition, and reinterpretation of the concept of mission. Mission should not start from discrimination, persecution, or proselytism, but should arise from biblical, historical, and theological ideologies and models that respond to the contextual challenges of the region.

Despite the positive observations I have just made, there remains much friction between different traditions—Catholics and non-Catholics, Protestants and Evangelicals, and so on. As we deal with these challenges, it is also necessary to work on the transition to the participation by and representation of new generations. Many of us here have participated in all three Global Gatherings. The key question is how we can invite new generations to take part so that they can have an experience like this one and bring different approaches and fresh perspectives to today's challenges. We need an ecumenism not of rhetoric, politics, or power, but of sincerity and vulnerability, and we need to transmit it to local and grassroots communities that can build on our work and contribute to the development of openness and mutual respect. We need to work together on a model of encountering each other and of community building that goes beyond innovation, entertainment, and emotions to recover the sense of the transcendent in our experience of faith.

We are experiencing today a growth in religious diversity and complexity, but also a predominance of absolutisms and fundamentalisms of various forms. Often these absolutisms have political or economic agendas that greatly affect social or political unity in the region. We should encourage collaborative work in addressing the challenges posed by humanitarian needs. Although we may not hear about it in the global media, our region is full of instances of forced migration, extreme violence, corruption, injustice, exploitation, and trafficking of women, as well as discrimination against a great number of groups. It is by passing on our experience to new generations that the Global Christian Forum can contribute toward fostering an openness to such consultations not only globally and regionally, but also at the national and local levels.

MIDDLE EAST

Joy Mallouh

As representatives of various churches, we have all recognized the positive role of the GCF in offering a platform for dialogue that is missing in our churches in the Middle East, which are suffering under persecution and war.

We have identified several challenges. There are three, but underneath each challenge we have several points.

First, the political instability due to:

(1) the Israeli-Arab conflict and occupation of land;

(2) wars in Iraq, Syria, Lebanon and, of course, Palestine resulting in a major refugee crisis;

(3) despair leading to emigration and affecting the Christian presence in the region;

(4) social injustice leading to Syria's problems; and

(5) lastly, underneath the political instability is the degradation of moral values.

Challenge number two is ecclesial and pastoral. Under this we identify the need to:

(1) strengthen relations between churches and increase collaboration in order to adopt a common strategy;

(2) empower youth and involve them in church life;

(3) empower also our educational and social institutions; and

(4) promote equal citizenship.

Challenge number three is due to the complexity of our social structure, including religious and cultural diversity, inter-faith relations, and church-government relationships.

But we have big hopes and we have identified three of them.

(1) Our hope is in steadfastness and witnessing accompanied with patience.

(2) Our hope is to revive the Middle East Council of Churches' role as an ecumenical body and for it to be inclusive, with the rapprochement of all church families so that they will cooperate and minister together.

(3) Our hope is in church commitment to inter-faith relations and the promotion of co-existence and social harmony with non-Christians.

I conclude with our commitment to continuing our ecumenical journey together and with the Global Christian Forum.

NORTH AMERICA

Allyson Banett-Cohen, Catherine Clifford

We were amused that the organizers of the Global Christian Forum decided that Canadians should be in charge of the North American regional groups. So there was a trinity of Canadians: a Roman Catholic, an Anglican and our Pentecostal brother who can't be with us at the moment. But we've all agreed on the message.

The challenges:

(1) Forming biblically literate, articulate disciples in our churches who can offer credible witness to gospel values together in our North American cultures.

(2) The positive experience so many of us have in these days of good energy, positive sharing and experiencing each other as fellow Christians in great diversity creates a challenge of communication. How do we replicate the experience of the Global Christian Forum and these values that we experience to our communities when we return home?

(3) To encourage greater participation in the Forum by indigenous peoples, Blacks, Latinos and others in North America, and by youth and women. There was a suggestion that perhaps the Forum could organize a meeting for younger leaders.

Among the hopes we identified and shared:

(1) We from North America see the growth of the churches in the Global South as a sign of hope. And we recognize that the growing presence of more recent immigrants to North America is a force to transform and renew the life and vitality of our churches. In this line also, an important sign of hope is the engagement in many ecumenical efforts of our churches to receive refugees and immigrants in North America.

(2) Without apologizing, with a passion to share the gospel, we hope that we can develop best practices of witnessing to the gospel with sensitivity to diverse contexts.

(3) The hope that all of our traditions will one day be able to recognize each other's baptism.

Comments from the plenary discussion after the regional reports

Editor's note: Since it has not been possible to identify every speaker, names of speakers are not included and the discussion summary may be incomplete.

Comment 1: Greater attention should be paid to indigenous peoples and the disabled.

Comment 2: There is a need for very local action, not only global ecumenism. The GCF should aid the organization of such local efforts.

Comment 3: More attention should be given to the churches of the Middle East, who are on the front line of the refugee crisis and the religious struggles.

Comment 4: The situation in the Middle East is quite diverse. For the first time in the ecumenical movement, it is recognized that the Middle East includes the Gulf states.

Comment 5: Priorities should be (1) ecumenical events for young people to participate in ministry in other contexts and church traditions; (2) pilgrimages of people, congregations and parishes visiting other people, congregations, and parishes, including those in other regions; and (3) lay people sharing with other lay people so that horizons can be widened on a global level.

Comment 6: Great and various challenges lay ahead. Locally, new proposals are being developed to overcome these challenges. But more exchange is needed, so that solutions can be found more quickly. There is a need for theological and missiological exchange at a global level.

Comment 7: Migration has been mentioned and the causes of migration in Africa are known. Migrant churches value the GCF as a platform for exchange with other Christians. But national ecumenical bodies often do not support migrant churches or offer help, for example to find resources and places for worship. The GCF could become a facilitator in this regard.

Comment 8: Achieving a sustainable environment with climate change is a major concern. Climate change will lead to more migration and more wars. Peace depends on our learning to live in a way that is simple, sharing, caring, and compassionate. We need to care for God's creation and try to enable all human beings to flourish, primarily in spiritual things, not so much in material things. There is a need to act now for the world of our grandchildren.

Comment 9: (1) The continuation of global ecumenical processes on the local level has always been a big challenge. This needs to be addressed through the theological education of pastors as key persons. (2) In the USA, some churches previously critical of climate change are changing their views. The church has to dissociate itself from this as a political issue and present it as a spiritual issue.

Comment 10: Violence in its multiple forms needs to be considered. Many churches are persecuted violently. But also, our violent discourse does violence to other confessions. Violent theological language towards other people needs to stop.

Comment 11: In Venezuela, brothers and sisters are suffering. Thousands are fleeing the country. Churches are not allowed to distribute food. Maybe the World Council of Churches needs to visit Venezuela and extend support similar to that offered to Chile under Pinochet.

Comment 12: The Bible needs to be read contextually, and also from the perspective of women.

Comment 13: Christians must be role models in this time, the last days. False prophets exist and must be avoided to preserve our integrity.

Comment 14: (1) Theology and liturgy come mostly from the Western world. How can contextualized Asian theology and liturgy be encouraged? (2) Pray not only for the Middle East, but also for religiously restricted countries in Asia.

Comment 15: (1) Focus on children, especially on violence against children. Churches need to be a strong voice to the government. (2) Religious fundamentalism infused with economics and politics wants to take power in Latin America. (3) The GCF should help to create a Latin American forum. Especially in the current economic crisis, support for such an idea would be very much appreciated.

Comment 16: Power is a key issue—in the church, in societies, in inter-personal relationships. We need to reflect on which paradigm we are operating in with regard to power, in order to avoid denying the example of Jesus, who humbled himself (see Philippians 2).

Comment 17: The issue for historical churches continues to be proselytism, which leads to doctrinal wars.

Comment 18: (1) Social justice causes are an issue. In the USA, the church often takes a neutral position. Churches should unify behind social justice causes, ideally without politicizing them. (2) Cooperation between white and migrant churches is largely lacking in the USA.

Colombian dance and music

DAY THREE: THURSDAY 26 APRIL
LET MUTUAL LOVE CONTINUE!
ENVISIONING THE JOURNEY AHEAD

AFTERNOON AND EVENING MEETINGS

16.30 Global Interchurch Groups

Conversations on Previous Sessions and Other Group Agenda from a Global Perspective

18.30 Evening Prayer in Global Interchurch Groups

20.30 In Colombia Together

Colombian Cultural Evening

16:30 Global Interchurch Groups

Conversations on Previous Sessions and Other Group Agenda from a Global Perspective

Evening Prayer in Global Interchurch Groups

The Gathering of the Community

The Leader welcomes the community and begins with a prayer

Silence

A song of praise

The Proclamation of the Word

The reading and rereading (multiple languages) of Luke 24:28–32

Silence

A sharing of a word or image that comes to heart and mind of participants

Prayer

Thanksgiving

Intercession

Lord's Prayer (each in own languages)

Conclusion

L: Let us go in peace. Alleluia!

Sign of peace.

20.30 In Colombia Together
Colombian Cultural Evening

Ms. Luz Marina Peña, Bishop Édgar Aristizábal Quintero, Archbishop Óscar Urbina Ortega (Colombia); Ms Elena Paquini (Italy)

DAY FOUR: FRIDAY 27 APRIL
LET MUTUAL LOVE CONTINUE!
FORWARD TOGETHER IN FAITH AND HOPE

MORNING PRAYER

Prepared by the Pontifical Council for Promoting Christian Unity and the Episcopal Conference of Colombia

Music:
   Catholic Church of Colombia

Morning Prayer

Welcome, everyone, to this moment of prayer. We have reached the last day of our meetings. Our hearts are full of joy for all we have lived and shared. We already feel nostalgic because we must leave, but we are motivated by the commitment and the Christian responsibility to continue advancing together in faith and hope, so that despite the distances that separate us 'our mutual love will continue'.

Brothers and sisters, every month the Holy See publishes a video in which the Pope's intentions about the current challenges for humanity are gathered, and he encourages the Church and everyone to join with him in prayer.

In January 2017 the theme was to pray for those who contribute to Chrstian unity. To set the mood for this moment, let us watch this video (*https://www.youtube.com/watch?v=gTBtCaEuOj4*). After the the video projection, we will join in singing.

Song: *Juntos como hermanos (Together as Brothers and Sisters)*

*Un largo caminar
por el desierto bajo el sol
no podemos avanzar
sin la ayuda del Señor.*

*Unidos al rezar, unidos
en una canción
viviremos nuestra fe
con la ayuda del Señor.*

*La Iglesia en marcha está
a un mundo nuevo vamos ya
donde reinará el amor
donde reinará la paz.*

Author: Father Cesáreo Gabaráin Azurmendi

President: We allow ourselves, with the conviction of our faith, to begin this moment with the trinary invocation, asking God to pour out on all of us his gifts and graces. In the name of the Father, the Son and the Holy Spirit. Amen.

Song:
(choir and first verse of 'Together as Brothers and Sisters')

We know that in Christ we are one and that love must remain in us. However, in everyday experience it is not always so. Without the Lord's help we cannot move forward; we ask God to forgive our sins of disunity and lack of love among us.

Silence (instrumental music)

Saint John in his first letter makes it clear to us: 'If we say: "We have no sin", we deceive ourselves and there is no truth in us. If we confess our sins, he is faithful and just and will forgive us our sins and purify us from all unrighteousness.' (1 Jn. 1:9)

Song: Señor 10 piedad – Kyrie eleison
Forgive us Lord, have mercy on your people
Forgive us Lord, teach us to forgive (2x)

Por el pecado del mundo
Padre ten piedad
por tanta desigualdad
en la reparticion del pan
y por nuestra indiferencia
Padre ten piedad
ante el dolor del que sufre
sin amor techo ni hogar.

Commentator: Let us sit down and prepare our hearts to accept the Word of God. May this seed find in us fertile ground in which it can germinate, grow, and bear abundant fruit.

Psalm 25 (24)

Commentator: This psalm is a plea from the believer in a situation of anguish. It is a very frequent prayer among the Jews to ask the Lord to guide them on the right path, the one of truth and justice. Also for us, today, may we ask for the gift of moving forward together in faith and hope.

After each stanza, we join with the antiphone in italics.

To you, O Lord, I lift up my soul;
in you I trust, O my God.

Do not let me be put to shame,
nor let my enemies triumph over me.
No one who hopes in you will ever be put to shame.

Muestranos Señor tu camino, y avanzaremos juntos en la fe y la esperanza (*Show us your way, Lord, and we will advance together in faith and hope*).

Show me your ways, O Lord,
teach me your paths;
guide me in your truth and teach me,
for you are God my Saviour,
and my hope is in you all day long.

Muestranos Señor tu camino, y avanzaremos juntos en la fe y la esperanza.

Remember, O Lord, your great mercy and love,
for they are from of old.
Remember not the sins of my youth
and my rebellious ways;
according to your love remember me
for you are good, O Lord.

Muestranos Señor tu camino, y avanzaremos juntos en la fe y la esperanza.

Good and upright is the Lord;
therefore he instructs sinners in his ways.
He guides the humble in what is right
and teaches them his way.

Muestranos Señor tu camino, y avanzaremos juntos en la fe y la esperanza.

All the ways of the Lord are loving and faithful
for those who keep the demands of his covenant.
For the sake of your name, O Lord;
forgive my iniquity, though it is great.

Muestranos Señor tu camino, y avanzaremos juntos en la fe y la esperanza.

Who, then, is the man that fears the Lord?
He will instruct him in the way chosen for him.
He will spend his days in prosperity,
and his descendants will inherit the land.

Muestranos Señor tu camino, y avanzaremos juntos en la fe y la esperanza.

The Lord confides in those who fear him;
he makes his covenant known to them.
My eyes are ever on the Lord,
for only he will release my feet from the snare.

Muestranos Señor tu camino, y avanzaremos juntos en la fe y la esperanza.

Turn to me and be gracious to me,
for I am lonely and afflicted.
The troubles of my heart have multiplied;
free me from my anguish.

Muestranos Señor tu camino, y avanzaremos juntos en la fe y la esperanza.

Look upon my affliction and my distress
and take away all my sins.
See how my enemies have increased
and how fiercely they hate me!

Muestranos Señor tu camino, y avanzaremos juntos en la fe y la esperanza.

Guard my life and rescue me;
let me not be put to shame, for I take refuge in you.
May integrity and uprightness protect me,
because my hope is in you.
Redeem Israel, O God,
from all their troubles!.

Glory be to the Father and to the Son and to the Holy Spirit. As it was in the beginning is now, and ever shall be, world without end. Amen.

Song: *Jesucristo me dejó inquieto (Jesus Christ left me restless)*

Jesucristo me dejo inquieto
Su palabra me llenó de luz,
Nunca más yo pude ver el mundo,
Sin sentir aquello que sintió Jesús (2x)

Reader: John 15: 8-17 (New International Version - NIV)

⁸This is to my Father's glory, that you bear much fruit, showing yourselves to be my disciples. ⁹As the Father has loved me, so have I loved you. Now remain in my love. ¹⁰If you keep my commands, you will remain in my love, just as I have kept my Father's commands and remain in his love. ¹¹I have told you this so that my joy may be in you and that your joy may be complete. ¹²My command is this: Love each other as I have loved you. ¹³Greater love has no one than this: to lay down one's life for one's friends.

¹⁴You are my friends if you do what I command. ¹⁵I no longer call you servants, because a servant does not know his master's business. Instead, I have called you friends, for everything that I learned from my Father I have made known to you. ¹⁶You did not choose me, but I chose you and appointed you so that you might go and bear fruit—fruit that will last—and so that whatever you ask in my name the Father will give you. ¹⁷This is my command: Love each other.

Assembly: How good and pleasant it is when God's people live together in unity! (Psalm 133:1)

Homily: Saint Clement of Rome, Letter to the Corinthians

Who will be able to explain the bond of divine love?

Love unites us to God, love covers a multitude of sins, love endures everything, supports it all with patience; nothing sordid or haughty is in it; love does not admit divisions, does not promote discord, but does everything in harmony; in love all of God's elect find their perfection, and without it nothing is pleasing to God. In love, the Lord welcomed us: because of his love for us; our Lord Jesus Christ, fulfilling the will of the Father, gave his blood for us, his flesh for our flesh, his life for our lives.

You see, beloved brethren, how great and admirable love is and how its perfection is unspeakable. No one is able to practice it properly if God does not give him this gift. Let us pray, therefore, and implore the divine mercy, so that we know how to practice love without blemish, free from all human partiality.

Blessed we are, dear brothers and sisters, if we fulfil the Lord's commands in the harmony of love, for this love will obtain for us the forgiveness of sins. It is written: Blessed is the one who is absolved of his guilt, whose sin has been buried; blessed is the man to whom the Lord does not point the crime and in whose Spirit there is no falsehood. This proclamation of happiness belongs to those who, through Jesus Christ our Lord, have been chosen by God, to whom be the glory for ever and ever. Amen.

Allow me, after having listened to Saint Clement of Rome, to quote some words from Pope Francis, who proposed three axes to advance in the common path of Christians and to deepen ecumenism. The Pope insisted, 'To continue our common journey, three words come to my mind: prayer, witness, mission.'

About prayer, he said: 'Let us not tire of asking the Lord for the gift of unity together.'

About witness, he said: 'The conviction has grown that ecumenism is not an impoverishment, but a richness; the certainty that what the Spirit has sown in the other produces a common harvest has matured.' He invited us to treasure that heritage and be aware that we are called to offer to the world every day, as Jesus asked us, the witness of our love and unity.

About mission, he recalled, 'There is a time for everything' (Eccl. 3:1) and this is the time in which the Lord is asking us in a particular way to come out of ourselves and our environment and bring his merciful love to a world thirsting for peace. Let us help each other to put the demands of the Gospel at the centre and to dedicate ourselves concretely to this mission.

Dear brothers and sisters, in this way the path to moving forward together in faith and hope is marked by the fulfilment of the mandate of the Lord's love, with these three central axes that the Pope proposed to us: prayer, witness, and mission.

Next, we continue with a moment of spontaneous prayers led by representatives of the Catholic Charismatic Movement (unrecorded).

Commentator: We stand, to conclude this moment of spirituality with our common prayer, praying for the unity of those who believe in Jesus Christ.

President: Let us unite our faith, our thoughts, our hearts and our voices so that together we can sing the prayer that Jesus the Lord taught us:

Song: Padre Nuestro (Our Father)

We hold each other's hands as brothers and sisters in prayer. We join in the song and we proclaim together the prayer of Our Father.

Song

Assembly:

> Our Father, who art in heaven,
> Hallowed be thy name;
> Thy kingdom come;
> Thy will be done on earth as it is in heaven.
>
> Give us this day our daily bread,
> Forgive us our sins as we forgive those who sin against us;
> lead us not into temptation, but deliver us from evil.

President: Let us pray:

> Father of love,
> You have called us to be one with your Son Jesus Christ,
> you ask us to bear abundant fruit by remaining in your love.
>
> We ask you that by the grace of your Spirit,
> we may love one another
> and stay in unity,
> advancing together by faith and hope in the ways of holiness.
>
> Through Jesus Christ Our Lord,
> Amen.

Song: *Iglesia Peregrina de Dios (Pilgrim Church of God)*
All united we form a single body
One people that at Easter was born:
Members of Christ by blood redeemed
Pilgrim Church of God

WE ARE ON THE EARTH
SEED OF ANOTHER KINGDOM,
WE ARE WITNESSES OF LOVE:
PEACE FOR WARS
AND LIGHT BETWEEN THE SHADOWS
PILGRIM CHURCH OF GOD

Vive en nosotros la fuerza del Espíritu
que el Hijo desde el Padre envió:
Él nos empuja, nos guía y alimenta
Iglesia peregrina de Dios.

Rugen tormentas y a veces nuestra barca
parece que ha perdido el timón.
Miras con miedo, no tienes confianza.
Iglesia peregrina de Dios

Una esperanza nos llena de alegría:
Presencia que el señor prometió.
Vamos cantando. Él viene con nosotros,
Iglesia peregrina de Dios.

Todos nacidos en un solo bautismo
unidos en la misma comunión
todos viviendo en una misma casa
Iglesia peregrina de Dios.

Todos prendidos en una misma suerte
ligados a la misma salvación
somos un cuerpo y Cristo es la cabeza.
Iglesia peregrina de Dios.

Author: Father Cesáreo Gabaráin

'My prayer is not for them alone. I pray also for those who will believe in me through their message, that all of them may be one, Father, just as you are in me and I am in you. May they also be in us so that the world may believe that you have sent me.' (Jn 17:20-21)

Prayer for the unity of Christians

Heavenly Father,
We thank you for the movement of unity
that you have raised up in our time
among the disciples of your Son, still separated.

We ask forgiveness for sins
that we have committed in the past
and that we continue to commit in the present
against the unity of the Church of your Son,
our Redeemer and Lord.

We beg you to grant us
the grace of the Holy Spirit,
so that we may seek
ardently and patiently for the unity
that your beloved Son wants for His Church.

Give us, Father, the Holy Spirit of prayer
that leads us, in truth and charity,
to perfect unity, so that the world may believe
that You sent your Son, who,
being the full truth and the true life,
is our way to you, Father.

To you be all honour and glory,
in communion with your Son Jesus Christ,
and the Holy Spirit, for ever and ever.

Amen.

DAY FOUR: FRIDAY 27 APRIL
LET MUTUAL LOVE CONTINUE!
FORWARD TOGETHER IN FAITH AND HOPE

9.30 PLENARY SESSION

Forward Together in Faith and Hope

Introduction to the Session and Invitation to the 25th Pentecostal World Conference

> ***David Wells*** (Canada), Vice-Chair, Pentecostal World Fellowship and GCF Committee Member for the PWF; General Superintendent, The Pentecostal Assemblies of Canada

Forward Together in Faith and Hope: Biblical Perspective

> ***George Mahlobo*** (South Africa), President, Apostolic Faith Mission; Pentecostal World Fellowship Advisory Committee Member

Forward Together in Faith, Hope, and Action: It is Possible!

William 'Billy' Wilson (USA), Global Co-chair, Empowered21; President, Oral Roberts University; Pentecostal World Fellowship Executive Committee Member

Introduction to the Plenary and Invitation to the Pentecostal World Conference

David Wells

Permit me to begin by saying that the leaders of the Pentecostal World Fellowship (PWF) would like to join the Global Christian Forum Committee in honouring Larry and Eleanor Miller for their tremendous service among us for the last seven years. On behalf of the PWF Executive and Advisory Committees, Prince Guneratnam, PWF President, and I want to extend our warmest appreciation to the Millers for their service over the past seven years. Frankly, they have been very instrumental personally in tying the Pentecostal World Fellowship more deeply into the Global Christian Forum. So it is very meaningful for us to come to Bogotá and offer our appreciation to the Millers. Dr Guneratnam has also shared an official welcome to Casely Essamuah as Secretary-elect. We were both involved in the GCF Committee meeting in France when it was determined that Casely would be called to service in this manner. We are enthused about you, Casely, and your upcoming leadership, your heart for God and his church. Be assured of the PWF's full engagement as we move forward together with our sisters and brothers.

Now on behalf of Dr. Guneratnam, the PWF Executive and Advisory Committee, I would like to invite you to join us in Alberta, Canada at the end of August 2019, for the 25th Pentecostal World Conference. Pentecostals do things a little more informally. But we are sincere about inviting brothers and sisters in Christ to join with us. We will have representation from the other bodies that are present here. But this is a broad invitation, including fellow Pentecostals that are in this gathering this morning. We invite you to join us for the work of the Spirit together, honouring Jesus, and also to enjoy some of God's most beautiful creation! I'm an Albertan and I know what I am talking about. Feel free to come and join us.

For this session on 'Mutual Love Continuing, Moving Forward together in Faith and Hope', we will have two leading Pentecostals from around the world contributing. It's really a great pleasure to be with one of our PWF Advisory Committee members who is the president of the Apostolic Faith Mission of South Africa, Pastor George Mahlobo. The Apostolic Faith Mission is an indigenous Pentecostal movement, one of the oldest in the world. We're very glad that he can come and speak with a biblical exposition on the theme of the day, bringing perspective from the African context. He will be followed by Dr Billy Wilson who will encourage us in faith as he shares with us the journey he is involved in as the Global Co-chair of Empowered21, which reaches globally with multiple movements. He is also currently the president of Oral Roberts University and therefore engaged with younger students as well. We look forward to hearing from you both, George and Billy.

Forward Together in Faith and Hope: Biblical Perspective

George Mahlobo

This morning I would like to present to you two pictures, namely the picture of Peter just after the resurrection of the Lord and the picture of the Christian community in Corinth. Let us look first at Peter.

Our text setting is at the Lake of Galilee, where the disciples had just had breakfast with the risen Lord Jesus Christ. Jesus pulls Peter aside and asks him three questions. But before I come to these three questions, let us note two things. When Peter is addressed by our risen Lord, he addresses him as 'Simon, son of Jonah'. At face value, there shouldn't be anything wrong with Jesus referring to Peter with his family name. But we must remember that when Peter encountered the Lord, Jesus gave him another spiritual reference, another spiritual identity—namely Peter, which means 'the rock'. Why is he now reverting to the family name?

The second thing I would like you to observe is that in this encounter between Jesus and Peter, the object of Peter's trade was fish and Jesus changed it to human beings. In the text it is clear that Peter has reverted back to his old job. In short, in his spiritual journey, Peter seems to be retreating rather than moving forward. He's retreating from his spiritual mandate to his mundane activity. It is therefore fitting that the Lord calls him 'Simon, son of Jonah' and not necessarily, 'Peter, the small rock'.

Three questions are posed in our first text. It is also significant that Jesus asks Peter one and almost the same question three times. We do not really know why Jesus asked Peter three times. Some, like Augustine and Chrysostom, suggest that the reason for the repeated question had to do with the restoration of Peter after he had denied the Lord three times.

However, let us look at the first question. The Lord Jesus asked Peter, 'Simon, son of Jonah, do you love me more than the others?' Now, it is interesting, when we look deeper, beyond the English rendering of the question. The Greek rendering of the question with reference to this particular word 'love', which is *agape*, seems to suggest that Jesus is looking at the kind of love that is willing to engage in self-sacrifice, the kind of love that is unconditional, the kind of love that is able to go through. And when the Lord asked him, 'Simon, son of Jonah, do you *agape* me?' Peter in his response did not say to the Lord, 'Yes, Lord, I *agape* you.' He says, 'Lord, I have a brotherly love for you. Lord, you are in my system.' He doesn't use the same word that Jesus is putting before him. This is a wonderful thing, and yet this is not exactly what Christ is asking. At the same time, this was a truthful answer on Peter's part. In that instant, he had not been given the grace required to be able to move forward to the higher level of *agape* love. Christ shows us the sort of friend and brother that he is. He demonstrates this by giving responsibility to Peter, to care for his lambs.

Now we see the same pattern with regard to the second question. When Jesus states the question, it is not only confined to how I feel, but it requires a deeper reflection. And again Peter does not rise to the occasion to say, 'Yes, Lord, I *agape* you.' Once again he says, 'Lord, I know you. I like you. Lord, I will follow you.' And the third time that Jesus asks the question, he doesn't use the word *agape* again. He goes down to the level where Peter is. 'Do you love (*philo*) me, Peter?' He goes down to that level.

Our text tells us that Peter was grieved that Jesus had asked him for the third time. But in his response, Peter declared a twofold truth: (1) that Jesus knows everything, and (2) that he knows that indeed he (Peter) is loving him.

The final remarks of Christ seem a little ominous, but really they are a beautiful promise—a fulfilment of the promise of beatitude to all who seek righteousness. Christ is telling Peter that he will be capable of *agape* in the future, that he will bring glory to God, that he will be able to love the Lord in the way he longed to love him. Now that Jesus has told Peter exactly what he is in for, he says, 'Follow me.'

The question with us today as a church is, 'How deep is our love for one another and for the Lord?'

Like Peter, we find ourselves helpless without that the Lord helping to elevate us to an *agape* love.

Now let's turn to the second text: the church in Corinth. In many ways, this Christian community represents many of our Christian communities all over the world. It is a community unable to go forward in faith and in hope. It is inward-looking. It is a community captured by fragmentation. It is fragmented on theological, ethical and liturgical issues, just to mention a few.

In 1 Corinthians 12, Paul is addressing them on one of the liturgical issues—the spiritual gifts. But in his address, as he is helping them to navigate and manage this important aspect of the spiritual gifts, it seems that his address is interrupted. Chapter 13 seems to be an interpolation that comes not by accident but intentionally, for after chapter 13 Paul continues with his discussion of spiritual gifts. But the importance of this interpolation must be sought in the recognition of a balancing act between the gifts of the Holy Spirit, as expressed in this Christian community, and the fruit of the Spirit. Their liturgy will be without effect without the fruit of the Spirit, which is encapsulated in *agape* love. Love, which is the fruit of the Spirit, would provide the required character that has been so lacking in this factionalized church. This love would enable them to make sure that their confession is compatible with their conduct. This love helps us, indeed, to walk the confession, to walk the talk. So Paul did well to balance the gifts of the Spirit with the fruit of the Spirit.

I want us to look at just a few powerful statements in the opening verses. The five powerful statements together mean that nothing matters if I do not have love. The first statement indicates that nothing that I *say*, nothing that I proclaim, nothing that I publish, nothing that I say about technology matters if I do not have love. At the conclusion of this Forum, nothing will matter about what we have been saying if the Lord does not lift us to an *agape* love. The second statement is that nothing that I *believe* matters if I do not have love. It doesn't matter whether my kind of faith is the kind that immediately brings the supernatural into the realm of reality. If I do not have this love, my faith doesn't matter. Third, nothing that I *give* or *sacrifice* will matter if it doesn't come from this love. These are some of the things that we do as we move forward together—we give and we sacrifice—but if it is not driven by this love, it doesn't matter. Paul says nothing that I accomplish will matter if I do not have love.

The best way to illustrate this point is a story of one woman deep in a rural area of South Africa who was informed, while she was by the river, that her little baby was in a burning hut. All the people were crying when this woman reached the spot. But she moved forward through the flames and got to the child, wrapped him, and came out with the child. The child was not burned, but the woman picked up serious burns. What kind of love was demonstrated? Self-sacrificing love. It would not help us as the GCF to do whatever we do around our hurting world without showing this love. As we move forward, we need this love.

As has been stated this morning, the Bible regards love as a command. John 13:34 says, 'A new commandment I give to you, that you love one another as I have loved you.' That you also love one another. Love is a form of conduct. In I John 3:18 we read, 'My little children, let us not love in word or in tongue, but in deed and in truth.'

Finally, love is a commitment. In I John 4:11–12, the Bible says, 'Dear friends, since God loved us that much, we surely ought to love each other. But if we love each other, God lives in us and his love is brought to its full expression in us.'

As we move forward together in faith and in hope, let us pray, 'Lord, help us to develop *agape*.'

Forward Together in Faith, Hope, and Action: It Is Possible!

William 'Billy' Wilson[1]

> My prayer is not for them alone. I pray also for those who will believe in me through their message, that all may be one, Father, just as you are in me and I am in you. May they also be in us so that the world may believe that you have sent me. I have given them the glory that you gave me, that they may be one as we are one—I in them and you in me—so that they may be brought to complete unity. Then the world will know that you sent me and have loved them even as you have loved me (John 17:20-23 NIV).

The type of unity that we see in John 17 is relational, missional, and spiritual. Usually 'power' is either fissional or fusional. Fission creates power by separating, fusion by joining together. The power of the John 17 type of unity can be called 'supernatural synergy'. It is this kind of power that inspires Empowered21.

Empowered21 is a movement seeking to empower a generation. The vision: 'That every person on Earth would have an authentic encounter with Jesus Christ through the Power and Presence of the Holy Spirit (…) by Pentecost 2033. The mission: to 'help shape the future of the Global Spirit-empowered movement throughout the world by focusing on crucial issues facing the movement and connecting generations for intergenerational blessing and impartation.'

Empowered21, based administratively in Oral Roberts University, is guided by a Global Council with 14 regional cabinets. These cabinets are pursuing initiatives and events in their area of the world to address the future of Spirit-empowered Christianity and find ways to connect the generations for spiritual impartation. Each regional cabinet operates under the same vision and purposes for Empowered21 in their region.

---

1 This text is the editor's interpretive summary of William Wilson's PowerPoint presentation.

Empowered21 organizes Work Groups to research, resource, and re-establish distinctives of Spirit-empowered ministry. The groups and their mandates are:

- NGN 21 — To build leaders, unites voices, resource others, connect movements, preach Jesus, and ignite the next generation of leaders in the global Spirit-empowered community.

- Scholars Consultation — To gather scholars from around the world to study the past, present, and future of the Spirit-empowered movement and address critical subjects facing the movement. Scholar consultation papers have been published as *Global Renewal Christianity* volumes 1-4, and most recently in *The Truth About Grace*.

- Discipleship Task Force — To form an outcomes-based model for Spirit-empowered discipleship and to create resources to equip believers from around the world.

- Evangelism Alliance — To identify and equip young Spirit-empowered evangelists from every continent as well as to find new and unique ways to connect and build relationships between these evangelists, providing mentorship partners and Spirit-empowered resources.

Empowered21 works because:

(1) It is meeting a need.

(2) Every voice is important (mutual respect and honor).

(3) It embraces the essentials. Diversity should not divide.

(4) Intergenerational connectivity releases blessing.

(5) Agreement on values is critical. Do something but limit activities.

(6) Contextualisation and decentralization match 21st-century realities.

(7) Leadership is the most important key to success.

For the earth will be filled with the knowledge of the glory of the LORD as the waters cover the sea (Habakkuk 2:14 NIV).

Metropolitan Geevarghese Coorilos

DAY FOUR: FRIDAY 27 APRIL
LET MUTUAL LOVE CONTINUE!
FORWARD TOGETHER IN FAITH AND HOPE

11.15 PLENARY SESSION

Facing Common Challenges Together in Faith and Hope

Moderator: **George Geevarghese Coorilos** (India), Moderator, Commission on World Mission and Evangelism, World Council of Churches; Metropolitan of Niranam Diocese, Malankara Syrian Orthodox Church

Prioritising Common Challenges: Listening and Responding to Global Gathering Conversations

- *Souraya Bechealany* (Lebanon), Secretary General, Middle East Council of Churches, Beirut
- *Raimundo Barreto, Jr.* (Brazil/USA), Assistant Professor of World Christianity, Princeton Theological Seminary, New Jersey, USA

- ***Wonsuk Ma*** (Republic of Korea/USA), Distinguished Professor of Global Christianity, Graduate School of Theology and Ministry, Oral Roberts University, Oklahoma, USA

Plenary Discussion of Panel Presentations and Panelist Responses

Third Global Gathering Message: First Reading

David Han (Republic of Korea/USA), Professor of Theology and Pentecostal Spirituality, Pentecostal Theological Seminary; GCF Committee Member for the Church of God (Cleveland);

Katherine Shirk Lucas (USA/France), Professor of Theology, Institut Catholique de Paris

Introduction to the Plenary

George Geevarghese Coorilos

Let's begin this session with a word of prayer.

Gracious and loving God, we come to you with hearts full of gratitude. We thank you for having brought us together for this great fellowship that we have in your name. Thank you for being with us on this journey for the last 20 years. As we look ahead, planning for our future, we continue to seek your guidance. As we begin this session, we pray that our reflections and deliberations will be guided by your Spirit and that they will bring glory to your name and your name alone. In Jesus' precious name we pray. Amen.

We have come to the final day of this very important gathering of the Global Christian Forum. To give you a sense of what will happen in this particular session, I want to locate it within the larger context of the global gathering.

On the first two days, we were urged to celebrate the 20 years of our journey together as the Global Christian Forum. We thanked God that we have been able to do this by His grace, that we have been able to foster mutual love and respect of others and of our churches. Since yesterday, we have changed gears. Since yesterday, our specific focus has been on the word 'continue' in 'Let mutual love continue'. We have been looking at questions like: What next? Where do we go from here? What should be the agenda for this year and the next few months or years to come?

We know that we have been able to gather some profound insights and challenges, including the beautiful Bible reflection that we had from Bishop Farrell, the plenary brainstorming that we had right here, our group work, and also this morning's Bible study. So the plenary focus now is on moving forward together in faith and hope.

The challenges and proposals that we have received, in terms of our future agenda, have been many and varied. Therefore, it is practically impossible to take all of them for the immediate future of the work of the GCF. What is crucial is that we prioritize them. And this is precisely what we have planned to do in this session. To help us do just that, we have asked three of our friends, our listeners, to reflect on what they have been hearing and give us some directions and priorities—to tell us, from their perspective, what will be the most important, the most pressing challenges that we cannot ignore and therefore must accept in our future work as GCF. In a sense, we are short-listing all those challenges and proposals that we have received so far.

I'm going to give ten minutes to each of our panellists. We have Dr Souraya Bachealany from Lebanon. She is a professor of ecclesiology and ecumenism, and also the acting General Secretary of the Middle East Council of Churches in Beirut, Lebanon. She will be followed by Professor Raimundo Barreto, a Brazilian theologian, currently teaching at Princeton Theological Seminary in the USA. He is assistant professor of World Christianity at Princeton and also the ordained pastor of a local Baptist church. Our last panellist will be Professor Wonsuk Ma from Korea. He is also teaching currently in the USA, as Distinguished Professor of Global Christianity at the Graduate School of Theology and Ministry of Oral Roberts University in Oklahoma. These three respondents will give us a sense of direction as we try to prioritize the challenges for our future work. After their time, we will open the floor for immediate reactions to what we have heard from them.

Facing shared challenges together in faith and hope

Souraya Bechealany

I wish to thank the Forum organizers for having entrusted us with the delicate task of producing a personal synthesis. We were asked to select three challenges and three hopes. While drafting my text, I noted that my hopes and challenges reflected back on each other, weaving a surprising dialogue. I therefore gave myself permission to break the rules and select four issues that are both challenges and hopeful expectations at the same time. I hope that, although I have bypassed the initial instructions, I have remained faithful to the original request.

1. *The translation of the Word of God: both a hope and a challenge*

The Word of God has been with us throughout our whole gathering. We meditated and prayed over it together. It was also the subject of Wednesday evening's talk. Mr. Perreau, Director General at United Bible Societies, spoke to us about what a challenge it is to translate the Bible. He told us that there are more than 6,000 languages in the world; the Bible has already been translated into 2,000 of them and is in the process of being translated into another 2,000. Such hope! But the challenge of the 2,000 remaining languages remains before us.

Dr Catherine Clifford commented yesterday, 'The Word takes the risk of being lost in translation.' Indeed! Did it not already take that risk by becoming a man and becoming lost to the point of total kenosis on the cross for us humans and for our salvation (Phil. 2)? Yes, the Word takes the risk of letting itself be translated into the language of humans to reach them wherever they are. The Word of God is not lost in cultures. On the contrary! Because it is alive, it evangelizes and is life-giving.

The video Mr. Perreau showed us was a wonderful example of this. Upon receiving the Bible in his native language, the elder of the tribe repeated Simeon's prayer in the Temple: 'Now, Lord, you have kept your promise, and you may let your servant go in peace. With my own eyes I have seen your salvation, which you have prepared in the presence of all peoples' (Lk. 2:29–30). Yes, the Word of God is alive and timely. What hope for humanity!

The translation of these remaining languages is a challenge for the GCF. The point is not for us to do what the United Bible Societies are in the process of accomplishing. The point is rather to get involved in the dynamics of this movement, encouraging it, backing and facilitating it, and even (why not!) contributing to it.

'So also will be the word that I speak; it will not fail to do what I plan for it; it will do everything I send it to do' (Isaiah 55:11). Like Paul, pray for us that the Lord's message may continue to spread rapidly (2 Thess. 3:1) and bring back to the Father his scattered children.

2. *Theology and bilateral and multilateral ecumenical agreements*

Just as the translation of the Word of God is a plural concept, so are theology and liturgy. During the Global Gathering, we heard a call ceaselessly repeated, encouraging new Asian and African theologies and liturgies. Another call was heard for a dialogue between the different ecclesial traditions.

We have also come to realize that the road to achieving ecumenical agreements does not end when texts are rejected or unfavourably received. The example of the extension of the agreement on 'justification' from two to five churches rekindles hope in us and prompts us to go further. It is a definite sign of hope.

There is also an obvious plea for a clear definition of words and concepts: proselytism, persecution, solidarity between churches, and discrimination. By no means is this a small challenge! Let us not lose sight of the fact that our two-thousand-year-old ecclesial history tells of numerous misunderstandings around words and concepts. We thus strongly urge that the document on mission and proselytism be completed, engaging in the process women and men affiliated with a wide range of ecclesial bodies and associated theologies.

Here again, the GCF is not to act in lieu of the existing ecclesial and theological bodies and organizations, or to shadow them. The GCF is the place where these multiple theologies and ecclesiologies enter into dialogue with the experiences of churches and Christians, emerging fortified every time.

In this way, the GCF can then become a genuine place for synodality and ecumenism, allowing the people of God to listen to each other and, beyond that, to listen together to the Word of God, agree courageously on what is possible, and humbly receive what seems less possible at this point in time.

Furthermore, Bishop Farrell's wish list could be a good starting point ('Envisioning the Journey Ahead: Six Proposals'). His items included calling the mainline churches take their young sister churches seriously; calling the new churches to deepen the theological basis of their Christian experiences; renouncing all types of proselytism; reverting to the roots of Scripture and the inspiration of the Holy Spirit to think and live ecumenically; moving on from sterile discussions about structures—'What were you arguing about on the road?' Jesus asked his disciples; and doing together much more than we actually do, such as biblical studies. We find ourselves faced here with quite a challenge, but one that draws us together along the road to hope!

3. The churches involved in the world to serve the Kingdom: denouncing evil, building justice and peace

Occupied territories (such as in the Palestinian-Israeli conflict), extremism, terrorism, deportation and emigration, corruption: these words describe dreadful situations of which we are all witnesses. But do we involve ourselves in them as true witnesses of Christ and of his Kingdom?

Brothers and sisters, I come from the Middle East where the political, social and economic situation, as you well know, is insecure and precarious, as well as a source of jeopardy for the entire world.

At home, we must first of all address evil together, denounce it, face it boldly, and identify it by name. That is a costly endeavour. After that, we must build peace and justice and venture to engage in the struggles of men and women—dare I say it, at the price of sometimes getting our hands dirty in the process.

Hosting displaced people and emigrants is a major challenge for Europe and the Americas these days. Helping them to remain in their original homes is an even greater challenge. How many ecclesial organizations glide over their personal economic interests nowadays in the course of offering relief to persecuted Christians?

What can the GCF offer in this case? As a place for global gatherings, it can foster, as it has been doing, both exchanges and the sharing of individual stories. Information distributed by the media is one thing;

the sharing of a painful personal experience, so indisputably true and authentic, is quite another. The GCF is the place to be to 'Come and see!' Listen closely and stay informed so that we can denounce evil and build peace together.

4. *The GCF and the risks of becoming institutionalized or hierarchical*

This challenge is for the GCF itself. How can it remain a place of coming together for regular, successful and well-organized gatherings and not slide towards becoming just one more rigid institution among many others?

First, I feel that it is important to keep our focus on the Forum's advocates and their original insights and intentions. What do they have to say about their initiative? How do they perceive it?

Second, let us work towards mutual acknowledgement of all baptized and turn them together towards the world. Remain a place for prayer and meetings freely open to all. Avoid overbooked programs, facilitate free exchanges between people, and encourage initiatives set up outside the Forum but deriving from its inspiration.

Finally, if necessary, be open to the possibility that the Forum may cease existing if the future opens other pathways for churches to engage and witness together.

And to conclude my synthesis on a wonderful note of hope: encourage a forum for young people. They are the future. And launch it at Taizé, that beautiful place of hope for the Church and for the world!

Prioritizing Common Challenges: Listening and Responding to Global Gathering Conversations

Raimundo C. Barreto Jr.

I wish to express my gratitude to all the organizers of this wonderful gathering for the kind invitation extended to me to participate in this session as a listener and respondent. I have structured what I will share at this time in the form of some images, questions, and suggestions concerning several topics I have heard throughout this gathering, topics that I hope will help us in our collective reflection about the next steps forward and future possibilities for the Global Christian Forum.

Some Images from This Global Gathering

Of the metaphors I have heard used in this gathering to describe the Global Christian Forum, the image of it as a window has stuck with me as one of the most meaningful ways to think about this forum as an open and creative space. It is a window that, once open, allows new air to come in and refresh the whole environment.

Another metaphor that has repeatedly appeared in our conversations is that of 'the journey.' Ecumenism is a long and unfinished journey. We partake in that journey together as siblings who need one another. In that common journey, we are reminded that we don't know everything, that our traditions and perspectives are limited, and that the word 'disciple' also means student or learner. The ecumenical journey is one of mutual and continuous learning. Therefore, it demands an attitude of openness and humility from all its participants.

Most of us in this gathering celebrate the Global Christian Forum as that space for mutual learning and renewed relationships. We are grateful for the vision and efforts that have allowed Christians who have not always seen eye-to-eye to sit around the same table and come into a broader fellowship and a common conversation. I also believe that most of us strongly affirm the Forum's methodology of storytelling, because it helps us connect with one another on the more fundamental level of our common humanity and on the basic aspects of our Christian faith. The relational nature of our interactions in this setting is certainly one of the fresh contributions the Forum has brought to the ecumenical movement.

Every time we gather, we learn more about one another, about ourselves, and about the journey itself. We all have been moved by the many testimonies we have heard over these last few days. The story that Pastor Lord Donkor of the Church of Pentecost and Brother Paolo of the Taizé Community shared about the beautiful relationship between an African Pentecostal church in the diaspora and a French monastic community has stuck with me as an example of a paradigmatic change in ecumenical relations nowadays. We have heard other stories like that in our small groups. One of the participants in the Southern Cone regional group kept reminding us that these stories usually do not get the attention of the larger public. Mainstream media will be more interested in stories of conflict and violence than in stories of mutual understanding and collaboration. It is our task, then, to find ways to tell these stories more broadly and to map such local or regional initiatives as part of our efforts to disseminate the spirit of the Global Christian Forum.

Some Questions We Have Raised

The GCF Global Gatherings provide unique opportunities for all of us to be together in one place from time to time. The gatherings have intentionally happened in Africa, Asia, and now Latin America. In our conversations here in Bogotá, we have asked some questions which deserve more attention. For instance, how can we maximize these opportunities to learn more from and about specific Christian experiences in the region where the Global Gathering takes place? Could we have learned more about the persistent witness of the churches in Colombia—along with their ecumenical international partners—for peace and justice, and the challenges of being peacemakers in such a context? Could we have heard more about the almost 6 million displaced persons in Colombia, or about other common challenges faced by Latin American Christians, like the humanitarian crisis in Venezuela, briefly mentioned last afternoon? Could we have learned more about the history of Christianity in Latin America, especially through the eyes of indigenous peoples and peoples of African descent? How could those narratives and perspectives have enriched our conversations and helped us understand our common global journey and challenges?

On Wednesday evening, we were reminded of the drastic demographic changes that have taken place in world Christianity in the past century. In the last 30 years or so, many scholars have spent a good amount of time trying to understand the implications of such a drastic shift for the future of our common faith journey. Cuban-American historian Justo Gonzalez says that we are approaching a significant change in the cartography and the topography of Christian history, rightly pointing out that 'it is impossible to follow history without an understanding of the stage on which it takes place.'[1] Gonzalez refers not only to geographical maps, but especially to the mental maps that inform our thinking and the way we see the world. The demographic and cultural shifts world Christianity has experienced particularly in the past 50 years demand a new mental map that moves away from Western captivity, embracing the rediscovered polycentric nature of world Christianity. Therefore, as we listen to each other's voices, we are actually engaging in a broad dialogical process that will potentially challenge assumptions we have operated with for a long time. The theological reflection Thomas Schirrmacher provided on the role of experience in theology on Wednesday morning exemplifies the need for us to revisit our constructed theologies within our respective traditions in light of the challenges that the new Christian maps pose to all of us.

Another important question that has emerged in some of our conversations this week is the need to pay attention to who is in this room and who is not. In our common journey, we should never stop asking who is at the table and who is missing, or about whose table it is, and who is setting the table. We have heard about how women and younger people are underrepresented in this gathering. What can be done to assure a greater presence of women and youth in future gatherings?

The absence of Latin American original or indigenous peoples—particularly in the voices of indigenous movements such as the Federación Evangélica Indígena de Ecuador (FEINE)—in this gathering has also been duly noted. Likewise, we have wondered why the presence of African Americans, Afro-Latin Americans, Afro-Caribbeans, and other brothers and sisters who have experienced in a particular and cruel manner the racialization of the modern world, and the persistence of racism and other sorts of discrimination, injustice, and violence, was so reduced in this place. We heard Ruth Padilla DeBorst

---

1   Justo Gonzalez, *The Changing Shape of Church History* (St. Louis, MO: Chalice Press, 2002), 7.

draw attention to the need for us to address power structures and relations. It is clear that we will need to move beyond 'polite ecumenism' in order to increase mutual understanding and promote opportunities for healing and reconciliation.

Suggestions for Our Next Steps

The situation of displaced peoples, refugees and forced migration has appeared a number of times in our conversations. Puerto Rican historian Luis Rivera-Pagan has drawn attention to the ecumenicity that exists in the experience of exile and diaspora.[2] This is a topic of common concern that can be addressed from a multi-contextual perspective. Christians from each region have specific contributions to make to such an important conversation. Furthermore, a focus on the problems at the root of displacement and forced migration also creates an opportunity for us to think about other related matters, such as discrimination and violence against religious minorities, xenophobia and racism, global capitalism and mass poverty, militarization and the war industry, the destruction of environmental resources and our need to care for our common great house. An emphasis on the topic of migration, displacement, and refugees would be in my view a good segue for the theme of this Global Gathering, 'Let mutual love continue,' based on Hebrews 13:1, since it would connect mutual love to loving the stranger, as urged in Hebrews 13:2.

Finally, since many of us have shown concern for linking the experience of this Global Gathering with the local and national realities of our churches and congregations, I suggest that we discuss the possibility of a coordinated effort to organize regional and national gatherings in the following years with a common focus on mutual love and love for the stranger in connection with matters of migration, displacement, and refugees, culminating with a global consultation like the one in Tirana (2015).

Thanks for your time and consideration.

---

[2] Luis N. Rivera-Pagan, 'The Plight of Puerto Rico: Coloniality, Diaspora, and Decolonial Resistance,' Herencia Lecture 2018, Princeton Theological Seminary, April 13, 2018.

The Growth of Global Christianity: Joy, Cost, and the Holy Spirit

Wonsuk Ma

Building relationships, sharing one's story of a spiritual journey, and embracing one another as brothers and sisters in the body of Christ have been the distinct ethos of the Global Christian Forum. This sharing of life often produces expressions of repentance for not treating each other as fellow Christians. And I have been personally enjoying this GCF mode of togetherness from the Hong Kong Asian forum (2005) up to this Bogotá gathering. Telling and hearing real stories is more than making time for exchange; it requires a mutual commitment to participate in other people's joy as well as sorrow.

This paradigm has also inspired newer gatherings. For example, the Global Forum of Theological Educators has adopted this format of 'wider and safe space' to share our stories among theological educators. (By the way, its second meeting will take place next year in Greece.)

My listening perspective has been shaped by my spiritual journey. I am a member of a newer church (Pentecostal), which is frequently mentioned when proselytism is discussed. I am also from the global South (South Korea), where Christianity has been known for its growth, missionary work, and megachurches. Furthermore, my keen interest in Christianity at the global level, in my role as a professor of global Christianity at Oral Roberts University, USA, influences my style of listening.

My single focus is the growth of Christianity in our generation. The simple truth is that there wouldn't be Christianity or churches without Christians. The following observations are based on the regional and interchurch group reports, complemented by plenary presentations. My focused attention on evangelism and the growth of Christianity has also been motivated by the relative silence about the topic at typical ecumenical gatherings such as the Global Christian Forum. While recognizing the evil of proselytism where it refuses to recognize other churches as part of Christ's body, we should not discourage those who are committed to actively witnessing to the saving grace of Christ. The fierce competition for souls, whether it is described in spiritual terms such as Paul's reference to 'principalities and powers' or in religious terms, does not give Christians a luxury of just 'polite witnessing'.

Rejoicing

At least three of the seven regional reports (Africa, Asia, and North America) identify the growth of global Christianity as the most important sign of hope. Gina Zurlo's presentation helps us to understand the significance of today's Christian growth. In 2018, Africa has the largest number of Christians in the world (631 million). In Asia, the rebirth and growth of Chinese Christianity is another example of the Holy Spirit's work, in spite of a harsh socio-political environment. (Han Chinese house churches are the fourth largest denomination in the world with 82.4 million people.)

Zurlo's presentation also demonstrates the steady redistribution of global Christians towards the south. In fact, the year 2018 marks global Christianity reaching one-third of the world's population. Around the 1910 Edinburgh Missionary Conference, Christianity reached almost 35 percent of global population, but soon after that it began a trajectory of decline. The recovery path is now set.

Equally significant is the radical shift in the north-south distribution of world Christians. In 1970, the North had 57 percent of world Christians, leaving 43 percent in the South. In 2018, the North has 34 percent and the South 66 percent. African and Asian reports mention the rise of new and fresh forms of churches, to address social changes. New contemporary Christian music (such as Hillsong) and lively worship have helped churches to reach out to younger generations. The new churches that embrace indigenous cultural and religious symbols (as opposed to missionary churches) have attracted a large following. The African Independent Churches are a fine example.

The impact of Pentecostal and Charismatic churches has significantly contributed to the growth of Christianity. This bloc now accounts for 27 percent of world Christians, making it the second-largest Christian bloc after the Roman Catholic Church. Also significant is its annual growth rate (as of the year 2000), which was the highest among Christian churches or all religious groups. The proportion of Pentecostal and Charismatic Christians relative to the total number of Christians is higher in the global South.

Two regional reports also identify the high proportion of youth and young adults in the church as an important sign of hope. It is further observed that churches that were formerly mission fields are now committing themselves to mission. Brazil, India, Nigeria, South Korea and other nations have become important missionary-sending countries.

Challenges

These positive global prospects, however, come with challenges to the church. First, there are regions where Christianity is steadily declining. The former Christian and missionary heartlands (that is, Western Europe and North America) have been losing members. Increasing secularism, religious pluralism, and postmodern relativism are often blamed.

However, there are signs of hope in spite of these challenges. The presence of the Taizé representatives at the GCF gathering is a strong reminder that the younger generation in secular Europe has a spiritual thirst which the church is expected to meet. The case of the Middle East, however, is painfully different. Political conflicts in the region have seriously impacted Christian communities, resulting in a drastic reduction of the Christian population. The abduction of two bishops and other Christian leaders in Syria was a stark reminder of this difficult reality. The consultation on 'Discrimination, Persecution, Martyrdom: Following Christ Together' proved to be timely and relevant.

The Asian report ranks, as the most important challenge, various issues arising from the religiously pluralistic context and the minority status of Christianity. Increasing religious nationalism, radicalization and intolerance are putting fellow believers in a difficult situation or even in an illegal status. At the same time, throughout history, Christianity when it possessed political power has oppressed people of other religions, and this history calls for repentance and solidarity.

The divided church has become a scandal in the face of our difficult challenges. First, our divisions deprive the churches of the opportunity to receive and give unique gifts bestowed on each church tradition so as to enrich each other and strengthen the whole body of Christ. As a consequence, the church is not able to raise a united voice in society. For this reason, three reports urge the Global Christian Forum to encourage ecumenical engagement at the regional and local levels.

Also, in their zeal of evangelism and mission, some churches have hurt other churches by engaging in sheep stealing. This act of proselytism is caused by ignorance of other churches, lack of interaction and fellowship, and spiritual arrogance.

However, more fundamentally, modern Christian mission was developed along with the Western colonial expansion. Because of this perceived linkage, the notion and practice of mission were built upon the assumption of power. Attitudes of cultural, political, social and racial superiority, whether actually expressed or only perceived, are the direct opposite of Jesus' way: kenosis (Phil. 2).

As the Christian number is reaching one-third of the world's population, the global church is called to be true followers of Christ who emptied himself of all power. And credibly witnessing to Christ requires his followers to walk and live like him! True followers of Christ should obey his commandment: 'Go (…) and make all the nations my disciples' (Matthew 28). This missionary mandate is urgent, because still today, two of every three persons in the world, and nine of every ten in Asia, are not his disciples. The Holy Spirit came to empower us to be true followers of Christ for effective witnessing to his saving love: 'When the Spirit comes upon you, you will be my witnesses in Jerusalem, all Judea, Samaria, and to the uttermost ends of the earth' (Acts 1:8).

Prioritising Common Challenges: Listening and Responding to One Another

Introduction to the discussion

George Geevarghese Coorilos

We are grateful to all three panellists for their excellent work. They have worked under tremendous time limitations, but I think they have done a great job in synthesizing all the reflections we have made in the last couple of days. I will not try to summarize what they have done, except to say that they have identified common concerns. For example, I think the three of them were saying that the Global Christian Forum should remain as a 'forum', an open forum for all of us to come together in mutual love. It should not get institutionalized. It should continue to be a window. So that is one common challenge that is emerging.

I also hear a common consensus around the need for churches to get involved in social action, the need to address social-justice concerns. That came up in all three presentations. The other common challenge that emerged is the changing global landscape of Christianity and therefore the challenges that it poses for the Global Christian Forum: the need to change our methodology in theologizing, new paradigm shifts in mission and evangelism, and so forth. One other thing that I heard, which is emerging as a kind of a common concern, is the need to decentralize the GCF. We need to focus on regional, national expressions of the GCF. We also heard the need to take Scripture seriously, especially in the context of the challenge that we still have in terms of translating the Word of God in different parts of the world. And we heard the challenge for the GCF to widen its umbrella, its horizon, in response to the whole question of who is here and who isn't, making the GCF more inclusive in terms of inviting more youth, women, people of disability, and marginalized peoples.

So these are some of the common concerns that I have heard in these three presentations. We are grateful to you for giving us these concrete directions.

At this point, I would like to ask all of us to take a few moments to respond to what you have heard from the three presentations. My suggestion is that we not add any new challenges unless you think they are really pressing. But if you can give us a sense of whether you can endorse some of the things you have heard, then it will help the organisers, the Committee, to prioritize the challenges for the future work. So I will open the floor for a few minutes.

Discussion

Editor's note: since it has not been possible to identify and transcribe every speaker, this discussion summary is incomplete and names of speakers are not included.

Comment 1: I would like to stress that since we have regional organisations around the support of migrants and refugees, we should somehow create a network so that, for example, as we are receiving Syrian refugees in Canada, we are in touch with the Syrian church leaders in order that we may know best how to assist the migrants. Perhaps their adaptation should be only temporary so that in the end we can encourage them to go home if their lands are once again in peace. Second, I would not like to lose the work on proselytism that was begun in the Global Christian Forum. I am sorry we did not hear more of where it had got to. I think it's urgent that this work continue.

Comment 2: I agree with most of the points that have been made. I would like to reaffirm one that we have heard over and over again. Sometimes, in many of our contexts and especially related to these types of meetings, we find a tension between action and the development of personal relationships. I believe that the genius and success of this meeting is based on the fact that, for example, hermeneutics fail us, theology fails us, institutions fail us. But 1 Corinthians 13:8 says: 'Love never fails', and that is what we have experienced here. I wonder what would happen if we had the opportunity to stay together for three, four, or five months. What would the Spirit of God do if we lived together like that?

Comment 3: The theme of the panel is: 'Facing challenges together'. I wonder how far can we go together. The challenge of the 19th century was slavery and there were Christians for and against it. Jumping to the 21st century, we still have racism. Now we have groups that do not have consideration for women or homosexuals. Among other things, you spoke of power structures. Do we have the capacity to face these challenges together or will we face them separately?

Comment 4: I was interested in the question, 'Are we true witnesses of justice and peace?' I have heard some conversation about that, but not much emphasis. I would love to encourage the Forum to think how we can promote justice, especially giving voice to women and children. We know that they are not represented equally now. How can we go about changing that?

Comment 5: I would like to encourage the Forum to reflect on the convergence between two movements: forced displacements, forced emigration of peoples, and also ecclesial displacements which play a role in the dynamics of proselytism or the free choice of people to associate themselves with other churches. We heard His Holiness Mor Aphrem speaking about the fact that the churches that now are completely destitute in Syria have fallen prey to aggressive proselytism. So when we find communities that are weakened or in contexts of conflict, or communities that have had to move through emigration, our responsibility is to surround them, to support them.

Comment 6: I want to start by just referencing something that Archbishop Anastasios of Albania has said. We have said a lot about justice and human rights, in different ways. But as Anastasios said, we must remember that the greatest treasure we have is the Word of God. And the greatest injustice in our world today is that a large part of the world has never had the opportunity to decide whether to choose Christ or not. There are many ways in which we can be involved, but a very large part of our world has never had the chance to choose Christ. I think that while we must work in many ways and in many areas, we must keep the central focus on making Christ known to every single person on the face of the earth. We will do these other things along the way. But there are other organisations that work for human rights. There are other organisations that work for peace. There are other organisations that work for many things, and we must come alongside and participate and do those things because we follow Christ and Christ loves them. But first and foremost, we must make Christ known to every single person on earth. We must be willing to sacrifice, even to die for that purpose.

Comment 7: We must not fail to recognize the tremendous work of the Spirit that has brought us together like this, in spite of the fact that many of the countries from which we come are at war with each other. Yet there is a tremendous peace of God that has us here without suspicion. On the matter of our proselytisation, I would like to say that suspicion still prevails. I'm wondering if we are honest enough to take back some of what we have heard from others about our own practices and theological understandings and put our own practices to the test so that there can be an increasing sense of understanding, which can only lead to a greater sense of accommodating one another and less suspicion, especially on the matter of proselytisation.

Comment 8: I a member of the committee of the Pentecostal Forum that we have been promoting for the past five years in Latin America. Following the words of Professor Wonsuk Ma who reported that today Pentecostals are 27% of Christianity, I would first like to congratulate us because this is the first global forum where Pentecostals are significantly represented. But secondly, I would like to ask you to reflect on that fact that even though Pentecostals achieved in one century the same number as Protestants did in five centuries, the growth rate makes it almost impossible for the whole world to become Christian in one generation. Perhaps the strategies should be changed and we should not delude ourselves by thinking that in one generation the whole world can become Christian.

Comment 9: I would like to align myself with most of the comments that have been made. However, I would like to add a comment on the issue of who is here and who is not here. Could the Forum look at creative ways of extending this Forum to the silent community, those who use sign language, so that they, too, could have a space where they could share their experiences? In my own experience in South Africa, we are one of the two denominations that are reaching out to such people, and in various ways we also encounter a challenge when it comes to Bible translation. I think there is a need for sensitivity that could also be explored. But I think it is critical, especially for Africa, that we create such a platform, because up to this point I think they have been marginalized by the society as well as by the church.

Comment 10: With many years of missionary experience in Latin America, I speak with some sense of trepidation. I resonate with so much of what has been said in this Forum, and I have participated in some of what this Forum has done at regional levels in Latin America. But I have to be honest and say I haven't heard much of anything said in the Forum about what I would call the cultural captivity of the church in the West, especially in the United States—the political captivity of the church, the compromised witness of the church in the United States of America. Not all the church, but certainly a large sector of the church. And I am speaking as a Pentecostal. So that makes me, very honestly, suspicious of programs that are hatched in the United States and then brought to the rest of the world as if they are a panacea, or some kind of special answer to the needs of the global church. It makes me very uncomfortable. I say this as a North American, a US citizen, yet as one who has spent many years in Latin America. I haven't heard this talked about much here in the Forum. Unfortunately for evangelicals and Pentecostals, certain kinds of Pentecostals in North America have been co-opted by Donald Trump and his party and his politics. But I am sure that similar things have happened in the history of the church in many other places. What can we in North America learn from church history, from the Catholic Church, from the Orthodox Church, and from many other confessions and churches, that will help us get through this very difficult time in the history of the church in the United States?

Comment 11: I am a Lutheran and a Palestinian Christian. I would like to reiterate what my sister said about the painful proselytism in the Middle East. Two things are important to understand. There are some evangelical or evangelistic groups who believe that the war going in Syria or Iraq is apocalyptic and eschatological. That is very dangerous. Even the Palestinian-Israeli conflict is seen within that perspective. This is the reason why—which is my second point—some people are following the tanks and those who are shooting, and distributing Bibles to the Christians and proselytizing them, taking them from their churches. This is harming the body of Christ in the Middle East. We are sometimes blamed because of irresponsible evangelistic campaigns by some groups in the Middle East. We ask you to remember that we have been Christians in the Middle East for 2,000 years. Support us so that we can continue. We don't need those who want to proselytize for their own personal interests and not for the interests of Christ.

Comment 12: At the risk of over-simplification, with this great emphasis on love and looking at all the other subjects—from proselytism to injustice to US involvement domestically and internationally—I wonder if it might be helpful to see these as streams of violence and to see gospel love as a Sermon on the Mount kind of love, as the opposing force, as active non-violence. So as we see the violence that is going on in the world, the things that are affecting our churches and our people and the poor, and the human trafficking and the horrid results of endless violence, I wonder if there would be a way for us to come together around helping each other to build a spirituality of non-violence—active non-violence—that doesn't stand indifferently, that stands with the victims, that stands with the people who are considered disposable so that the day comes, as Father Boyle says, when we stop throwing people away. I'm part of an initiative in the Catholic Church with big goals, called the Catholic Non-Violent Initiative. Pax Christi and the Pontifical Council were trying to see if we could ask Pope Francis to write an encyclical on Jesus and non-violence. We are trying to look in-house and see how we at every level and every aspect of our church can form our own people in gospel non-violence.

Responses from the Panel

George Geevarghese Coorilos

Thank you all for your active participation and the rich contributions you have made. I did not hear any particular question of clarification—perhaps there was one—but I will still give our panellists two minutes each to make a response.

Raimundo Barreto

There was a question addressed to me. The speaker mentioned that we have faced structural problems for a long time—slavery, racism, gender, sexuality—and the question was whether it is possible to overcome these structural injustices together or if we have to do so separately. I think it is a deep question, a very welcome question for us to consider. My sincere hope is that we will do it together. I am a firm believer in what is happening here. I hope we will not give up on each other. The reason why I mentioned this subject was actually something in the message from the General Secretary of the World Council of Churches on the first day, about avoiding the comfort of polite ecumenism.

I hope that we will not have meetings to feel good about ourselves. And to be honest, I am feeling good, very good to be with you all this week. It has been wonderful. Some people have even expressed that they would like to spend more time. But this is not the goal. It's good to feel good. It's good to get to know one another. But we should build trust, and this has been happening for more than ten years now. Some of you have been in three big gatherings and many other smaller gatherings; this is a journey already. By now we should be able to have some trust built in this Forum. Those of us who are coming and joining, we are learning. We are getting into this environment where there has to be enough trust for us to talk to one another and listen to one another even when we have to talk about difficult topics where we don't see eye to eye. There are many things where many of us are not in agreement. But we should keep talking.

When I mentioned Justo Gonzáles, a historian whom many people know, I did so not only to throw a scholar's name at you. He is someone I have a high respect for as a Christian and a historian. Those who know him know that he is a sincere Christian. In a very small book that he wrote many years ago, he tried to help us understand that the idea of dialogue is central to all Christian traditions. He plays with the idea that there are four gospels, not only one, and we need four narratives. We need to keep talking and listening to one another. We will probably enlarge our perspectives and challenge one another. For example, what I heard from Thomas Schirrmacher was a challenge to his own tradition. I have been an evangelical for many years, and I heard what he said as a challenge to his own tradition. I think each of us could do that as we learn from one another. The difficult questions will remain, but I hope we will keep working both individually and together. I hope that we will keep talking to one another to the point that some time we will be able to join efforts and understand that we need to talk theologically together to get away from the captivity of talking ideologically. We need to go back to talking theologically. If we do that, I think we will be able to understand each other a little more.

Souraya Bachealany

I would like to make two important points. First, there is the point made by Dr Catherine Clifford about displacements. The arrival of Eastern churches and Christians in the West is a grace for the West. We Orientals have lived for 2,000 years in pluralism and diversity. In our countries, we do not know uniformity. It is an opportunity for churches to develop their ecclesiologies in the midst of pluralism and to welcome these different theologies as a chance to move themselves to the new places to which Christ calls us.

Second, I touched on the matter of the political ambitions behind some of the Western organizations located in the Middle East. I beg you not to make us victims. We are in control of our history. We have contributed as best we can to the history of our Middle East. If we need you, it is not for your charity, but to rebuild with us the torn body of Christ in the Middle East. When you arrive in the Middle East, do not replace us. Help us to be the Orientals of our own land in order to help you to be yourselves in your own lands. Some institutions that have a lot of money are coming to help us. They say to us, 'You do not know how to do your own business. We have the power to do it for you.' As General Secretary, I can give only one answer: you can have the power of money, but the authority of the church remains ours forever and ever.

Wonsuk Ma

My offering will be theological. I hope that we do not see a divided mission and a divided house, as if on the one hand there is singling out of proclamation and evangelism as the whole of mission, while on the other there is singling out of justice as the whole mission. I think the same Holy Spirit empowers the Church to bring the justice and good news of Jesus Christ to the world that is suffering, to those who do not know Jesus. Therefore, I celebrate how the new methodological emphasis in recent years, for example through the World Council of Churches, has brought to light the powerful and broad range of the work of the Holy Spirit. The Holy Spirit leads us in authentic discipleship, in the self-giving love and justice of God's Kingdom, in empowered witnessing, in faithful living, in joyously sharing one's encounter with Christ, and in going and proclaiming even to the ends of the earth. It's the same Holy Spirit, if we are attentive enough to his voice and if we are honest enough to say, 'Yes, the Holy Spirit has been working dynamically in your tradition all these years but differently from how he has been working in mine.' If we repent and ask forgiveness for our ignorance, I believe that the Lordship of Jesus Christ will be realized among us as we celebrate. But also, we can go out joyously together to the broken world.

George Geevarghese Coorilos

Once again, our profound thanks to our three respondents who have helped us in moving the agenda forward, in synthesizing the reflections that we have heard in the last two or three days, and in giving us a sense of the direction in which the GCF should be moving ahead. Thank you so much once again for your input.

This discussion is not yet over. As I understand, we will come back to this discussion one more time in the afternoon, and hopefully in that session we will get a much clearer picture of what challenges we should really take up as the GCF. So we can still continue our discussion as we move along. At this stage, our last ten minutes will be devoted to the message committee. They have been working very hard. The first draft of the message is now ready for us to hear. So I invite David Han and Katherine Shirk Lucas to come forward and read to us the first draft of the message. We will not have time to discuss it yet. We will listen to it and then reflect on it during break time. In the next session we will come back to it for plenary discussion.

Revd Nicta Lubaale

DAY FOUR: FRIDAY 27 APRIL
LET MUTUAL LOVE CONTINUE!
FORWARD TOGETHER IN FAITH AND HOPE

14.30 PLENARY SESSION

Where is the Spirit Leading Us?

Moderator: **Nicta Lubaale** (Uganda/Kenya), General Secretary, Organization of African Instituted Churches; GCF Committee Member

Testimony: Hopes and Challenges of the Third Global Gathering Youth Delegates

Stacey Duensing (USA), Pastor, Reformed Church in America

Third Global Gathering Message: Second Reading

David Han (Republic of Korea/USA), Professor of Theology and Pentecostal Spirituality, Pentecostal Theological Seminary; GCF Committee Member for the Church of God (Cleveland)

Katherine Shirk Lucas (USA/France), Professor of Theology, Institut Catholique de Paris

Thank You, Larry and Eleanor Miller — Global Christian Forum Committee Members

- *Kathryn L. Johnson* (USA), Lutheran
- *Ganoune Diop* (Senegal/USA), Seventh-day Adventist
- *Dimitra Koukoura* (Greece), Orthodox
- *Brian Farrell* (Ireland/Vatican City), Catholic
- *Anne-Cathy Graber* (France), Mennonite
- *Nicta Lubaale* (Uganda/Kenya), African Instituted
- *Wesley Granberg-Michaelson* (USA), Reformed

Response

Larry Miller

Prayer

Brian Farrell

Youth Testimony: Hopes and Challenges[1]

Stacey Duensing

Introduction

Grace and peace to you from God our Father and the Lord Jesus Christ. My name is Revd Stacey Duensing, and I serve as a pastor in the Reformed Church in America. I speak to you on behalf of the youth delegates who asked me to compile their reflections and present this report to you.

I would like to start by thanking the leaders of the Global Christian Forum for intentionally inviting youth delegates to this global gathering. Thank you, Dr. Casely Essamuah, for making time to meet with the youth delegates, to share with us, and to listen to us. Thank you also to the church leaders here who have invited us into this space. We, as youth, are filled with gratitude to be received into this gathering in the true spirit *and practice* of mutual love. For in the act of being welcomed as youth delegates, the Forum has practiced mutual love. Thanks be to God!

We, as youth, are here on the journey with you. We are eager to learn and to participate. We are committed to the work of mutual love; not only here at this gathering of the Global Christian Forum, but also in the future.

Hopes and Challenges

On Thursday evening during dinner, Dr. Casely hosted youth delegates to discuss our hopes from the Forum as well as challenges we see for the future. During our conversation, it was established that at this meeting of the Global Christian Forum, the term *youth* corresponds to delegates under the age of 40. We also met with Archbishop Angaelos, who reminded us that Christianity is never about an us-and-them mentality. This applies also to youth delegates and their receptiveness to the seasoned wisdom of older leaders present here. We

---

1 See the 'Youth Forum Programme' in the appendices of this book.

must work together, listening and learning together, if we are to let mutual love continue.

First, I will share two sources of hope that we discussed in our meeting.

(1) We are filled with hope from what we have experienced here: Christians from different communions, cultures and countries gathering together to seek our common unity in Christ and to practice mutual love.

(2) We are filled with hope from the welcome we have received as youth to participate and learn alongside you. We are hopeful that youth participation will continue and grow in the future, so that young leaders may learn from the wisdom of established leaders and also add to the Global Christian Forum the diversity of their perspective.

This hope for continued youth involvement leads to our challenge: how are youth to be included in the future? The youth delegation discussed this challenge and would like to contribute the following ideas concerning the participation and representation of youth delegates:

(1) Youth participation in the global gathering promotes inter-generational learning and discussion. This is of deep value to us as we practice mutual love. We must work together. In addition to our time together with the Forum, the youth delegates have also enjoyed their conversations together as youth. We suggest continued opportunities for the youth to gather together by themselves while also still participating in the full forum. One suggestion that arose was that youth delegates could arrive a day before the forum for fellowship and learning, and to grow in unity of voice. After this meeting, the youth could then participate in the full forum.

(2) With regard to the representation of youth delegates: In the spirit of mutual love, sharing, and unity, we encourage the continued participation of youth delegates in the Global Christian Forum. We would like to encourage each of the GCF's four 'pillars' to bring to the next global gathering *at*

least four youth delegates. In addition, we encourage the participation of youth on the Global Christian Forum Committee—at the very least, one representative from each of the four pillars. We further encourage, should this action be taken, that these youth representatives be chosen with mindfulness of diversity in all areas, including ethnicity, world region, and gender.

On behalf of the youth delegation, I thank you for your warm welcome of youth delegates here and our inclusion. Let mutual love continue.

Thank You to the Millers

Kathryn L. Johnson

My own history with Larry and Eleanor Miller began before Larry came to lead the Global Christian Forum, when he was general secretary of the Mennonite World Conference. From that initial encounter, I have a persistent gratitude and a tiny story.

On Wednesday, we saw pictures of reconciliation among a number of communions that have been separated since the sixteenth century. Around the edges of those pictures I saw hovering the spirit of Larry Miller. Larry was part of the intense conversation between Anabaptists/Mennonites and my own Lutheran tradition as they recognized that our two traditions could not discuss differences in theology and practice, such as baptism, unless they first addressed the legacies of violent persecution on our side towards Anabaptists.

In this painful conversation, Lutherans lovingly were helped along to the painful realization that our only possible response was repentance. Then, on the Mennonite side, Larry guided the process by which Mennonites gracefully extended forgiveness. This reconciliation was a gift, I believe, to the whole church, and this experience was fresh in our minds as approached the 500th anniversary of the Reformation. Cardinal Kasper, a Catholic observer, said of that process, 'Here we can find inspiration for how to come to 2017.' Larry, the entire church is in your debt for this characteristically unobtrusive contribution to learning how to deal with the wounds of our differences.

But after that reconciliation, differences like baptism remained. Both Catholics and Lutherans were eager to pursue this topic with Anabaptists, and here we come to the story. Larry proposed to Bishop Farrell and to the Lutheran World Federation that we three pursue this topic together. 'Larry', I said, 'are you sure? Do you want to be in a dialogue that could be two against one?' And Larry said at once, 'Which two?' In that response was the confidence that trusting relationships could open the imagination to new possibilities and insights not defined by past history, and also the commitment to taking risks on behalf of unity which we have seen consistently in Larry's time as Secretary of the Global Christian Forum. For this we say 'Thank you!'

Others want to thank you also, as representatives of the whole GCF. A little cloud of witnesses has assembled here to thank and bless you.

Ganoune Diop

Larry and Eleanor, among the Christian values and virtues that your Anabaptist-Mennonite faith has intentionally championed since you came on to the scene of Christian history, there are two which you have remarkably embodied and modeled in the context of your leadership at the Global Christian Forum. One is brotherhood. The other one is non-violence.

Of course, we could expand on your contributions and mention your emphasis on separation of church and state, which could have avoided the seeming cultural captivity of the church in some nations. We could also mentioned your humility anchored in the values that you are in the world but not of the world.

I testify that clearly you have been successful to prove to all who have the privilege to partner with you that you and Eleanor are a brother and a sister to us. Your attitude reflected a deep commitment to peacemaking. Therefore you are blessed according to our Lord Jesus' beatitude.

Thank you for having created a space, a welcoming space for all of us to feel at home with you.

May the peace of God which surpasses all understanding keep your hearts and minds in Christ Jesus our Lord and Saviour.

In gratitude.

Dimitra Koukoura

Larry and Eleanor are a devoted couple, both to their family and to the Forum. This flows from their deep commitment to Christ and to serving His prayer for unity. Larry has been an efficient learner. He followed the mandate of the Forum, which is learning from one another. But at the same time, he has been a great practitioner of inviting people from various Christian families together. This gathering is the proof. Obviously, over the period of his tenure, he has been hardworking, sleepless day and night, and anyone can observe the impact from the success of this Third Global Gathering as you have experienced it. Laurent et Eleanor, on vous remercie beaucoup!

Brian Farrell

Most of you will be aware that in the Catholic Church one of the biggest, most solemn celebrations we have is the canonization of a holy person. I think that the day we start canonizing Mennonites, Larry would be one of the great candidates. But let me tell you, Larry, you wouldn't be number one on the list. The number one position would be for Eleanor.

Personally, I've known the Millers since 2003. I don't know if you remember, Larry, but we met for the very first time at the Conference of Secretaries of Christian World Communions, at a meeting in Cyprus, I believe. I had just been appointed to my position, and I had no idea what the ecumenical world was like. So Larry took me a bit under his wing and presented and explained in very clear and precise terms what I was supposed to do in that group.

Over the years, we have had wonderful moments at all kinds of ecumenical meetings. But I do want to say that Larry will, in a sense, go down in the history of relationships between us because he was instrumental in starting the Catholic-Mennonite dialogue and getting it done. And that has produced some extraordinary results. I would invite you all to read the document produced by this dialogue, *Called Together To Be Peacemakers*. The idea of the peace churches and the old, traditional, historical churches that have been engaged in wars forever—it was a fascinating dialogue. The document is highly illuminating.

So, Larry, there are many things we could say about you. You are, to use a word that has been used here, one of the pillars of ecumenical work and building relationships. And you have done it because you have put your heart and soul into it. You are totally convinced that this is what the Lord is calling us to. You have given your time and your energy—and that's why I say Eleanor is the saint in the family, because you have given your heart and soul to this business. So thank you, Larry. May God bless you in your future. We will always remember with gratitude what you have done.

A Parable of Ecumenical Fraternity
Anne-Cathy Graber

Let me tell you a little story. It is short and concrete, and it really happened a few years ago. It is the kind of story that could go unnoticed. However, this story is a parable.

It's the story of a man who arrived in a faraway land, in Africa, after a long voyage, with considerable jet lag, to lead his first meeting of the Global Christian Forum Committee.

During the trip from the airport to the meeting place, the car broke down! It was getting dark and they were in the middle of the countryside. The driver suggested that he call a taxi so that the man might journey on to the meeting place in time for supper, and to get some sleep. As for the driver, he would wait for the service people. The man, however, refused and said that he would wait with his host until the service truck arrived.

So what does this little story have to do with our thanksgiving today?

As you will have guessed, the man is Larry Miller (and the result would have been the same thing had Eleanor been there!). The driver was also a member of the Global Christian Forum Committee.

This little story speaks in a simple way about what the work towards communion between our churches asks of us. It is about choosing to remain with the other during a breakdown, difficulty or challenge that stops us both, even in the middle of the night. It would have been, in fact, more logical, faster and more comfortable to have taken the taxi. But this choice would have left the other alone to wait in the dark. Ecumenical fraternity has a cost: we cannot be content with immediate and easy solutions (such as taking a taxi).

Ecumenical fraternity means choosing to remain with the other. It means to believe and hope, whatever the circumstances and obstacles on the way. To wait together by the road is itself to make a solution, even in the middle of the night.

Thank you, Larry and Eleanor, for this true story. Thank you for the gift of your witness to ecumenical fraternity.

Nicta Lubaale

I first met Larry at a meeting of the Conference of Secretaries of Christian World Communions. He's one of those people who welcomed me and helped me to understand. It's good to know that even Bishop Farrell was helped by Larry, so I was not the only ignorant person he helped! But later we got into conversations and talked about the beginnings of Mennonites, and I talked about the beginnings of African Instituted Churches. We concluded that the Mennonites are the African Instituted Churches of Europe, because of our shared history. And that brought us together even before he took on the role of secretary of the Global Christian Forum.

Thank you, Larry, for the hard work you put in, for the Christian concern for all Christian traditions in this Forum. Larry has been working with Magali Moreno, Kim Cain in communications, Joséphine Nthinyuzwa, and Eleanor. But really, the full-time person running the work day-to-day has been Larry. And it's been like that from the beginning, even under Huibert van Beek. So Casely, you know what is ahead of you!

Thank you so much, Larry, for putting us together with all the emails, the passion of detail, and for being a very conscientious person who has kept us going on this journey as a committee. Thank you very much, Larry and Eleanor.

Now we are getting to the point of saying thank you and for our gifts to be given. In the photos, we saw Larry giving gifts of a pottery plate with the Christian symbol of three fish linked inseparably together. We did not know what to give you as a gift for the work you have done. But still we want to give you something we think of as a humble gift. It may not communicate all the thank-yous, but we want to give this gift on behalf of this whole gathering of the Global Christian Forum.

Wesley Granberg-Michaelson

There really is no way to adequately express gratitude for the countless hours (even during these days), the sleepless nights, the continual concern, and the stewardship for the Global Christian Forum you have shown. There is one small way of saying thanks that we want to give you, and these are cards which each member here in Bogotá has signed for both of you, that you can keep and treasure.

If you look at the cards, you'll see that the art is distinctive, because it is from the St. John's Bible. The St. John's Bible is produced at the St. Joseph Abbey over countless years and has been called an absolutely priceless treasure, conveying the Word of God both in word and in dramatic graphic detail. One version of the St. John's Bible and its volumes has been published, and we would like to give that to you as a small token of our boundless gratitude. Pictures of it are on the screen. Larry, we did not bring it on the plane with us, but it will arrive at your new home.

Response

Larry Miller

I'm sorry it's time to leave this gathering. I hear you saying so many nice things. But I'm a bit concerned about where we are and what's happening. These are the sorts of things you say at someone's funeral! So if you don't mind, we'll simply run the video of this session when that day comes.

Over the past few days, I have for the first time begun to feel just a bit nostalgic about leaving the Forum—in spite of the sleepless nights. But the reason is that I know I will not see many of you again, and you are the reasons for which these years have been a gift of God to me, and I think to Eleanor as well. We thank you. So may God make his face to shine upon you and bless you and give you peace in the days ahead. We're not leaving the journey, but we will not see you as often. Thank you for these years.

Brian Farrell

Larry, I think that the best gift that we can give to you and Eleanor is to implore the Lord's grace upon you for all the years ahead and all the great things you will do, built on the foundations of all that you have done already for which we are so grateful. So we ask the Lord to bless Larry and Eleanor in their future. We send you with prayer and in song, prayed and sung corporately:

> *Oh God, you have called your servants to ventures of which we cannot see the ending, by paths as yet untrodden, through perils unknown. Give us faith to go out with good courage, not knowing where we go, but only that your hand is leading us and your love supporting us; through Jesus Christ our Lord.*

Song:

Laudate omnes gentes, laudate Dominum. Laudate omnes gentes, laudate Dominum! Text: Taizé Community

Archbishop Angaelos

DAY FOUR: FRIDAY 27 APRIL
LET MUTUAL LOVE CONTINUE!
FORWARD TOGETHER IN FAITH AND HOPE

CLOSING PLENARY SESSION

Where is the Spirit Leading Us?

Moderator: **Wesley Granberg-Michaelson** (USA), GCF Committee Member representing the World Alliance of Reformed Churches; President, Global Christian Forum Foundation

Panel of Perspectives: What Next?

- *Angaelos* (Egypt/United Kingdom), Archbishop of London, Coptic Orthodox Church
- *Ruth Padilla DeBorst* (Costa Rica), Coordinator, Networking Team, International Fellowship of Mission as Transformation
- *Angela Berlis* (Switzerland), Vice-chair, Department of Old Catholic Theology, University of Bern; Member, Faith and Order Commission, World Council of Churches

- *Casely Essamuah* (Ghana/USA), Secretary-elect, Global Christian Forum

Third Global Gathering Message: Final Reading and Reception

David Han (Republic of Korea/USA), Professor of Theology and Pentecostal Spirituality, Pentecostal Theological Seminary; GCF Committee Member for the Church of God (Cleveland);

Katherine Shirk Lucas (USA/France), Professor of Theology, Institut Catholique de Paris

Introduction

Wesley Granberg-Michaelson

Dear friends in Jesus Christ, we are coming to the end of our pilgrimage together during these days. At the end of this time, we focus on being sent out. We are sent out in two ways.

First, we will be sent out with words from four of us who have been a part of our community and are also journeying together to their homes. Those four are here on the platform with me. One of them is Archbishop Angaelos, an archbishop of the Coptic Orthodox Church who shepherds his part of the flock in England. He is also the president of the United Kingdom Bible Society. We also have Ruth Padilla DeBorst, whom we've already heard from, who is from the Christian Reformed Church and a vital part of the wider evangelical theological community of Latin America. Then we have Angela Berlis, who is a professor of theology from the Old Catholic Church and on the Faith and Order Commission of the World Council of Churches. Finally, we have a person whose face you will already recognize, Casely Essamuah, who will be on July 1 the new Secretary of the Global Christian Forum.

First, we will ask these four to share with you briefly what they are going home thinking about and willing to do, how this time will change them, what they will share with others, and how they feel their being here will make a difference. What are the things that are on their hearts as they leave, and as they help you prepare to leave? Then we'll have some time to talk together and to share briefly. We will conclude at about six o'clock, when we will gather for a second way to end our pilgrimage together—in worship. Lastly, we will share food and fellowship around the table at the end of the meeting.

Now we begin by hearing from each one of your colleagues, starting with Archbishop Angaelos.

Archbishop Angaelos

Christ is risen! I am sure that is the reason why we are here. We are not here because he was risen two thousand years ago. We are here because he is well and truly risen today. As risen, he gives hope, he gives life, and he is the core of what we believe we are.

Now I'm going to break a few stereotypes. The first is to rejoice in Christ. Although we do suffer as Christians—and we have heard so much about this from His Holiness the patriarch and brother bishops in our own Coptic Orthodox Church, throughout Syria, Iraq, India and the whole Middle East—I want us, as we go forward, to tread carefully, not to think of us or them as victims but as witnesses. They carry our message, the message of Christ, and they bring forth light into a region that would be truly dark without them. The presence of Christians is reconciling, healing, proclaiming and inspiring.

Now, I have my own view; you may differ. I do not think that the Middle East will be void of Christians, because there will always be Christians there. But I do know for a fact, however, that the numbers have fallen dramatically in Iraq and Syria, and thus also for Christians across the Middle East. There will be a greater minority and the pressure will increase on that minority, which means that it is now necessary for us to stand together as the body of Christ. I'm sure that if the great St John the Evangelist were to get royalties for every time we used chapter 17 of his gospel, the Church would be in a very different place. But when we say 'that they may be one', that's scary because many of us don't want to be one. It is different if we go to the depth of Trinitarian theology. There are three persons, Father, Son and Holy Spirit, intrinsically distinct yet one in the Trinity. So with regard to the oneness we speak about in the church, our role is very particular. It's not that we become one body administratively, but one in faith, unified. If we go from this place knowing that we want to be unified, that is the greatest message we can give to the world. You see, there is a myth out there that Christians are divided.

I want to share a story. I served as assistant to the previous pope of the Coptic Orthodox Church. In his residence, there was a wonderful bed of roses in various colours. Someone said, 'Look at all those different colours.' And His Holiness said, 'Those colours aren't different, they are variants'. We here do not wish to differ. But we are variants in our expressions and in our lives. We will disagree. We should never come down to a homogeneous grey shapeless matter of the lowest common denominator. But we should know what we stand for and who we are. We should know that we believe in the Triune God, the incarnate Son, his death, his resurrection, his ascension, and in the fact that he awaits us in his heavenly kingdom.

Now that won't cover everything. But it will cover most of it, and our ministry now is a ministry on the ground. I personally am involved, as I know are many you in this room are, in theological dialogues. And they are important because in some things we can't all be right, as much as we don't like to hear that. But we can stand up at the same time, looking at how we can make a difference in the world, in being light in that way. People will think that what we do is a waste. But it is certainly not a waste to be here in this fellowship and with you as sisters and brothers.

Now I want to close with a passage that I am sure you will recognize and that I think will inspire us.

'How then shall they call upon him in whom they have not believed? And how shall they believe in him of whom they have not heard? And how shall they hear without a preacher? And how shall they preach unless they are sent?' Now this is our word: 'How beautiful are the feet of those who preach the gospel of peace and bring glad tidings of good news.' We can move from here and focus on what separates us, or we can move beyond what separates us and go from here with glad tidings of good news.

Ruth Padilla DeBorst

Jesus is Lord. We say that often as a religious expression. For the first followers of Jesus Christ, saying 'Jesus is Lord' was far more than that.

It meant that it is not Caesar who is Lord, not Herod, not Caiaphas, and not me.

Sociologists talk about us as animals who not only tell stories but live into the stories we see ourselves cast into. We are told by the stories we believe. So a question that I think is before us is: what story do we see ourselves living into? Who is Lord in that story? Is it a story of unlimited progress that leaves millions behind and breaks the best of creation to pieces? Is it a story that erects walls, weaponizes relationships and forces millions to wander because of rising waters or untold violence? Is this the story that as Christians we see ourselves embedded into? Are we allowing our imaginations to be co-opted by the myth of progress, this pagan myth of consumerism that is consuming our very souls? All of us, I believe, need to continue every day seeking prayerfully to allow God's Spirit to be revealed to us, and to ask in what ways we are living out that story. Or do we belong to another story?—namely, the good news about a good creation, of a God who created out of love and not out of violence, of a Spirit who sustains with love, a community of love who undergirds our very existence and a Lord who rules out of self-giving.

We talked about the shift of Christianity to the Global South, and a challenge that I think still stands before us as a Forum and as particular churches and individuals is this: in what way is that shift really being reflected in the power structures of our churches, and in the agendas that are set? Who is setting the table for our gatherings? Is the money determining the agenda? Who sits around the table? Whose voices are being heard? So as we go home, we need to ask ourselves, 'What story are we living into?'

And just one little, very practical challenge. I grew up in Buenos Aires, as a Baptist. Since then I have had three children baptized in an Anglican Church. I've been a missionary in the Christian Reformed Church. And currently we have a local community, a monastic family community, and a house church. But this small Baptist church in Buenos Aires began 25 years ago to meet with the other churches in the neighbourhood—Presbyterian, Anglican, Methodist, Roman Catholic, Lutheran. The pastors began to meet once a month to pray together. Once a month for 25 years, whoever the pastor was in those churches, they met to pray. Today, every single month there is an ecumenical service in that neighbourhood. And the Protestant Reformation was remembered and talked about in the Roman Catholic cathedral with presentations by a Baptist pastor, a Presbyterian minister and a Lutheran minister. Just a challenge to each of us: how do we take all these big dreams we have been talking about and make them concrete on the ground?

May God be with us, and may we, through our lives and the story we live into, confess that Jesus is Lord. Amen.

Angela Berlis

When I go home, my husband will be waiting expectantly. We have been married for 30 years. He will be very curious because he was involved in earlier meetings of the Global Christian Forum. He envied me when I told him that I would be here. In our life together, we have always distributed different roles. He has been involved in the charismatic movement in The Netherlands as well as the Global Christian Forum. I have participated more in ecumenical dialogues. We share different qualities in our house and that is very good. But now it is very good for me also to share a little of his experience.

He told me that it is usual in the Global Christian Forum to share faith stories. I said to my group that I was not used to doing this. But I enjoyed it deeply. I was glad to hear many stories from other people, too many stories to report in these few minutes. I will take those stories home not only as stories from individuals, but also as stories which unite us as Christians in global Christianity.

For me going home will mean several things. I will reflect more on the meaning of the Global Christian Forum and the way this Forum was created as an open space, as a place for free speech. I think it is very important to be a place for free speech, a place where you can talk with each other without having to wonder what the other person might be thinking about you. In the ancient world, a forum—an *agora*—was a space for free people who have free speech. This is a very important idea that I experienced here in the past days: a space of encounter, a space where we can share, united in the unity which is already given in Christ.

What unity do we seek? In the ecumenical dialogues where I am involved—I am also here as a representative of the Faith and Order Commission of the World Council of Churches—we are also looking for unity, for grace, to put it into words, into new words, which are fitting for the world today. When I go home I will tell my husband that I have now experienced some things which he had already experienced. But I will also say that it is important to continue my work reflecting on unity so that I am not only practicing unity on a local level or a personal level. I will continue to think about what these things can mean: how we can put them into theological thinking, into reflective unity, but also a unity which is experienced.

I will go home and go to other meetings. I will talk with my students in Switzerland about my experiences here. I will tell them that they have to look at a broader horizon. They have to go forward with their ideas, their thinking, their experiences of Christianity, but not only with experiences of Christianity in Switzerland. I will try to tell them to broaden their horizon to include all the other faith stories and all the other experiences of faith.

There are many things that I will take with me. I was very glad that we talked so much about the persecuted church in Syria and the Middle East. These are things I will take into my prayers. But we also have to continue to reflect. There are many places and things I will take with me, including the Scripture readings of Luke 24 in our evening prayers. Did they not burn in our hearts all the time?

Casely Essamuah

My dear Christian friends, the first word today should be 'thank you' to Larry and Eleanor for their faithful service to the Global Christian Forum all these years. We give thanks to God, not only for the work they did but also for emulating the Spirit of Christ. I would wish that I could have 10%, not a double portion, of the spirit with which Larry worked. Thank you very much. Because of your diligent work, the Church of Christ has greater and fuller unity than when you started.

We all celebrate the growth of the Christian faith throughout the world. That growth is based on the sacrifice of generations of missionaries who went to places that seemed strange to them, and sought to share a message of hope and love—of new life in Jesus Christ. Some of them, like those that came to my part of the world, in West Africa, came, having packed all their earthly belongings in coffins, and knowing that they would most likely not return to their homelands alive. They embodied what the writer to the Hebrews stated in such graphic terms:

Hebrews 11:33-39

> [33]*who through faith conquered kingdoms, administered justice, and gained what was promised; who shut the mouths of lions,* [34]*quenched the fury of the flames, and escaped the edge of the sword; whose weakness was turned to strength; and who became powerful in battle and routed foreign armies.* [35]*Women received back their dead, raised to life again. There were others who were tortured, refusing to be released so that they might gain an even better resurrection.* [36]*Some faced jeers and flogging, and even chains and imprisonment.* [37]*They were put to death by stoning; they were sawed in two; they were killed by the sword. They went about in sheepskins and goatskins, destitute, persecuted and mistreated—* [38]*the world was not worthy of them. They wandered in deserts and mountains, living in caves and in holes in the ground.* [39]*These were all commended for their faith, yet none of them received what had been promised.*

How do we respond as older churches? With great and justifiable pride that our heritage is marked by sacrifice that has borne fruit. How do we respond as younger churches? With gratitude and humility that the baton has been passed on to us to reach others also. How do we respond as the global body of Christ? In partnership with one another, knowing that we are stronger together than apart.

We leave Bogotá with two clear mandates: first, that GCF needs to engage the youth. And second, that we replicate these life-affirming and exceptionally successful Global Gatherings at the national and regional levels. In both cases, the how and when and what have been left unsaid, as together we rely on God's Spirit to lead the way. We have been called to repentance, that henceforth none of us should say, 'I have no need of you'. We are Christ's body, one body, and cannot function as though mutilated.

For 25 years, I have lived my vocational calling with Matthew 28:18-20 and Acts 1:8 and also knowing that the fields are white and the labourers are few (Matt. 9:37). Now the Lord is calling me to take on John 17:21, that all may be one so that the world may believe. Our unity is to add credence to our witness to a world that so desperately needs the gospel. God in Christ by offering salvation has done His part. It is now our duty and joy to do ours.

Thank you and God bless you all.

Revd Dr Casely Essamuah, Revd Nicta Lubaale, Revd Wesley Granberg-Michaelson

DAY FOUR: FRIDAY 27 APRIL
LET MUTUAL LOVE CONTINUE!
FORWARD TOGETHER IN FAITH AND HOPE

CLOSING PRAYER & COMMISSIONING SERVICE

Commissioning of Revd Dr Casely Essamuah as Secretary of the Global Christian Forum, and of the Participants in the Third Global Gathering for Service in Mission

1. The Gathering of the Community

A leader[1] welcomes the community and begins with a prayer

Song: Entremos y ensalcemos al Señor[2]

2. The Proclamation of the Word

The reading and re-reading (multiple languages) of Luke 24:33-53

Sermon in four parts:

Luke 24:36-43: The risen Christ appears to the disciples

Ioan Sauca (Romania/Switzerland, Orthodox)

Dear brothers and sisters, trying to stay short as requested and to relate my reflection to the mission and work of the Global Christian Forum, I can identify three main learnings from this passage.

1. Jesus came personally to meet the apostles and to convince them of his resurrection. He stood in their midst, entered into dialogue with them, listened to their worries and questions, received with patience and love their very doubts without anger or judgement, and responded with palpable proofs and logical answers.

In Christ, God became one of us and spoke to us face-to-face as Emmanuel, no longer through messages or through manuscripts or books, but through personal encounter. Consequently, those who live in Christ are called to share in the dialogical and communitarian life of God and to be open to dialogue and communion. While remaining faithful to their own identities, they must listen with patience and love to the doubts and questions of others and always look for the road to unity and harmony. This I see to be the basis for the goal and vocation of those participating in the Global Christian Forum.

---

1 Leaders of the prayer and commissioning service were Pirjo-Liisa Penttinen, Andrezj Choromanski, John Gibaut, and for the commissioning, Nicta Lubaale and Wesley Granberg-Michaelson. Anne-Cathy Graber and John Gibaut led in preparation and organization of the service.

2 Brother Paolo and local friends of the Taizé Community sang and led music during the service.

To be open to dialogue is therefore not an option but an obligation if we wish to remain faithful to what we are as Christians, reflecting God's very image. In Greek, there is another verb which is opposed to *dialogo*, and that is *diaballo*. From that verb derives the word *diabolos*—the devil, who is the father of lies, of cheating, of scattering, of disunity. It is up to us which master we follow—the one asking for dialogue or the one pleading for scandal, disunity, disintegration.

2. The risen Lord was not a ghost or a spirit, but neither was he a resuscitation of a corpse. Lazarus, the son of the widow of Nain, and others who experienced the resurrection of a corpse died again. Christ's resurrected body will be alive for eternity, because his resurrected body, though still material, was fully penetrated and imbued by the Spirit. He had a body like any human, but he came into the midst of the apostles through closed doors.

Christ's resurrection is an eruption of the reality of the Kingdom to come, the Kingdom of the future, in history. He is the first one resurrected, the prototype of what we will all be in the eschaton. For this reason the early Christian writers called the Sunday of the resurrection the eighth day—the day beyond history. With that fully spiritualized, risen body, Christ ascended to heaven and is seated at the right hand of the Father. But he did not leave us as orphans. He sent us the Holy Spirit on the day of Pentecost. In the coming of the Spirit, Christ is fully present, and where Christ is present the Father is present too. For this reason the first Christians considered themselves to be *christophoros* or *theoforos*, which means bearers of Christ or of God, and the Church was said to be full of Trinity. If we are to be temples of the Holy Spirit and bearers of Christ, we are called to do God's and Christ's mission, not our own. And the risen Christ will always be with his Church.

3. Their personal encounter with Christ after the resurrection was not enough to motivate and encourage the apostles to go out and share the good news, because the Christian faith is not a result of study and research but a gift of the Holy Spirit. Though convinced about His resurrection, the apostles were still afraid and stayed behind locked

doors. But when the Spirit had come, their hearts were burning and they went out witnessing about Christ's resurrection.

The coming of the Spirit transforms those who receive it. Witnessing, supporting missionary entities and acting as missionaries will in turn be signs that one lives in the Spirit. Thus *marturia* (witness or mission) is not something we do but something into which we become. Referring to the coming of the Holy Spirit, Christ says that 'you will be my witnesses' and the verb used is *einai* (*esesthe*, Acts 1:8).

Therefore, the Church and each Christian individually have to be witnesses. The conversion, however, is not our business but entirely God's affair. The end of chapter two in the book of Acts says that following the witness of the apostles 'God added to their numbers every day' (Acts 2:47).

In the Orthodox Church, from the day of the resurrection until the day of Pentecost, the epistles that are to be read every Sunday are taken from the Acts of the Apostles. I see in this choice of the book of Acts by the early church two important affirmations which I hope to be also guiding principles of those involved in the Global Christian Forum:

- (a) A church that has lost its passion for mission has given up its very vocation and reason for existence.

- (b) A church that no longer experiences the vitality of the church of the book of Acts and no longer feels the presence of the Lord in answering the real needs, sufferings and longings of the people of our times is already a dead church. Christ is alive forever and His presence should be manifested in the churches today as in the days after the resurrection and Pentecost.

Song: Bless the Lord (1x)

Luke 24:44-47

Ganoune Diop (Senegal/USA, Seventh-day Adventist)

In the Gospel of Luke 24:44, Jesus told his disciples: 'These are my words that I spoke to you while I was still with you, that everything written about me in the Law of Moses and the Prophets and the Psalms must be fulfilled.' Then he opened their minds to understand the Scriptures.

Earlier he had told Pharisees that the Scriptures testify of him (John 5:39).

Looking at the Scriptures, one of the most fascinating revelations is how Jesus embraced the story of the whole human family. He fulfils our stories.

He came to embrace our destiny in order to defeat death from inside. He came to deliver us from evil.

To do so he chose to live our story and our stories.

The only righteousness that there is has thus infiltrated a world where no one could claim to be righteous.

Jesus came to relive our stories in amazing ways. He came to succeed where humanity had failed and gotten entangled in the spiral of evil.

It is not by chance that Jesus is designated by means of several titles. These titles and actions demonstrate how Jesus embraced both the history of Israel and our stories for the purpose of offering us his destiny of life eternal.

(1) He is called the second Adam. He came to relive the history of Adam. He succeeds where Adam failed.

(2) He is called the son of David, the promised king (see 2 Samuel 7).

(3) He is called the Son of Abraham, the ultimate priest who brings the blessings to the whole human family (Genesis 22).

(4) He is the Israel of God. He relives the history of Israel. He came to succeed where Israel did not fulfil its mission.

(5) Israel went to Egypt. Jesus went to Egypt

(6) Israel came out of Egypt. Jesus came out of Egypt: 'I called my son out of Egypt.'

(7) The water changed into blood. Jesus changed water to wine at Cana.

(8) Israel was tempted in the wilderness for 40 years. Jesus was tempted for 40 days and nights.

(9) There were 12 tribes. There were 12 apostles.

(10) There were 70 elders. 70 disciples were sent out (according to some manuscripts).

(11) Moses went on a mountain, Mount Sinai, to receive the Torah. Jesus went on a mountain, the Mount of Beatitudes, to give the true interpretation of the Torah. All prophets used to say, 'thus says the Lord.' Jesus said: 'Amen, I tell you this' because He is the Lord.

(12) God made a covenant with Israel on Mount Sinai through Moses. Jesus came to make a new covenant with peoples of all nations, tribes and tongues.

(13) When the covenant was ratified at Sinai, Moses took the blood and sprinkled it on the people of Israel. When Jesus ratified the covenant, he took bread and wine to establish the new covenant. He said, 'This is my blood of the covenant. This is my body.'

(14) Moses and the Israelites crossed through a divided Red Sea. God had to make a miracle in parting the waters so that his people could cross over. Jesus did not have to part the waters. He masters the whole universe. He can walk on waters.

(15) Jesus made more miracles than all the prophets combined. He healed the sick, resurrected dead people. He even opened

the eyes of the blind, which was unheard of in the Old Testament.

Israelite institutions also find their fulfilment in Jesus. Jesus is Emmanuel, God with us, God dwelling in our midst, God pitching God's tent or tabernacle with us and in us through God's Holy Spirit. Jesus then is the sanctuary of God.

Israelite festivals also find their fulfilment in our Lord and Saviour. Christ our Passover lamb has been sacrificed. He is also our freedom. He is the one who brings true liberation: 'If the Son makes you free you shall be free indeed,' he said.

Jesus is our Jubilee, our only hope for atonement, our freedom and reconciliation.

His name is Jesus, Yehoshua. There are two components in his name:

(1) One from the verb *yasha,* to save, to take out of a danger zone, to rescue.

(2) The other at the beginning of his name 'Yeho' is an abbreviation of Yahweh from the verb *haya,* to be. This means that Jesus is the eternal one, the everlasting one, God.

His name then means the eternal one, the everlasting one, the one who causes to be, that is the creator who has come to save us.

A creature did not come to save us. God the creator came to save us. His name is Jesus. The name above all names, but also the name for all names.

Song: *Bless the Lord* (1x)

Luke 24:48-49

Souraya Bechealany (Lebanon, Maronite Catholic)

In verse 48, Jesus says, 'You are witnesses of these things.' What things are being mentioned? The passage has just explained: the suffering and resurrection of Christ for the remission of sins and the salvation of all people.

Being witnesses marks us with an identity. It makes us what we are: a living testimony, a martyr—confirmed by the shedding of blood if needed—, a sacrament and a spiritual offering. That is what we are: witnesses to Life.

Yet how can we be witnesses to Life when everything in us, around us, between us often speaks of death? We bear the weight of divisions between our churches and from others. We are tried and tested, made vulnerable.

We could not be witnesses if Christ had not fortified us by the gifts and graces of his resurrection. That is why verse 49 announces a promise made true: 'And I myself will send upon you what my Father has promised. But you must wait in the city until the power from above comes down upon you.'

'And I myself': this expression marks God's 'today' (the *nunc*), this today that does not move on. We have received the strength of the Spirit. It comes to us from the Father. We are then enabled to be witnesses. That, for us, is the greatest challenge and the greatest hope!

Brothers and sisters, the Lord is asking us to stay in the city and to wait for the power, the Spirit. The city is here and now (*hic et nunc*) in Bogotá. This week, Bogotá has been our shared city. We experienced here a beautiful Pentecost of the Spirit, I hope. We who have already been empowered by the Holy Spirit at our baptism are gathered together here in Bogotá, invoking the Spirit, sharing our faith and hope, and witnessing to our mutual love.

Lord Jesus Christ, crucified and raised to give us life, renew in us the baptism of the Spirit. Grant us each to return home tonight or tomorrow to our respective cities and to live there as witnesses of the mutual love that unites us. And of this, may we be your witnesses. Amen.

Song: Bless the Lord (1x)

Luke 24:50-53

Laura Saa (Ecuador, Pentecostal)

This passage is a hinge between the gospel of Luke and the book of Acts. Jesus has risen and been reunited with his disciples. He has corrected their erroneous thoughts about the restoration of the Kingdom and has given them a very important promise about the coming of the Comforter, the Holy Spirit, who would give them the power to preach the Good News, in his name, to all nations.

In these verses, Jesus takes the disciples out of Bethany—we could say, away from their everyday distractions—and takes them to the Mount of Olives. There he blesses them, with a blessing that is not simply routine but empowers them with well-being, peace and hope. Then, almost instantly, they see Jesus ascending to heaven with their own eyes. They worship him, recognizing his deity. In this spirit they return with joy to Jerusalem.

Aren't they supposed to mourn the loss of a great friend? No. On the contrary, they understand that they have been commissioned for a great task—the proclamation of the Gospel—and that they would receive the power to do it. Thence their joy. This is what they would do while awaiting Jesus' return. They have the joy of knowing that they are not alone, for Jesus accompanies them and his Spirit goes before them to fulfil the mission of reconciling the world with him.

Now we are here, far from our homelands. We have left our own Bethany, taking up a new vision that allows us to grasp very closely the will of God for his people: the unity of Christians.

We have heard about persecution, discrimination, poverty, violence and so many other signs of suffering around us, yet we have been blessed with new hopes. Our discussions have insisted on the need to work more on what is important to build a better world and to put aside our differences by becoming better followers of Christ. For the world needs a church that responds to the challenges of our time.

He has empowered us to bring good news to our communities: understanding, solidarity, communion and reconciliation. He has opened our eyes so that we can enjoy his love and sense his desire that as disciples we might fulfil the demands of the gospel.

He has blessed us. And now let us as his body, his church, bless one another. Let us instil joy in those who feel discouraged, support and console those who suffer for various reasons, contextualize the gospel and respect each other with joy. May the communion of the Father guide us, may the love of Christ shown on the cross unite us, and may the Holy Spirit help us in the fulfilment of our mission.

Song: Bless the Lord (4x)

3. Prayer

Leader: Holy Spirit, Creator,

In the beginning you moved over the waters.

From your breath all creation draws life.

You raised Jesus from the dead, and you raise us up in him.

Without you, life turns to dust.

We thank you for your presence among us these days.

Song: Veni lumen cordium

Leader: Holy Spirit, Counsellor,

by your inspiration, the prophets spoke and acted in faith.

You clothed them in power to be bearers of your Word.

Send us forth with your power as we journey home.

Song: Veni lumen cordium

Leader: Holy Spirit, Power,

you came as fire to Jesus' disciples;

you gave them voice before the rulers of this world.

Give us your voice to speak peace to our own nations and peoples.

Song: Veni lumen cordium

Leader: Holy Spirit, Sanctifier,

> you created us children of God;
>
> you make us the living temple of your presence;
>
> you intercede within us with sighs too deep for words.
>
> May your prayer within each of us in this global gathering be made visible in mission, justice and peace.

Song: Veni lumen cordium

Leader: Holy Spirit, Giver of life,

> You guide and make holy the church you create;
>
> you give gifts—
>
> > the spirit of wisdom and understanding,
> >
> > the spirit of counsel and fortitude,
> >
> > the spirit of knowledge and piety,
> >
> > the spirit of the fear of the Lord,
> >
> > the spirit of unity,
>
> that the whole creation may become what you want it to be,
>
> and that your will be done on earth as it is in heaven.

Lord's Prayer (each in own languages)

4. Welcoming the new Global Christian Forum Secretary

Leader:

My brothers and sisters in Christ, Casely has been chosen to be the Secretary of the Global Christian Forum. He will enter fully into this ministry on 1 July 2018. This ministry continues the good work done through the years in by Huibert and Larry, and is part of the work and witness of the whole church.

It is a new beginning because Casely brings particular gifts to our ministry together. As we stand in God's presence, let us pray that grace will be given to Casely and to all of us in the work of the Global Christian Forum, that we may fulfil the responsibilities which are ours together.

Leader asks the new Secretary to stand, and says:

> **Casely, do you, in the presence of this Global Gathering, commit yourself to the responsibility entrusted to you?**

The new Secretary replies:

> **I do.**

The Leader asks the members of the Global Christian Forum Committee to stand and says:

> **Do you, members of the Global Christian Forum Committee, commit yourselves to share with Casely in the ministry of the Forum?**

Global Christian Forum Committee:

> **We do.**

The Leader asks all members of the Global Gathering to stand, and says:

> **As brothers and sisters in the body of Christ, will you support Casely and the Global Christian Forum in this ministry together?**

People:

> **We will.**

Leader:

Sisters and brothers in Christ, we are called to proclaim the story of God's love and, above all, the Gospel of our Saviour Christ. I ask your prayers for Casely who has come among us to lead us and to serve with us.

Silent prayer for Casely

All members of the Global Gathering:

> *For this reason we kneel before the Father, from whom every family in heaven and on earth derives its name. We pray that out of his glorious riches he may strengthen you with power through his Spirit in your inner being, so that Christ may dwell in your hearts through faith. And we pray that you, being rooted and established in love, may have power, together with all the Lord's holy people, to grasp how wide and long and high and deep is the love of Christ, and to know this love that surpasses knowledge—that you may be filled to the measure of all the fullness of God.*
>
> *Now to him who is able to do immeasurably more than all we ask or imagine, according to his power that is at work within us, to him be glory in the church and in Christ Jesus throughout all generations, forever and ever! Amen.*

Song: Laudate omnes gentes

5. Commissioning the Members of the Third Global Gathering for Service in Mission

Leader:

Dear friends, with the disciples on the Road to Emmaus, in the mission of Jesus Christ we are constantly brought together and sent out. We are gathered by God's word and table, and we are sent out to do God's work of unity, healing, justice, and peace.

Leader:

We bless you, O God, and we praise your name. You anointed your own Son with the Holy Spirit to preach good news to the poor, to heal the broken-hearted, to comfort the sorrowful and to overcome division.

Leader:

Look kindly on your servants whom we send forth as messengers of reconciliation, salvation, unity and peace. Guide their steps, and with the power of your grace strengthen them in spirit.

Make their words the echo of Christ's voice, so those who hear them may be drawn to his Gospel.

Leader:

Through them may your Holy Spirit touch the hearts of all they meet. May their love for one another be the sign that they are your disciples. We ask this through Christ our Lord, who lives and reigns with you and the same Holy Spirit, one God, now and forever.

All: Amen.

Song: In the Lord I'll be ever thankful (El Señor)

Leader: Let us go in peace.

All: **Alleluia!**

The exchange of a sign of peace.

The GCF Committee in its first meeting following the Third Global Gathering (Malaysia, February 2019)

Postscript: Ministry During COVID

No one could have foreseen that barely twenty-two months after the Third Global Gathering of the Global Christian Forum in Bogotá, Colombia, the world would come to a complete standstill. Stopped in their tracks by a microscopic virus, most countries forbade gatherings of any size for some months. Almost six months after the shutdown, as I write this postscript, the world is slowly adjusting to a new day, one where social distancing and travel restrictions hinder much in-person human connection.

In such circumstances, how can the mandate of a non-institutional body like the GCF be implemented? Granted, many have benefitted tremendously from digital and online communication during this season, but we all yearn for in-person gatherings where the fulness of humanity can be enjoyed—where we can continue to practice mutual love. The global pandemic and the resulting shutdown make the memories of events such as Bogotá 2018 all the more endearing. The GCF faces a special challenge because it is not an organization or institution, but a *forum* and a platform. By its very nature, it does not have a membership but only participants. However, its nimbleness also allows it some creativity.

How do we measure the impact of the GCF, and especially of its global gatherings? Traditional measurements cannot answer this question. We recognize that the fruits of the GCF's labours will not be seen on its own tree. Instead, they will spread throughout areas of collaboration, dimensions of partnerships, and personal relationships fostered that build bridges for greater works by the churches.

Sharing Faith Stories

Other than convening a table that brings together the widest possible representation of global Christianity, the DNA of the Forum is its predilection for the sharing of faith stories. That is a unique charism that fosters relational unity even in the midst of the lack of doctrinal uniformity. Over the years, these faith stories have been a window through which we have seen Christ in each other and each other in Christ. They have substantially increased mutual trust and been foundational in building bridges for a more authentic communication around the issues on which we do not all yet agree. As Kathryn Johnson put it, 'Every Christian has his or her relationship with Jesus Christ; every Christian life is a journey with Jesus. Telling that story is a way of introducing ourselves to each other, Christian to Christian.'

The beauty of sharing faith stories is that it enriches both the one telling the story and the one listening. To quote Kathryn Johnson again, 'We are invited at this Gathering to listen as if we do not already know; to listen generously with open minds, hearts and spirits; to listen with our theological disquiets put for the moment on the side; to listen for the surprising work of the Spirit of God. ... Each had to listen with ears open to the faithfulness which that perspective expressed, listening for Christ's presence where it was not expected to be' (41).

Through this means, 'Stories reverently offered and prayerfully heard can provide bridges over which we can move to a new place, where the paths of our journeys with Jesus are not so far apart. We share with each other the companionship of Christ' (42).

Spontaneous testimonies or recollections of a church's faith story, as they were shared in small groups, cannot easily be captured in a book, but a few snippets can whet our appetite for the transformational potential of such stories. Brian Stiller, Global Ambassador for the World Evangelical Alliance, recalled the following from his group:

> *Of those in our circle, Rosalee, raised in Brazil, educated and now living with her husband and children in the UK, walked us through her early coming to faith. She now heads the global office of the Theological Commission of the WEA. Said, living in the unrest and struggle of Lebanon, told us how he and his family survived and thrived in the midst of gun battles and Syrian refugees. Paolo, serving in the Taizé community in France, through worship led us in their plaintive and inspiring music. Stefan from Moscow (we had met at the 500th anniversary service of the Protestant Reformation last October in Moscow) told of his early knowing of God's presence. Joseph from Ghana learned of the Gospel as a child. We learned from Rauli, a Finlander, of his early adventures into the former Soviet community. We laughed and prayed as we learned the ways of the Spirit. [Source: https://dispatchesfrombrian.com/2018/06/]*

Wesley Granberg-Michaelson, former General Secretary of the Reformed Church of America and a GCF committee member, offered this recollection:

> *My group in Bogotá reflected the mix of the whole gathering, with several evangelicals and Pentecostals, and others who were Catholic, Orthodox, and versions of Protestantism, from diverse regions. Some of the stories still haunt me, spiritually. A Pentecostal described reluctantly attending a revival as a young man when an unknown preacher powerfully prophesied that he would be called into ministry and travel the world to build unity in the body of Christ. Decades later, that has described his life. An Anglican priest told of being strangely overcome by an experience of God's love, like John Wesley, while in an economics class. A Vatican official shared how as a boy he was stunned when a non-Catholic friend told him he wasn't allowed to come into a Catholic church*

for a funeral. God spoke, and he works globally for Christian unity. [Source: https://sojo.net/articles/open-window-mutilated-body]

Takeaways from Bogotá

The 'Message from Bogotá' collaborative letter, written by participants, expressed the wish that we could bring such a spirit of unity home to our various nations, and regions. The young participants desired more such gatherings, especially ones dedicated to their age group and its unique concerns.

A small group of GCF Committee members joined the Forum's Facilitation Group (executive committee) for a meeting in Thessaloniki, Greece, barely five months after the Bogotá Global Gathering. Their first act was to give thanks to God for an exceptionally successful Gathering, and immediately several said that Bogotá was the first Global Gathering after which the very existence of the GCF was not questioned. It is increasingly obvious that everyone sees the need for a complementary inter-church forum which provides a safe space for encounter for all, especially those who would rather not speak with one another. A place to see Christ in each other—that is what the Global Christian Forum is and aspires to be.

Within 18 months after Bogotá 2018, the Secretariat had set two dates for regional consultations: November 2020 in Nairobi, Kenya for Africa, and April 2021 in Lima, Peru for Latin America. But none of us had anticipated a pandemic. Sadly, our projected meetings have been shelved until we can hold large in-person gatherings. Other means of ensuring human connection and promoting friendship are being pursued.

The sharing of faith stories has continued, but now around the issues of how churches have responded to the COVID-19 pandemic. We have heard from leaders from all over the world concerning the material and physical challenges they have faced, as well as the spiritual and innovative opportunities this pandemic has created for their ministries and people. We have posted several of these on our website and YouTube channel as well as our Facebook page.

The work thus continues, albeit in a different format.

Measuring Global Christian Forum Impact Post-Bogotá

Olav Tveit, then General Secretary of the World Council of Churches, remarked in his paper at Bogotá that the WCC's General Assembly in Busan was more representative as a result of the work of the GCF. During the 2019 General Assembly of the Pentecostal World Fellowship in Calgary, Alberta, Canada, workshops were held on Christian unity; discussions of that topic were hitherto unprecedented at such gatherings. The PWF has now constituted a Christian Unity Commission to interface with other Christian denominations, marking another historic development. Leaders of the so-called four pillars frequently address the General Assemblies of each other's denominations.

The factors that motivated the initiation of the Global Christian Forum are still present: massive growth of Christian believers in the global South, mainly among Evangelical and Pentecostal churches, who are mostly uninvolved in any fellowship beyond their own church affiliations; and the needs of a world that continues to divide along many different fault lines. More and more, we need our churches to take to heart John Wesley's 'the world is my parish' approach instead of inverting this concept into 'my parish is my world'. We need more authentic global citizenship. The pandemic has revealed that our borders are human conceptions. We are all in this together, and the earlier we heed the words of the apostle Paul, the better for us all: 'If one part suffers, every part suffers with it; if one part is honored, every part rejoices with it' (1 Cor 12:25, NIV).

We left Bogotá with many other subthemes calling for our attention: evangelism and mission, discipleship of the nations, pilgrimages of justice and peace, climate justice, outreach to and with vulnerable populations. In the face of such seemingly insurmountable hurdles, how do we serve towards the goal of working with God's Spirit to provide abundant life for all?

Where is the hope? Our hope firmly remains in Jesus Christ, and in what he has already accomplished on the cross and through his resurrection from the dead. But our hope is also in realizing that when we unite, we are a stronger force for good in this world. Our pilgrimage from division to unity continues as we make the Global Christian Forum a truly global network in all aspects. From its very beginning, those who conceived of the Forum sought to broaden the circle of existing ecumenical bodies, without creating another institution. We are to be a complementary platform rather than an alternative movement. In a sense, then, our work is never done. There is yet more to be done. And that is our prayer and aspiration.

    Casely Baiden Essamuah
    Global Christian Forum Secretary
    September 2020

Global Gathering Stewards from Colombia

LET MUTUAL LOVE CONTINUE!

APPENDICES

Greetings - Russian Orthodox Church

Greetings - Focolare Movement

Sharing of Faith Stories in Groups: Guide for Participants

Sharing of Faith Stories in Groups: Guide for Facilitators

'Discrimination, Persecution, Martyrdom: Following Christ Together' Consultation Message

Youth Forum Schedule / Programme

Participants, Churches, Organisations and Roles

Greetings from the Russian Orthodox Church

Hilarion, Chairman, Department of Church Relations (DECR), Moscow Patriarchate

Dear Dr Miller

On behalf of His Holiness Patriarch Kirill of Moscow and All Russia, I would like to thank you for the invitation to send a delegation of the Russian Orthodox Church to the 3rd international meeting of the Global Christian Forum to take place in Bogotá, Colombia.

We hope that the next global meeting of representatives of various Christian confessions will contribute to the cause of Christian witness before the whole world.

Please be informed that, with the blessing of His Holiness, participating in the work of the forum from the Russian Orthodox Church will be Archimandrite Philaret (Bulekov), DECR vice-chairman, and Hieromonk Stephan (Igumnov), DECR secretary for international Christian relations. Archpriest Mikhail Gundyaev, who is a member of the organizing committee of the Global Christian Forum, is also included in the official delegation of the Russian Orthodox Church.

Using this opportunity, I wish you God's help in preparing the forthcoming event.

Respectfully,

+Hilarion
Chairman
Department of Church Relations
Moscow Patriarchate

Greetings from the Focolare Movement

Maria Voce, President, Focolare Movement

Reverend Dr Larry Miller

Thank you sincerely for your kind and welcome invitation to participate in the third *Global Christian Forum*, which will be held from April 24 to April 27, 2018, in Bogotá, Colombia.

To my regret, it is not possible for me to attend because of concurrent commitments. Therefore I delegate Miss Beatriz Sarkis Simoes, member of the 'UNO' Centre, our international secretariat for ecumenism, to represent the Focolare Movement.

Rest assured that I am with you spiritually, even from the preparatory stage of this important ecumenical appointment.

Hoping and praying that the Lord Himself guide every step of the Convention's endeavour to make us Christians more and more brothers and sisters united in His Spirit of love and unity, I respectively send you my very best wishes.

Maria Voce

Sharing of Faith Stories in Groups
Guide for All Participants

Sharing with one another the stories of our journeys with Jesus Christ: The process

Gathering in small, diverse groups to listen and to speak about this holy topic has been a characteristic practice of the Global Christian Forum from its beginning. At this Global Gathering also, telling our stories has a prominent place.

> *In early days of the Forum, making space for faith stories was a way to extend a welcoming hand to all participants. Although Christians do not all delight in theological discussions or worship in the same ways, all Christians journey with Jesus Christ. Everyone thus has a story to tell. Together, these narratives bear witness to the astonishing range of God's ways of working with us. As our own stories join the others in the group, we can see them, and our communities, with fresh eyes.*
>
> *As this practice embraces the story of every person, it also honors the graceful variety of the formative communities to which participants belong. While the journeys are as distinct as the persons around the circle, they bear witness also to the roles of the diverse communities of practices and praise in which we live.*
>
> *In reflecting on the experience of sharing faith stories, the Forum has said that they invite us to hear Spirit in new ways and leads us back to the continuing guidance of the Word of God.*[1]

At this Global Gathering, Tuesday afternoon will be devoted to groups for faith stories. The Tuesday morning plenary will conclude with an introduction to help you prepare for these sessions.

---

1   See 'Our Unfolding Journey with Jesus Christ: Reflections on the Global Christian Forum Experience,' 2013, available in English, French, and Spanish at http://www.globalchristianforum.org/papers.html.

Your group will include about 15 other people, who are diverse in their church memberships and traditions, in age and gender, in country and region, and in other ways. The groups will be composed also with attention to mother tongues; translation help will be available as needed.

Each group will have an experienced facilitator to introduce and guide the process, and to be sure you know when your time nears its end. The facilitator will also give the first example of telling a faith story.

Preparing for the sessions to 'tell the stories of our journeys with Jesus Christ'

In the group, each person is asked to speak for about 7 minutes. It is not expected that you would plan in advance every word you would say. But, if your life permits, you can give some prayerful thought to how you will tell your story.

> *For some of you, testimonies are a regular part of your Christian life; others may find this assignment more unfamiliar and perhaps even a bit intimidating.*
>
> *No matter how many times you have related your faith story before, you are invited here not simply to repeat what you might have said in other contexts but to respond to this specific moment: at this time, with these people, with this purpose, you will join your story to the others in your group.*
>
> *Remember that these stories are your stories, but since they are about your relation with Christ, their purpose is also—it is first!— to give praise to Christ, our common Lord. Thus, they serve the purpose of the session: through these stories, 'to recognize one another in Christ and Christ in one another.'*

Telling your faith story

Please plan to speak for no more than 7 minutes. In your group, the facilitator will provide a simple way for you to know when you have about one minute remaining.

Begin with a very brief introduction, no more than a sentence or two:

- your name and home country;
- your church family and (if applicable to you) your current work.

Then speak about a few aspects of your story—not the entire story, but a few selected incidents or aspects, shaped for the purposes of this gathering.

This is not an introduction to your entire life; the time is too brief and too focused. And it is not a resume or *curriculum vitae*, with a focus primarily on professional positions or accomplishments.

That means you need a clear idea of what focus—what few incidents or themes—you want to shape your faith story. This could be how you came to faith, how faith shaped your journey at a crucial point, perhaps a point of clarity or of struggle; or a specific story of encounter with Christ in recent life.

It is helpful to think also how you would speak not only of you 'in yourself' in relation to Jesus Christ but also about you in your community of faith.

In any case, be assured that you can speak in your own 'language of faith,' the words and ways of speaking most congenial to you. Listening to the range of these styles is one of the gifts of the Forum.

Listening to the stories of others

Expect the Holy Spirit to be at work both as you speak and as you listen. **Listening is as important as speaking!**

Ask God to open your eyes and ears, your mind and your heart.

Seek to contribute to an atmosphere of respectful listening and a spirit that allows for humor and gentle laughter.

As each person speaks, ask yourself: How do I see here encounter with Christ? How do I hear in these words the living Word of God at work among God's people?

There may be members of the group whose Christian experience is much different from your own. There may be people from Christian traditions or communities with which you are unfamiliar, or about which you are even a bit wary. Be especially attentive to these stories: How can you here be 'discovering our shared relationship to our Lord Jesus'?

As you listen, you might have questions, because you come from different cultures and church traditions. The faith sharing is not meant to become a discussion. The rest of the Gathering will give you opportunities to approach a speaker, perhaps during one of the breaks, and continue a conversation.

After the sessions:

Give thanks for the stories you have heard, especially for the places where you were surprised or challenged.

Pray for each of your group members.

Reflect on how your own perspective on your story may have changed by its interaction with the other stories of your group.

Sharing of Faith Stories in Groups

Guide for Facilitators

Gathering to share faith stories—both to tell one's own story and to listen to the stories of others—is a treasured practice at Global Christian Forum events. It is an opportunity to recognize in one another the encounter with Jesus Christ.

Each faith-sharing group is composed of about 15 people, who are diverse in their church memberships and traditions, in age and gender, in country and region, and in other ways.

There is a Guide to this process for all participants in the welcome packets, and so your group members should have a general idea of what to expect. But an attentive facilitator is crucial to the process—for the experience of each person and for the group as a whole. Thank you for taking on this important task!

Your principal responsibilities are:

- To take the lead in setting a warm tone of welcome and of reverent and respectful listening, a tone that makes room for gentle laughter and for surprise;

- To describe briefly what will happen in the session;

- To provide your own faith story as an inviting example, a model in both focus and length; and

- To take primary responsibility for shaping the use of time, first by example and then, if necessary, by graceful intervention.

Before your group meets:

- With the help of the Guide for participants, think about how you will, very briefly, emphasize key points at the beginning of the first session.

- Give some prayerful thought to your own presentation—both to its content and its length (no more than 7 minutes!).

- Decide how to approach managing the time for stories to observe the 7-minute limit.
  - Time keeping needs to be both firm and unobtrusive, to give all members of the group their full share of time and to ease the anxiety of speakers about how they will know when begin to stop.
  - **A good strategy is to agree with another participant to be timekeeper.** This person could simply raise two fingers when two minutes remain, and then raise a single finger, and keep it raised, during the final minute.
  - Decide if you want to discourage people from using their phones to keep time for themselves; at least discourage glancing at one's own phone during the stories of others.
- Arrive in the assigned room a few minutes early. Be sure that the chairs are arranged in a circle, square or rectangle, so that all persons can see each other's faces.

During the sessions:

- Begin with a welcome, perhaps a very brief prayer for the Spirit's guidance, and an introduction to the process. You might want to underline points like these:
  - **Listening is as important as speaking.** Look for Christ in the other; listen for the Holy Spirit.
  - Your story is your time to point to your encounter with Christ in your life so far. Since there is not time to tell your whole life story, it is good to focus on one or two concrete examples. Aim to help the group see something both of the direction of your personal journey and of the way that journey has been shaped by your church community or tradition.
  - Everyone should be comfortable in using their own 'language of faith': some people are accustomed to speaking in very personal terms, whereas others are more comfortable with a different style. All of us will want to welcome the words of those not speaking

        - in their mother tongues; if some are speaking with translation, the group will make room also for that.
        - Please do not interrupt a speaker or start a discussion at the end of a story.
        - **Speak for no longer than 7 minutes**. (Describe how you have decided to indicate when their time is almost gone.)
- Then begin the storytelling with your own faith journey.
- Then ask who wishes to come next. As the process continues, you may want to encourage those who are reticent, perhaps by looking to the one seated next to the previous speaker or with an encouraging nod or word.
- Be alert to a point in the session when it might be good to propose a brief break to sing a hymn or spend a few minutes in silent prayer. There is a lot to digest in such an intensive encounter!
- If there is time after all the stories, you might decide to give opportunity to those who wish to add something briefly. Propose that there are opportunities throughout the Gathering to pursue conversation!
- Close with a word of thanksgiving for the time together and for the work of Christ that has been witnessed. Point the group toward Evening Prayer, which will be in the same place. Depending on the time, you may want to take a brief break or to continue directly with the prayer, and then have some minutes of free time before moving to dinner.

After the sessions:

- The Forum continues to learn about 'best practices' for these groups. Reflect on what happened in your group: What was especially memorable? What could have been done in a better way?
- A time for facilitators to reflect together on the process is planned. Look for the announcement.

CONSULTATION MESSAGE

Discrimination, Persecution, Martyrdom:
Following Christ Together
Tirana, Albania, 2–4 November 2015

4 November 2015

"If one member suffers, all suffer together; if one member is honoured, all rejoice together." (1 Corinthians 12:26)

1. For the first time in the modern history of Christianity high level leaders and representatives of the various Church traditions gathered together to listen to, learn from, and stand with discriminated and persecuted Churches and Christians in the world today.

2. This global gathering of 145 people took place from 2–4 November, 2015, in Tirana, Albania, a country that was declared by its constitution to be an atheist state in 1967, and now has flourishing churches in a framework of religious freedom even though some discrimination may remain.

3. The Consultation, entitled **Discrimination, Persecution, Martyrdom: Following Christ Together**, was convened by the

Global Christian Forum together with the Pontifical Council for Promoting Christian Unity (Roman Catholic Church), the Pentecostal World Fellowship, the World Evangelical Alliance, and the World Council of Churches. It was organized in close collaboration with the Orthodox Autocephalous Church of Albania, the Albanian Bishops' Conference, and the Evangelical Alliance of Albania.

4. We have come together because discrimination, persecution and martyrdom among Christians and people of other faiths in the contemporary world are growing due to a complex variety of factors in different realities and contexts.

5. As we follow Christ, Christians can be exposed to any form of persecution, suffering and martyrdom, because the sinful world is against the Gospel of salvation. But from earliest times Christians experienced the hope and reality of the Resurrection through walking the way of the Cross. Together we follow Christ as we "hunger and thirst for righteousness" (Matthew 5:6) for all.

6. The life of the Church for centuries has been a constant witness in two ways: the proclamation of the Gospel of Christ, and the testimony through the shedding of the martyr's blood. The 21st century is full of moving stories of faithful people who have paid for their dedication to Christ through suffering, torture and execution. Christian martyrs unite us in ways we can hardly imagine.

7. We acknowledge that solidarity among Christian churches is needed to strengthen Christian witness in the face of discrimination, persecution, and martyrdom. In the 21st century, we need to urgently strengthen the solidarity of all Christians, following up on what has been accomplished with insight and discernment from this Consultation.

8. We repent of having at times persecuted each other and other religious communities in history, and ask forgiveness from each other and pray for new ways of following Christ together.

In communion with Christ we commit ourselves:

- (a) **To listen more** to the experiences of Christians, Churches, and of all those who are discriminated against and persecuted, and deepen our engagement with suffering communities.

- (b) **To pray more** for Churches, Christians, and for all those suffering discrimination and persecution, as well as for the transformation of those who discriminate and persecute.

- (c) **To speak up more** with respect and dignity, with a clear and strong voice together, on behalf of those who are suffering.

- (d) **To do more** in mutual understanding to find effective ways of solidarity and support for healing, reconciliation, and for the religious freedom of all oppressed and persecuted people.

9. Listening to the experience of those going through challenging times, praying and discerning together ways of following Christ in these harsh realities, the Consultation calls on:

- (a) **All Christians** to include more prominently in their daily prayers those who are discriminated against, persecuted, and suffering for the fulfilment of God's Kingdom.

- (b) **All Christian organisations on regional, national and local levels** from various traditions to learn, pray and work together in their localities for the persecuted to ensure they are better supported.

- (c) **All Churches** to engage more in dialogue and co-operation with other faith communities, and be "as wise as serpents and innocent as doves" (Matthew 10:16) by remaining vigilant, watchful and fearless in the face of discrimination and persecution.

(d) **All persecutors** who discriminate against and oppress Christians and violate human rights to cease their abuse, and to affirm the right of all human beings to life and dignity.

(e) **All governments** to respect and protect the freedom of religion and belief of all people as a fundamental human right. We also appeal to governments and international organisations to respect and protect Christians and all other people of goodwill from threats and violence committed in the name of religion. In addition, we ask them to work for peace and reconciliation, to seek the settlement of on-going conflicts, and to stop the flow of arms, especially to violators of human rights.

(f) **All media** to report in an appropriate and unbiased way on violations of religious freedom, including the discrimination and persecution of Christians as well as of other faith communities.

(g) **All educational institutions** to develop opportunities and tools to teach young people in particular about human rights, religious tolerance, healing of memories and hostilities of the past, and peaceful means of conflict resolution and reconciliation.

(h) **All people of good will** to work for justice, peace and development, knowing that poverty and disrespect of human dignity are major contributing factors to violence.

10. We recommend that the Global Christian Forum evaluates within two years the work of this event, and reports to all four bodies for their follow up.

May God the Father who created us equal by His grace, strengthen our efforts to overcome all forms of discrimination and persecution.

May His Holy Spirit guide us in solidarity with all those who seek peace and reconciliation.

May He heal the wounds of the persecuted and grant us hope as we look forward to the glorious coming of our Lord Jesus Christ who will make all things new.

Youth Forum Programme

Time & Venue
- Tuesday April 24, 13.00-14.00 Lunch
- Thursday April 26, 19.00-20.30 Dinner

Objectives
(i) To offer a brief orientation to newer/younger members of the GCF family.

(j) To ensure that they know each other and can build bridges for interchurch cooperation while at the conference and beyond.

Session One – Tuesday Lunch
(11) Welcome – Casely Essamuah

(12) Introductions – Name, Church, Country

(13) Youth Forum presentations – 10 minutes each:

    (i) My Call to Ecumenism – Dr. Mel Robeck (Pentecostal/USA)

    (ii) Mega Churches and the Ecumenical Movement – Dr. Hana Kim (Presbyterian/Korea)

    (iii) The GCF Holland Experience – Anmar Hayali

(4) Questions/Answers and Interaction (10 minutes)

Session Two – Thursday Dinner
(1) Welcome – Casely Essamuah

(2) Forum Presentation - GCF in local contexts, 15 minutes each:

(i) The Significance of GCF in Today's World – Archbishop Angaelos (Orthodox/UK)

(ii) Sam Murillo (Mexico/Methodist)

(3) Forum Interaction, each participant:

(i) What have I learned at this Global Gathering?

(ii) What will I do with my experience here?

(iii) Who will I initiate contact with across ecclesial lines?

(iv) How will I tell this story to others?

(v) What do I want to tell GCF?

Magali Moreno, GCF Events Coordinator

Participants, Churches, Organisations and Roles

Third Global Gathering participant lists are here provided in three distinct formats in order to highlight different perspectives from which the same information can be viewed.

- In the **Participants** list, all Global Gathering participants are named alphabetically, by surname, with church or organisation and country of residence following. This list includes not only official representatives of churches and organisations but everyone else present, usually to serve in some special capacity during the Gathering. These roles or functions are identified in parentheses. If one is looking for an individual participant, this is the list to consult.

- The **Churches and Organisations** list shows the composition of the Gathering according to church family and church or organisation or movement. If one would like to catch a glimpse of the ecclesial profile, scope, and balance of the Gathering, this is the list to examine, remembering that the groupings are bodies of different sorts and that some participants claim more than one confessional or organisational belonging even though usually only one is indicated in the list. (GCF staff and stewards are not included in this list.)

- The **Roles** list provides a sense of the organisational framework of the Gathering by listing the groups responsible for it or active in it.

Participants

ABRAHAMS Ivan, Bishop, World Methodist Council, South Africa

ADAM William, Revd Dr, Anglican Communion, United Kingdom

AGUILERA Agustín, Revd, Latin American Evangelical Alliance / Evangelical Alliance of Bolivia, Bolivia

ALTIZER Ricky, Mr, Evangelical, USA (*Communications Team*)

ÁLVAREZ Diego, Mr, Lutheran World Federation Colombia, Colombia (*Communications Team*)

ANDISON Jennifer, Revd Canon, Anglican Communion, Diocese of York-Credit Valley, Canada

ANDRIOPOULOS Iakovos, Archimandrite, Church of Greece, Greece

ANGAELOS H.E. Archbishop, Coptic Orthodox Church, Diocese of London, United Kingdom

APHREM II Ignatius, H.H. Patriarch Mor, Syriac Orthodox Patriarchate of Antioch and All the East, Syria

ARIZTIZABAL Edgar, Msgr, Episcopal Conference of Colombia, Colombia

ATTA-BAFFOE Victor, Rt Revd Dr, Anglican Communion, Diocese of Cape Coast, Ghana

AUDO Antoine, Bishop, Chaldean Catholic Diocese of Aleppo, Syria

BAAH Robert, Revd Dr, Church of Pentecost, USA

BAAWOBR Richard, Bishop, Catholic Church, Diocese of Wa, Ghana

BACON Nathanael, Deacon, InnerChange, Guatemala

BACON Jennifer, Mrs, InnerChange, Guatemala

BAILEY Coleman, Mr, Church of God (Cleveland), USA (*Youth Delegate*)

BAILEY Alvin R., Revd Dr, Evangelical Association of the Caribbean, Jamaica

BALI Joseph, Fr, Syriac Orthodox Patriarchate of Antioch and All the East, Syria

BARNETT-COWAN Alyson, Revd Canon Dr, Anglican Church of Canada/Canadian Council of Churches, Canada

BAROLIN Rogelio D., Revd, World Communion of Reformed Churches, Uruguay

BARRETO Raimundo, Prof Dr, American Baptist Churches USA, USA

BARRIGA Jairo, Revd, Presbyterian Church of Colombia, Colombia (*National Organising Committee*)

BEACHAM Doug, Dr, Pentecostal World Fellowship/International Pentecostal Holiness Church, USA

BECHEALANY Souraya, Prof Dr, Middle East Council of Churches, Lebanon

BERLIS Angela, Prof Dr, World Council of Churches, Switzerland

BERNAL Cristian, Mr, Lutheran Church Colombia, Colombia (*Steward*)

BLANZAT Pierre, Revd, French Protestant Federation/Francophone Christian Forum, France

BONILLA Luisa, Ms, Mennonite Church Colombia, Colombia (*Steward*)

BRERETON Ann, Mrs, International Catholic Charismatic Renewal Services, Australia

BROWN Elijah, Revd Dr, Baptist World Alliance, USA (*GCF Committee Member*)

BUSTAMANTE Jorge, Fr, Catholic Church, Episcopal Conference of Colombia, Colombia (*National Organising Committee*)

CAIN Kim, Revd, Global Christian Forum, Australia (*Staff/Communications Team*)

CAJÍAS Fernando, Mr, Catholic Church, Episcopal Conference of Colombia, Colombia (*Communications Team*)

CAMPOS José, Dr (MD), Latin American and Caribbean Pentecostal Forum, Ecuador

CARDONA Juan Alberto, Bishop, Methodist Church of Colombia, Colombia (*National Organising Committee*)

CARNASSALE Helio, Revd, Seventh-day Adventist Church, Brazil

CARVAJAL Jesiel, Mr, World Vision Ecuador, Ecuador

CASTAÑO Edgar, Revd, Colombian Evangelical Council (CEDECOL), Colombia (*National Organising Committee*)

CASTILLO Fabián A., Revd, Syro Orthodox Church of Antioch, Colombia

CASTRO Lina, Ms, Young Women's Christian Association Colombia, Colombia

CHAMOUN Michael, H.E. Archbishop, Syriac Orthodox Patriarchate of Antioch and All the East, Syria (*GCF Committee Member*)

CHEN Selma, Revd, Lutheran Church of Taiwan, Taiwan

CHIMHUNGWE Paul S., Dr, World Convention of Church of Christ, Swaziland

CHOROMANSKI Andrzej, Revd Dr, Catholic Church, Pontifical Council for Promoting Christian Unity, Vatican City (*Planning Group & GFC Committee Member*)

CLIFFORD Catherine, Prof Dr, Saint Paul University, Canada

COLÓN Eduardo, Mr, Catholic Church, Colombia

COORILOS Geevarghese Mor, Metropolitan, Syriac Orthodox Patriarchate of Antioch and All the East/World Council of Churches Commission on World Mission and Evangelism, India

CORRELL Claire, Mrs, Evangelical/Baptist, USA (*Observer*)

CORRELL Thomas, Revd, National Association of Evangelicals USA/World Evangelical Alliance, USA

CORVALÁN Oscar, Dr, Latin American and Caribbean Pentecostal Forum, Chile

COY Marian, Ms, Lutheran Church Colombia, Colombia (*Steward*)

CRUZ Diana, Ms, World Student Christian Federation Colombia, Colombia (*National Organising Committee*)

CUBILLOS Esteban, Mr, Mennonite Church Colombia, Colombia (*Steward*)

DANET Anne-Laure, Revd, French Protestant Federation/ Francophone Christian Forum, France

DEYOUNG Lee, Mr, Reformed Church in America, USA

DÍAZ Alexander, Captain, The Salvation Army Colombia, Colombia

DIOP Ganoune, Revd Dr, Seventh-day Adventist Church General Conference, USA (*Planning Group, GCF Committee Member*)

DONKOR Lord E., Revd Dr, Church of Pentecost, United Kingdom

DUENSING Stacey, Revd, Reformed Church in America, USA (*Youth Delegate*)

DUQUE Francisco, Bishop, Anglican Church Colombia, Colombia (*National Organising Committee*)

DURÁN Arnulfo, Revd, Baptist Church in Colombia, Colombia (*National Organising Committee*)

ELLIOTT Maurice, Revd Canon Dr, Anglican Communion, Ireland

EMBERTI GIALLORETI Leonardo, Prof Dr, Community of Sant'Egidio, Italy

ESSAMUAH Angela, Mrs, Evangelical/Non-denominational, USA (*Guest*)

ESSAMUAH Casely, Revd Dr, Global Christian Forum, USA (*Staff*)

ESSAMUAH Zachary, Mr, Evangelical/Non-denominational, USA, (*Guest*)

ESSAMUAH Zikomo, Mr, Evangelical/Non-denominational, USA, (*Guest*)

ESSAMUAH Zinhle, Ms, Evangelical, USA (*Communications Team*)

FABUSORO David, Archbishop, The Church of the Lord (Prayer Fellowship) Worldwide, Nigeria

FARRELL Brian, Bishop, Catholic Church, Pontifical Council for Promoting Christian Unity, Vatican City

FERGUSON Chris, Revd Dr, World Communion of Reformed Churches, Germany

FIGUEROA DE GÓNGORA María Eugenia, Mrs, Catholic Church, International Catholic Charismatic Renewal Services, Guatemala

FISCHER Christoph, Revd, Pentecostal/Lutheran, Germany

FODAY-KHABENJE Aiah, Revd Dr, Association of Evangelicals in Africa, Kenya (*GCF Committee Member*)

FREIRE DE ALENCAR Gedeon, Dr, Latin American Network of Pentecostal Studies, Brazil

GASTELLU CAMP Adriana, Revd, Church of Sweden, Sweden (*Observer*)

GEORGE Abraham, Revd, International Justice Mission, USA

GHAZARYAN DRISSI Ani, Dr, World Council of Churches Commission on Faith and Order, Switzerland

GIBAUT John, Revd Canon Dr, Anglican Communion, United Kingdom (*Planning Group, GCF Committee Member*)

GÓMEZ Eduardo, Revd, Latin America Evangelical Alliance, Colombia

GÓMEZ Ruth Vanessa, Ms, Lutheran Church Colombia, Colombia (*Steward*)

GOROPEVSEK Timothy, Mr, World Evangelical Alliance, USA (*Communications Team*)

GOUGAUD Emmanuel, Fr, Catholic Bishops Conference of France/Francophone Christian Forum, France

GOUNDIAEV Mikhail, Archpriest, Russian Orthodox Church, Switzerland (*Planning Group, GCF Committee Member*)

GRABER Anne-Cathy, Revd Dr, Mennonite World Conference, France (*Planning Group, GCF Committee Member*)

GRAFE Chishilde, Ms. Evangelical Lutheran Church of Colombia, Colombia

GRANBERG-MICHAELSON Wesley, Revd, World Communion of Reformed Churches, USA (*Planning Group, Message Committee, GCF Committee Member*)

GROETING Patricia, Ms, Argentina (*Interpreter*)

GULFO Gamaliel, Mr, Colombia (*Nurse*)

HACHEM Gabriel, Fr Prof Dr, Greek Melkite Catholic Church of Antioch, Lebanon

HAM Carlos, Revd Prof Dr, Matanzas Evangelical Theological Seminary, Cuba

HÄMÄLÄINEN Arto, Revd Dr, Pentecostal World Fellowship/ Pentecostal Church of Finalnd, Finland

HAN David Sang-Ehil, Prof Dr, Church of God (Cleveland)/ Pentecostal Theological Seminary, USA (*Planning Group, Message Committee, GCF Committee Member*)

HAWXHURST Jean, Revd Dr, The United Methodist Church, USA (*Observer*)

HAYALI Anmar, Mr, Together Church in the Netherlands, Netherlands

HEATH Richard, Mr, Bay Area Community Church, USA

HERNÁNDEZ Atahualpa, Bishop, Evangelical Lutheran Church of Colombia, Colombia (*National Organising Committee*)

HERNÁNDEZ César, Mr, Seventh-day Adventist Church, México

HILLERT Albin, Mr, Church of Sweden/World Council of Churches, Sweden (*Communications Team*)

HINKELMANN Frank, Revd Dr, European Evangelical Alliance, Austria

HINTIKKA Kaisamari, Revd Dr, Lutheran World Federation, Switzerland

HOEKZEMA Trevin, Mr, Bay Area Community Church, USA

HOLLOWAY Gary, Dr, World Convention of Churches of Christ, USA

HOPPE Nathan, Prof Dr, Orthodox Autocephalous Church of Albania, Albania

HOWELL Richard, Revd Dr, Asia Evangelical Alliance/World Evangelical Alliance, India (*Planning Group, GCF Committee Member*)

HUNTER Harold, Revd Dr, International Pentecostal Holiness Church, USA

IGUMNOV Stefan, Hieromonk, Russian Orthodox Church, Russia

JACKSON Amanda, Ms, World Evangelical Alliance, United Kingdom

JACOME Parrish, Revd, Latin America Baptist Union, Ecuador

JANSON LIDAK Noemi, Ms, Baptist Church in Colombia, Colombia

JIMÉNEZ Francisco, Mr, Church of God (Cleveland)/Seminario Sudamericano, Ecuador

JIMÉNEZ Judy, Mrs, Young Women Christian Association Colombia, Colombia (*National Organising Committee*)

JOHNSON Kathryn, Dr, Lutheran World Federation, USA (*Planning Group, GCF Committee Member*)

JOSEPH Michael, Mr, Colombia (*Interpreter*)

JUNGE Martin, Revd Dr, Lutheran World Federation, Switzerland

KÄÄRIÄINEN Kimmo, Revd Dr, Evangelical Lutheran Church of Finland, Finland

KENGNE DJEUTANE, Georgine, Ms, World Student Christian Federation, Cameroon (*GCF Committee Member*)

KENNY Peter, Mr, Ecumenical News, Switzerland (*Communications Team*)

KIM Hana, Revd Dr, MyungSung Presbyterian Church, Republic of Korea

KINZER Mark, Rabbi Dr, Union of Messianic Jewish Congregations, USA (*Observer*)

KOMAKOMA Joseph, Revd Fr, Symposium of Episcopal Conferences of Africa and Madagascar, Ghana

KOSKELA Harri, Dr, Pentecostal World Fellowship/Pentecostal Church of Finland, Finland (*Communications Team*)

KOUKOURA Dimitra, Prof Dr, World Council of Churches/ Ecumenical Patriarchate, Greece (*Planning Group, GCF Committee Member*)

KROCHAK Andrij, Mr, Ecumenical Patriarchate, France (*Youth Delegate*)

KÜMMERLE Andreas, Dr, Evangelical Lutheran Church in Württemberg, Germany

KUPCIS Ivars, Mr, World Council of Churches, Switzerland (*Communications Team*)

KURTÉN Kristina Sofia, Ms, Evangelical Lutheran Church of Finland, Finland (*Observer*)

LANGLOIS John, Mr, World Evangelical Alliance, United Kingdom

LARA Daniel, Mr, Lutheran Church Colombia, Colombia (*Steward*)

LEHTONEN Rauli, Revd, Filadelfia Church Stockholm, Sweden

LEITES Marcelo, Mr, World Student Christian Federation Latin America, Argentina

LEIVA Eduardo, Mr, Methodist Pentecostal Church, Chile

LESSING Hanns, Revd Dr, World Communion of Reformed Churches, Germany

LÓPEZ Magda, Ms, Young Women's Christian Association Colombia, Colombia (*Youth Delegate*)

LÓPEZ Pedro Manuel, Mr, Assemblies of God, Peru

LÓPEZ Simeón, Hieromonk, Serbian Orthodox Church in Colombia, Colombia

LUBAALE Nicta, Revd, Organization of African Instituted Churches, Kenya (*Planning Group, GCF Committee Member*)

MA Wonsuk, Prof Dr, Oral Roberts University, USA

MAÇANEIRO Marcial, Fr Prof Dr, Pontifical Catholic University of Paraná, Brazil

MACHADO Felix Anthony, Archbishop, Catholic Church, India

MACHUCA Viviana, Ms, World Vision Colombia, Colombia (*National Organising Committee*)

MACMILLAN Christine, Commissioner, World Evangelical Alliance, Canada (*Message Committee*)

MADEGA Mathieu, Bishop, Symposium of Episcopal Conferences of Africa and Madagascar, Gabon

MAHLOBO M. George, Revd, Pentecostal World Fellowship/ Apostolic Faith Mission of South Africa, South Africa

MALAVÉ Carlos, Revd, Christian Churches Together USA, USA

MALLOUH Said, Revd, Church of God in Lebanon and Syria, Lebanon

MANNOIA Kevin, Revd Dr, Wesleyan Holiness Connection, USA

MATEAR Elizabeth, Commissioner, The Salvation Army International, United Kingdom (*GCF Committee Member*)

MATEUS Odair Pedroso, Revd Dr, World Council of Churches, Switzerland

MATTHEWS Victoria, Rt Revd, Anglican Communion, New Zealand

MÉAR Christine, Mrs, France (*Interpreter*)

MEJÍA Milton, Revd, Latin American Council of Churches, Colombia (*National Organising Committee*)

MENDIETA Arturo, Bishop, Church of God Colombia, Colombia (*National Organising Committee*)

MENDOZA Richar, Bishop, Church of God Ecuador, Ecuador

MERMEJO César, Revd, Evangelical Alliance of Venezuela, Venezuela

MICH Tadeusz, Dr, World Vision International, USA (*GCF Committee Member*)

MILLER Eleanor, Mrs, Global Christian Forum, France (*Staff*)

MILLER Larry, Revd Dr, Global Christian Forum, France (*Staff, Planning Group*)

MODÉUS Martin, Rt Revd Dr, Church of Sweden, Sweden

MORENO Magali, Ms, Global Christian Forum, Paraguay (*Staff*)

MORFI Xanthi, Ms, World Council of Churches, France (*Communications Team*)

MPERE-GYEKYE William, Very Revd, Methodist Church Ghana, Ghana

MUEHLSTEDT Corinna, Dr, ARD Germany, Italy (*Press*)

MURILLO Samuel, Revd, World Methodist Council, Mexico (*Youth Delegate*)

MURPHY James A., Mr, Catholic Church, International Catholic Charismatic Renewal Services, USA

NATES Francisco, Mr, Mennonite Church Colombia, Colombia (*Steward*)

NTIHINYUZWA Joséphine, Mrs, Global Christian Forum, France (*Staff*)

NYGAARD Birger, Mr, Evangelical Lutheran Church in Denmark, Denmark

OBENG Victor Revd, Langham Preaching Ghana, Ghana

OKOH Daniel, Archbishop, Organization of African Instituted Churches, Nigeria

OLANG Jim, Mr, Association of Evangelicals in Africa, Kenya (*Communications Team, Youth Delegate*)

OLEA Jorge, Revd, Evangel World Prayer Center, Canada

ONYANGO ABOGNO Habakuk, Archbishop Dr, Church of Christ in Africa, Kenya

ORELLANA Luis, Dr, Latin American and Caribbean Pentecostal Forum, Chile

ORTEGA DOPICO Joel, Revd, Cuba Council of Churches, Cuba

OSITELU Rufus, The Most Revd Dr, The Church of the Lord (Prayer Fellowship) Worldwide, Nigeria (*Message Committee*)

OYEWOLE Adejare, Apostle, Unification Council of Cherubim and Seraphim Churches, United Kingdom

PADILLA DEBORST Ruth, Dr, International Fellowship for Mission as Transformation, Costa Rica

PAOLO Brother, Taizé Community, France

PAPANIKOLAOU Gabriel, Metropolitan, Church of Greece, Greece

PASQUINI Elena, Ms, Catholic Church, Gloriosa Trinità, Italy

PEI Lianshan, Revd, China Council of Churches, China

PEKRIDOU Katerina, Ms, Conference of European Churches, Belgium (*Message Committee*)

PENTTINEN Pirjo-Liisa, Revd, Young Women's Christian Association/Evangelical Lutheran Church Finland, Finland (*GCF Committee Member*)

PÉREZ Atenágoras, Archimandrite, Greek Orthodox Metropolis of Mexico, Central America, Colombia, Venezuela and the Caribbean Islands, Cuba

PÉREZ Miyer, Mr, Mennonite Church Colombia, Colombia (*Steward*)

PERILLA Jaime, Mr, Seventh-day Adventist Church Colombia, Colombia

PERREAU Michael, Mr, United Bible Societies, United Kingdom

PERZYŃSKI Andrzej, Fr Prof Dr, Catholic University in Warsaw, Poland

PESARE Oreste, Mr, International Catholic Charismatic Renewal Services, Italy

PETERSON II Eric, Mr, Oral Roberts University, USA

PHILIP Mary, Prof, Martin Luther University College, Canada

PICO Jeimy Katherine, Ms, Lutheran Church Colombia, Colombia (*Steward*)

PLÜSS, Jean-Daniel, Dr, Pentecostal Assemblies of Switzerland/ Fondation du Forum Chrétien, Switzerland (Planning Group)

PLUTSCHINSKI Timo, Mr, World Evangelical Alliance, Germany

PRECIADO Felipe, Mr, Mennonite Church Colombia, Colombia (*Steward*)

PROAÑOS Felipe, Mr, Mennonite Church Colombia, Colombia (*Steward*)

RAMÍREZ Paola, Ms, Presbyterian Church Colombia, Colombia (*Steward*)

RAMÍREZ Raimy, Mrs, Global Christian Forum, Colombia (*Staff*)

RIHANI David, Revd, Jordan Evangelical Council, Jordan

RITSI Martin, Very Revd, Orthodox Christian Mission Center (Ecumenical Patriarchate), USA (*Message Committee*)

RIVERA AGOSTO Angel, Revd, Disciples of Christ Global Ministries, USA

ROBECK Cecil M., Jr., Prof Dr, Fuller Theological Seminary, USA (*GCF Committee Member*)

RODGERS Robert, Revd Dr, Evangel World Prayer Center, USA

RODRÍGUEZ Jeferson, Prof, Assemblies of God Colombia/Latin American and Caribbean Pentecostal Forum, Colombia (*National Organising Committee*)

RODRÍGUEZ Martha Yaneth, Mrs, World Vision Colombia, Colombia

RODRÍGUEZ Santiago, Revd, Assemblies of God Colombia, Colombia

ROSERO Mayra, Ms, Mennonite Church Colombia, Colombia (*Steward*)

ROUSSINEAU Gabriel, Fr, Chemin Neuf Community, France (*Communications Team*)

RUIZ David, Revd, World Evangelical Alliance, Guatemala

RYTKÖNEN Aaro, Revd, Gulf Churches Fellowship, Oman

SAA Laura, Revd, Latin American and Caribbean Pentecostal Forum, Ecuador

SÁNCHEZ Mayerly, Ms, World Vision Colombia, Colombia (*Communications Team*)

SÁNCHE Michael, Mr, Mennonite Church Colombia, Colombia (*Steward*)

SANTANA Antonio Revd, Cuba Council of Churches, Cuba

SANTIAGO Helen, Dr, Latin American and Caribbean Pentecostal Forum, Puerto Rico (*Message Committee*)

SANTIZO Claudia, Ms, World Methodist Council, Guatemala (*Youth Delegate*)

SARKIS Beatriz, Ms, Focolare Movement, Italy

SAUCA Ioan, Fr Prof Dr, World Council of Churches, Switzerland

SAXENA Samuel, Revd, Asia Evangelical Alliance, India (*Youth Delegate*)

SCHIRRMACHER Thomas, Bishop Prof Dr, World Evangelical Alliance, Germany (*Planning Group, GCF Committee Member*)

SCHIRRMACHER Esther, Ms, World Evangelical Alliance, Germany (*Youth Delegate*)

SCOTT Janet, Dr, Friends World Committee for Consultation, United Kingdom

SEGURA Harold, Revd, World Vision Latin America, Costa Rica

SELBACH Christopher, Mr, Brot für die Welt, Germany (*Observer*)

SEYENKULO Daniel, Bishop Dr, Lutheran Church in Liberia, Liberia

SHIRK LUCA Katherine, Prof, Institut Catholique de Paris, France (*Message Committee*)

SIEMIENIEWSKI Andrzej, Bishop, Catholic Archdiocese of Wrocław, Poland

SINTADO Myriam, Ms, Switzerland (*Interpreter*)

SINTADO Carlos, Dr, Switzerland (*Interpreter*)

SKUPCH Sonia, Revd, Evangelical Church River Plate, Argentina

SOOBRAYDOO Gilbert, Mr, Chemin Neuf Community, France, (*Communications Team*)

STILLER Brian, Dr, World Evangelical Alliance, Canada

STUCKY Peter, Revd, Mennonite Church Colombia, Colombia (*Observer*)

SUAREZ Anthony, Revd, National Hispanic Christian Leadership Conference, USA

SWANSON, James E., Bishop, The United Methodist Church, USA

TAHAAFE-WILLIAMS Katalina, Revd Dr, World Council of Churches Commission on World Mission and Evangelism, Switzerland (*Message Committee*)

TANG Shiwen, Revd, China Council of Churches, China

TCHE Paul, Revd, Disciples Ecumenical Consultative Council, USA

THEVENET Daniel, Revd, Union of Evangelical Churches of the Revival/Francophone Christian Forum, France

THOMAS Gabrielle, Prof Dr, Receptive Ecumenism Project, University of Durham, United Kingdom

TORRES Timoteo, Archimandrite, Greek Orthodox Church in Colombia, Colombia (*National Organising Committee*)

TRIVIÑO Humberto, Captain, The Salvation Army Colombia, Colombia (*Youth Delegate*)

TSCHIRSCH Agustina, Ms, Baptist World Alliance, Argentina (*Youth Delegate*)

UETI Paulo, Dr, Anglican Communion, Brazil

URBINA ORTEGA Oscar, Archbishop, Catholic Church Episcopal Conference of Colombia, Colombia

URIBE Javier, Dr, Latin American and Caribbean Pentecostal Forum, Mexico

USMA-GOMEZ Juan, Msgr, Catholic Church, Pontifical Council for Promoting Christian Unity, Vatican City

VAN BEEK Huibert, Mr, Global Christian Forum, Switzerland (*Staff*)

VAN BEEK Maria Mrs, Global Christian Forum, Switzerland (*Guest*)

VELLOSO EWELL Rosalee, Revd Dr, World Evangelical Alliance, United Kingdom

VENEGAS Gabriela, Ms, Mennonite Church Colombia, Colombia (*Steward*)

VERCAMMEN Joris, Archbishop Dr, International Old Catholic Bishops Conference of the Union of Utrecht, Netherlands

VIEIRA Raissa, Ms, World Communion of Reformed Churches, Brazil

VILLARREAL Gabriel, Mr, Seventh-day Adventist Church, Colombia

VUORENSOLA-BARNES Saara, Ms, Lutheran World Federation Colombia, Colombia

WALDROP Richard, Dr, Church of God (Cleveland), USA

WANG Limin, Fr, China Council of Churches, China

WARNECKE Martin, Mr, World Evangelical Alliance, Germany (*Staff*)

WATSON Colin, Mr, Christian Reformed Church in North America, USA

WATSON Michael, Bishop, The United Methodist Church, USA

WELLS David, Revd Dr, Pentecostal World Fellowship/Pentecostal Assemblies of Canada, Canada (*Planning Group, GCF Committee Member*)

WELLS Jonathan, Mr, Pentecostal World Fellowship, Canada (*Youth Delegate*)

WENNER Rosemarie, Bishop, World Methodist Council/The United Methodist Church, Germany (*GCF Committee Member*)

WILSON William, Revd Dr, Pentecostal World Fellowship/Empowered 21/Oral Roberts University/Church of God, USA

YOUNAN Munib, Bishop Dr, Evangelical Lutheran Church in Jordan and the Holy Land, Israel

ZURLO Gina, Dr, Center for the Study of Global Christianity, USA

Churches and Organisations

African Instituted Churches

Church of Christ in Africa, ONYANGO ABOGNO Habakuk, Archbishop Dr, Kenya

Church of the Lord (Aladura) Worldwide, OSITELU Rufus, The Most Revd Dr, Nigeria

Church of the Lord (Aladura) Worldwide, FABUSORO David, Archbishop David, Nigeria

Organisation of African Instituted Churches, LUBAALE Nicta, Revd, Kenya

Organisation of African Instituted Churches, OKOH Daniel, Archbishop, Nigeria

Unification Council of Cherubim and Seraphim Churches, OYEWOLE Adejare, Apostle Nigeria

Anglican Communion

Anglican Church of Canada Diocese of York-Credit Valley, ANDISON Jennifer, Rt Revd Canon, Canada

Anglican Church of Canada/Canadian Council of Churches, BARNETT-COWAN Alyson, Revd Canon Dr, Canada

Anglican Church of Colombia, DUQUE Francisco, Very Revd Bishop, Colombia

Anglican Church of Ghana Diocese of Cape Coast, ATTA-BAFFOE Victor, Rt Revd Dr, Ghana

Anglican Church of New Zealand Diocese of Christchurch, MATTHEWS Victoria, Rt Revd Bishop, New Zealand

Church of Ireland Theological Institute, ELLIOTT Maurice, Revd Canon Dr, Ireland

The Anglican Communion, ADAM William, Revd Dr, United Kingdom

The Anglican Communion, GIBAUT John, Revd Canon Dr, United Kingdom

The Anglican Communion, UETI Paulo, Dr, Brazil

Baptist

American Baptist Churches USA, BARRETO Raimundo, Prof Dr, USA

Baptist Church in Colombia, DURÁN Arnulfo, Revd, Colombia

Baptist Church in Colombia, JANSON LIDAK Noemi, Ms, Colombia

Latin America Baptist Union, JACOME Parrish, Revd, Ecuador

Baptist World Alliance, BROWN Elijah, Revd Dr, USA

Baptist World Alliance, TSCHIRSCH Agustina, Ms, Argentina

Catholic Church

Archdiocese of Wrocław, SIEMIENIEWSKI Andrzej, Bishop, Poland

Catholic Bishops Conference of France, GOUGAUD Emmanuel, Fr, France

Catholic Church of Colombia, COLÓN Eduardo, Mr, Colombia

Catholic University in Warsaw, PERZYŃSKI Andrzej, Fr Prof Dr, Poland

Chaldean Catholic Church (Diocese of Aleppo), AUDO Antoine, Bishop, Syria

Community of Sant'Egidio, EMBERTI GIALLORETI Leonardo, Prof Dr, Italy

Diocese of Wa, BAAWOBR Richard, Bishop, Ghana

Episcopal Conference of Colombia, ARIZTIZABAL Edgar, Msgr, Colombia

Episcopal Conference of Colombia, BUSTAMANTE Jorge, Fr, Colombia

Episcopal Conference of Colombia, CAJÍAS Fernando, Mr, Colombia

Episcopal Conference of Colombia, URBINA ORTEGA Oscar, Archbishop, Colombia

Focolare Movement, SARKIS Beatriz, Ms, Italy

Gloriosa Trinità, PASQUINI Elena, Ms, Italy

Institut Catholique de Paris, SHIRK LUCAS Katherine, Prof Dr, France

International Catholic Charismatic Renewal Services, BRERETON Ann, Mrs, Australia

International Catholic Charismatic Renewal Services, FIGUEROA DE GÓNGORA María Eugenia, Mrs, Guatemala

International Catholic Charismatic Renewal Services, MURPHY James A., Mr, USA

International Catholic Charismatic Renewal Services, PESARE Oreste, Mr, Italy

Pontifical Catholic University of Paraná, MAÇANEIRO Marcial, Fr Prof Dr, Brazil

Pontifical Council for Promoting Christian Unity, CHOROMANSKI Andrzej, Revd Dr, Vatican City

Pontifical Council for Promoting Christian Unity, FARRELL Brian, Bishop, Vatican City

Pontifical Council for Promoting Christian Unity, USMA-GOMEZ Juan, Msgr, Vatican City

Saint Paul University, CLIFFORD Catherine, Prof Dr, Canada

Symposium of Episcopal Conferences of Africa and Madagascar, KOMAKOMA Joseph, Revd Fr, Ghana

Symposium of Episcopal Conferences of Africa and Madagascar, MADEGA Mathieu, Bishop, Gabon

Churches of Christ / Disciples of Christ

Disciples of Christ Global Ministries, RIVERA AGOSTO Angel, Revd, USA

Disciples Ecumenical Consultative Council, TCHE Paul, Revd, USA

World Convention of Churches of Christ, HOLLOWAY Gary, Revd Dr, USA

World Convention of Churches of Christ, CHIMHUNGWE Paul S., Dr, Zimbabwe

Evangelical

Asia Evangelical Alliance / World Evangelical Alliance, HOWELL Richard, Revd Dr, India

Asia Evangelical Alliance, SAXENA Samuel, Revd, India

Association of Evangelicals in Africa, FODAY-KHABENJE Aiah, Revd Dr, Kenya

Association of Evangelicals in Africa, OLANG Jim, Mr, Kenya

European Evangelical Alliance, HINKELMANN Frank, Revd Dr, Austria

Evangelical Association of the Caribbean, BAILEY Alvin R., Revd Dr, Jamaica

Evangelical Alliance of Venezuela, MERMEJO César, Revd, Venezuela

International Fellowship for Mission as Transformation, PADILLA DEBORST Ruth, Dr, Costa Rica

Langham Preaching Ghana, OBENG Victor Revd, Ghana

Latin America Evangelical Alliance, GÓMEZ Eduardo, Revd, Colombia

Latin American Evangelical Alliance / Evangelical Alliance of Bolivia, AGUILERA Agustín, Revd, Bolivia

National Association of Evangelicals USA/World Evangelical Alliance, CORRELL Revd Thomas and Mrs Clare USA

National Hispanic Christian Leadership Conference, SUAREZ Anthony, Revd, USA

World Evangelical Alliance, GOROPEVSEK Timothy, Mr, USA

World Evangelical Alliance, JACKSON Amanda, Ms, United Kingdom

World Evangelical Alliance, LANGLOIS John, Mr, United Kingdom

World Evangelical Alliance, MACMILLAN Christine, Commissioner, Canada

World Evangelical Alliance, PLUTSCHINSKI Timo, Mr, Germany

World Evangelical Alliance, RUIZ David, Revd, Guatemala

World Evangelical Alliance, SCHIRRMACHER Esther, Ms, Germany

World Evangelical Alliance, SCHIRRMACHER Thomas, Bishop Prof Dr, Germany

World Evangelical Alliance, STILLER Brian, Dr, Canada

World Evangelical Alliance, VELLOSO EWELL Rosalee, Revd Dr, United Kingdom

World Evangelical Alliance, WARNECKE Martin, Mr, Germany

Friends

Friends World Committee for Consultation, SCOTT Janet, Dr, United Kingdom

Holiness

Church of God in Lebanon and Syria, MALLOUH Said, Revd, Lebanon

Wesleyan Holiness Connection, MANNOIA Kevin, Revd Dr, USA

Lutheran

Church of Sweden, GASTELLU Adriana, Revd, Sweden

Church of Sweden, MODÉUS Martin, Rt Revd Dr, Sweden

Evangelical Lutheran Church of Finland, KÄÄRIÄINEN Kimmo, Revd Dr, Finland

Evangelical Lutheran Church of Finland, KURTÉN Kristina Sofia, Ms, Finland

Evangelical Church River Plate, SKUPCH Sonia, Revd, Argentina

Evangelical Lutheran Church of Colombia, HERNÁNDEZ Atahualpa, Bishop, Colombia

Evangelical Lutheran Church of Colombia, GRAFE Chishilde, Ms, Colombia

Evangelical Lutheran Church in Denmark, NYGAARD Birger, Mr, Denmark

Evangelical Lutheran Church in Jordan and the Holy Land, YOUNAN Munib, Bishop Dr, Israel

Evangelical Lutheran Church in Württemberg, KÜMMERLE Andreas, Dr, Germany

Lutheran Church in Liberia, SEYENKULO Daniel, Bishop Dr, Liberia

Lutheran Church of Taiwan, CHEN Selma, Revd, Taiwan

Lutheran World Federation, HINTIKKA Kaisamari, Revd Dr, Switzerland

Lutheran World Federation, JOHNSON Kathryn, Dr, USA

Lutheran World Federation, JUNGE Martin, Revd Dr, Switzerland

Lutheran World Federation (Colombia), ÁLVAREZ Diego, Colombia

Lutheran World Federation (Colombia), VUORENSOLA-BARNES Saara, Ms, Colombia

Martin Luther University College, PHILIP Mary, Prof, Canada

Mennonite

Mennonite Church Colombia, STUCKY Peter, Revd, Colombia

Mennonite World Conference, GRABER Anne-Cathy Revd Dr, France

Methodist

Methodist Church of Colombia, CARDONA Juan Alberto, Bishop, Colombia

Methodist Church of Ghana, MPERE-GYEKYE William, Bishop, Ghana

The United Methodist Church, Jean Hawkhurst, Dr, USA

The United Methodist Church, SWANSON James E., Bishop, USA

The United Methodist Church, WATSON Michael, Bishop, USA

World Methodist Council, ABRAHAMS Ivan, Bishop, South Africa

World Methodist Council, MURILLO Samuel, Revd, Mexico

World Methodist Council, SANTIZO Claudia, Ms, Guatemala

World Methodist Council, WENNER Rosemarie, Bishop, Germany

Old Catholic

International Old Catholic Bishops Conference of the Union of Utrecht, VERCAMMEN Joris, Archbishop Dr, Netherlands

Orthodox – Eastern

Church of Greece, PAPANIKOLAOU Gabriel, Metropolitan, Greece

Church of Greece, ANDRIOPOULOS Iakovos, Archimandrite, Greece

Ecumenical Patriarchate, KOUKOURA Dimitra, Prof Dr, Greece

Ecumenical Patriarchate KROCHAK Andrij, Mr, France

Ecumenical Patriarchate/Orthodox Christian Mission Center, RITSI Martin, Very Revd, USA

Greek Orthodox Church in Colombia, TORRES Timoteo, Archimandrite, Colombia

Greek Orthodox Church in Cuba, PÉREZ Atenágoras, Archimandrite, Cuba

Orthodox Autocephalous Church of Albania, HOPPE Nathan, Prof Dr, Albania

Serbian Orthodox Church in Colombia, LÓPEZ Simeón, Hieromonk, Colombia

Russian Orthodox Church, GOUNDIAEV Mikhail, Archpriest, Switzerland

Russian Orthodox Church, IGUMNOV Stefan, Hieromonk, Russia

Orthodox – Oriental

Coptic Orthodox Church, Diocese of London, ANGAELOS, H.E. Archbishop, United Kingdom

Syriac Orthodox Patriarchate of Antioch and All the East, APHREM II Ignatius Mor, H.H. Patriarch, Syria

Syriac Orthodox Patriarchate of Antioch and All the East, BALI Joseph, Fr, Syria

Syriac Orthodox Patriarchate of Antioch and All the East, CASTILLO Fabián, Colombia

Syriac Orthodox Patriarchate of Antioch and All the East, CHAMOUN Michael, H.E. Archbishop, Syria

Syriac Orthodox Patriarchate of Antioch and All the East/ World Council of Churches Commission on World Mission and Evangelism, COORILOS Geevarghese Mor, Metr., India

Pentecostal

Assemblies of God Colombia, RODRÍGUEZ Santiago, Revd, Colombia

Assemblies of God Jordan/Evangelical Council of Jordan, RIHANI David, Revd, Jordan

Assemblies of God Perú, LÓPEZ Pedro Manuel, Mr, Perú

Assemblies of God Switzerland/Foundation du Forum Chrétien Mondial, PLÜSS Jean-Daniel, Dr, Switzerland

Church of God (Cleveland), BAILEY Coleman, Mr, USA

Church of God (Cleveland)/Pentecostal Theological Seminary, HAN David Sang-Ehil, Prof Dr, USA

Church of God (Cleveland)/Seminario Sudamericano, JIMÉNEZ Francisco, Mr, Ecuador

Church of God (Cleveland)/Shalom Project International, WALDROP Richard, Dr, USA

Church of God Colombia, MENDIETA Arturo, Bishop, Colombia

Church of God Ecuador, MENDOZA Richar, Bishop, Ecuador

Church of Pentecost, BAAH Robert, Revd Dr, USA

Church of Pentecost, DONKOR Lord E., Revd Dr, United Kingdom

Evangel World Prayer Center, OLEA Jorge, Revd, Canada

Evangel World Prayer Center, RODGERS Robert, Revd Dr, USA

Filadelfia Church Stockholm, LEHTONEN Rauli, Revd, Sweden

International Pentecostal Holiness Church, HUNTER Harold, Revd Dr, USA

Methodist Pentecostal Church Chile, LEIVA Eduardo, Mr, Chile

Oral Roberts University, PETERSON II Eric, Mr, USA

Oral Roberts University, MA Wonsuk, Prof Dr, USA

Pentecostal, FISCHER Christoph, Germany

Pentecostal/Fuller Theological Seminary, ROBECK Cecil Mel, Prof Dr, USA

Pentecostal Forum of Latin American and the Caribbean/ Pentecostal Church Ecuador, CAMPOS José, Dr (MD), Ecuador

Pentecostal Forum of Latin American and the Caribbean/ Pentecostal Church Chile, CORVALÁN Oscar, Dr, Chile

Pentecostal Forum of Latin American and the Caribbean/ Pentecostal Church Brazil/ Latin American Network of Pentecostal Studies, FREIRE DE ALENCAR Gedeon, Dr, Brazil

Pentecostal Forum of Latin American and the Caribbean/ Pentecostal Church Chile, ORELLANA Luis, Dr, Chile

Pentecostal Forum of Latin American and the Caribbean/ Assemblies of God Colombia, RODRÍGUEZ Jeferson, Prof, Colombia

Pentecostal Forum of Latin American and the Caribbean/ Foursquare Church Ecuador, SAA Laura, Revd, Ecuador

Pentecostal Forum of Latin American and the Caribbean, SANTIAGO Helen, Puerto Rico

Pentecostal Forum of Latin American and the Caribbean, URIBE Javier, Dr, Mexico

Pentecostal World Fellowship/International Pentecostal Holiness Church, BEACHAM Doug, Dr, USA

Pentecostal World Fellowship/Pentecostal Church of Finland, HÄMÄLÄINEN Arto, Revd Dr, Finland

Pentecostal World Fellowship/Pentecostal Church of Finland, KOSKELA Harri, Dr, Finland

Pentecostal World Fellowship/Apostolic Faith Mission of South Africa, MAHLOBO M. George, Revd, South Africa

Pentecostal World Fellowship/Pentecostal Assemblies of Canada, WELLS David, Revd Dr, Canada

Pentecostal World Fellowship, WELLS Jonathan, Mr, Canada

Pentecostal World Fellowship/Empowered 21/Oral Roberts University/Church of God, WILSON William, Revd Dr, USA

Union of Evangelical Churches of the Revival/Forum Chrétien Francophone, THEVENET Daniel, France

Reformed

Christian Reformed Church in North America, WATSON Colin, Mr, USA

MyungSung Presbyterian Church, KIM Hana, Revd Dr, Republic of Korea

Presbyterian Church of Colombia, BARRIGA Jairo, Revd, Colombia

Reformed Church in America, DEYOUNG Lee, Mr, USA

Reformed Church in America, DUENSING Stacey, Revd, USA

World Communion of Reformed Churches, BAROLIN Rogelio D., Revd, Uruguay

World Communion of Reformed Churches, FERGUSON Chris, Revd Dr, Germany

World Communion of Reformed Churches, GRANBERG-MICHAELSON Wesley, Revd, USA

World Communion of Reformed Churches, LESSING Hanns, Revd Dr, Germany

World Communion of Reformed Churches, VIEIRA Raissa, Ms, Brazil

Salvation Army, The

Salvation Army Colombia Territory, DIAZ Alexander, Captain, Colombia

Salvation Army Colombia Territory, TRIVIÑO Humberto, Captain, Colombia

Salvation Army International Headquarters, MATEAR Elizabeth, Commissioner, United Kingdom

Seventh-day Adventist Church

Seventh-day Adventist Church General Conference, DIOP Ganoune, Revd Dr, USA

Seventh-day Adventist Church Latin America Division, CARNASSALE Helio, Revd, Brazil

Seventh-day Adventist Church Colombia, PERILLA Jaime, Mr, Colombia

Seventh-day Adventist Church Colombia, VILLARREAL Gabriel, Mr, Colombia

United and Uniting Churches

China Christian Council, PEI Lianshan, Revd, China

China Christian Council, TANG Shiwen, Revd, China

National Organisations and Movements

Canadian Council of Churches, BARNETT-COWAN Alyson, Revd Canon Dr, Canada

China Christian Council, PEI Lianshan, Revd, China

China Christian Council, TANG Shiwen, Revd, China

Christian Churches Together in the USA, MALAVÉ Carlos, Revd, USA

Christian Council of Cuba, ORTEGA DOPICO Joel, Revd, Cuba

Christian Council of Cuba, SANTANA Antonio, Revd, Cuba

Colombia Evangelical Council (CEDECOL), CASTAÑO Edgar, Revd, Colombia

French Protestant Federation, BLANZAT Pierre, Revd, France

French Protestant Federation, DANET Anne-Laure, Revd France

Together Church in the Netherlands, HAYALI Anmar Hayali, Mr, Netherlands

Regional Ecumenical Organisations and Movements

European Conference of Churches, PEKRIDOU Katerina, Ms, Belgium

Francophone Christian Forum, BLANZAT Pierre, Revd, France

Francophone Christian Forum, DANET Anne-Laure, Revd France

Francophone Christian Forum, GOUGAUD Emmanuel, Fr, France

Francophone Christian Forum, THEVENET Daniel, Revd, France

Gulf Churches Fellowship, RYTKÖNEN Aaro, Revd, Oman

Latin American Council of Churches, MEJÍA Milton, Revd, Colombia

Middle East Council of Churches, BECHEALANY Souraya, Prof Dr, Lebanon

Middle East Council of Churches, Fr Prof Dr Gabriel Hachem, Lebanon

International Movements and Organisations

Brot für die Welt, SELBACH Christopher, Mr Germany

Center for the Study of Global Christianity, ZURLO Gina, Dr, USA

Chemin Neuf Community/Net for God, ROUSSINEAU Gabriel, Fr, France

Chemin Neuf Community, SOOBRAYDOO Gilbert, Mr, France

InnerChange, BACON Nathanael, Deacon, Guatemala

InnerChange, BACON Mayra Ávila, Mrs, Guatemala

International Fellowship for Mission as Transformation, PADILLA DEBORST Ruth, Dr, Costa Rica

International Justice Mission, GEORGE Abraham, Revd, USA

Receptive Ecumenism Project, THOMAS Gabrielle, Prof Dr, University of Durham, United Kingdom

Taizé Community, Brother Paolo, France

Union of Messianic Jewish Congregations, KINZER Mark, Rabbi Dr, USA

United Bible Societies, PERREAU Michael, Mr, United Kingdom

World Council of Churches, SAUCA Ioan, Fr Prof Dr, Switzerland

World Council of Churches Central Committee, KOUKOURA Dimitra, Prof Dr, Greece

World Council of Churches Commission on Faith and Order, BERLIS Angela, Prof Dr, Switzerland

World Council of Churches Commission on Faith and Order, GHAZARYAN DRISSI Ani, Dr, Switzerland

World Council of Churches Commission on Faith and Order, MATEUS Odair Pedroso, Revd Dr, Switzerland

World Council of Churches Commission on World Mission and Evangelism, COORILOS Geevarghese, Metropolitan Dr, India

World Council of Churches Commission on World Mission and Evangelism, TAHAAFE-WILLIAM Katalina, Revd Dr, Switzerland

World Council of Churches Communications, HILLERT Albin, Mr, Sweden

World Council of Churches Communications, KUPCIS Ivars, Mr, Switzerland

World Council of Churches Communications, MORFI Xanthi, Ms. Switzerland

World Student Christian Federation, KENGNE DJEUTANE Georgine, Ms, Cameroon

World Student Christian Federation Colombia, CRUZ Diana, Ms, Colombia

World Student Christian Federation Latin America and the Caribbean, LEITES Marcelo, Argentina

World Vision International, MICH Tadeusz, Dr, USA

World Vision International (Colombia), MACHUCA Viviana, Ms, Colombia

World Vision International (Colombia), RODRÍGUEZ Martha Yaneth, Ms Colombia

World Vision International (Colombia), SÁNCHEZ Mayerly, Ms, Colombia

World Vision International (Ecuador), CARVAJAL Jesiel, Mr, Ecuador

World Vision International (Latin America and the Caribbean, SEGURA Harold, Revd, Costa Rica

World Young Women's Christian Association, PENTTINEN Pirjo-Liisa, Revd, Finland

World Young Women's Christian Association (Colombia), CASTRO Lina, Ms, Colombia

World Young Women's Christian Association (Colombia), JIMÉNEZ Judy, Ms, Colombia

World Young Women's Christian Association (Colombia), LÓPEZ Magda, Ms, Colombia

Roles

Global Christian Forum Committee

BROWN Elijah, Revd Dr, Baptist World Alliance, USA

CHAMOUN Michael, H.E. Archbishop, Syriac Orthodox Patriarchate of Antioch and All the East, Syria

CHOROMANSKI Andrzej, Revd Dr, Catholic Church, Pontifical Council for Promoting Christian Unity, Vatican City

DIOP Ganoune, Revd Dr, Seventh-day Adventist Church, USA

GENNADIOS OF SASSIMA, H.E. Metropolitan. Prof Dr, Ecumenical Patriarchate, Turkey

FODAY-KHABENJE Aiah, Revd Dr, Association of Evangelicals in Africa, Kenya

GARDNER Paul, Revd Dr, World Council of Churches, Jamaica

GIBAUT John, Revd Canon Dr, Anglican Communion, United Kingdom

GOUNDIAEV Mikhail, Archpriest, Russian Orthodox Church, Switzerland

GRABER Anne-Cathy, Revd Prof Dr, Mennonite World Conference, France

GRANBERG-MICHAELSON Wesley, Revd, World Communion of Reformed Churches, USA

GUNERATNAM Prince, Revd Dr, Pentecostal World Fellowship, Kuala Lumpur

HAN David Sang-Ehil, Prof Dr, Church of God (Cleveland), USA

HOWELL Richard, Revd Dr, Asia Evangelical Alliance/World Evangelical Alliance, India

JOHNSON Kathryn, Dr, Lutheran World Federation, USA

KENGNE DJEUTANE Georgine, Ms, World Student Christian Federation, Cameroon

KOUKOURA Dimitra, Prof Dr, World Council of Churches, Greece

LUBAALE Nicta, Revd, Organization of African Instituted Churches, Kenya

MATEAR Elizabeth, Commissioner, The Salvation Army International, United Kingdom

MICH Tadeusz, Dr, World Vision International, USA

PENTTINEN Pirjo-Liisa, Revd, Young Women's Christian Association/Evangelical Lutheran Church Finland, Finland

ROBECK Cecil M. Jr., Prof Dr, Fuller Theological Seminary, USA

SCHIRRMACHER Thomas, Bishop Prof Dr, World Evangelical Alliance, Germany

WELLS David, Revd Dr, Pentecostal World Fellowship, Canada

WENNER Rosemarie, Bishop, World Methodist Council, Germany

National Organising Committee

BARRIGA Jairo, Revd, Presbyterian Church of Colombia, Colombia

BUSTAMANTE Jorge, Fr, Episcopal Conference of Colombia, Colombia

CARDONA Juan Alberto, Bishop, Methodist Church of Colombia, Colombia

CASTAÑO Edgar, Revd, Colombian Evangelical Council (CEDECOL), Colombia

CRUZ Diana, Ms, World Student Christian Federation Colombia, Colombia

DIAZ Alexander, Captain, Salvation Army Colombia, Colombia

DUQUE Francisco, Bishop, Anglican Church Colombia, Colombia

DURÁN Arnulfo, Revd, Baptist Church in Colombia, Colombia

HERNÁNDEZ Atahualpa, Bishop, Evangelical Lutheran Church of Colombia, Colombia

JIMÉNEZ Judy, Mrs, Young Women Christian Association Colombia, Colombia

MACHUCA Viviana, Ms, World Vision Colombia, Colombia

MEJÍA Milton, Revd, Latin American Council of Churches, Colombia

MENDIETA Arturo, Bishop, Church of God Colombia, Colombia

RODRÍGUEZ Jeferson, Prof, Assemblies of God Colombia/ Latin American and Caribbean Pentecostal Forum, Colombia

TORRES Timoteo, Archimandrite, Greek Orthodox Church Colombia, Colombia

TRIVIÑO Humberto, Captain, The Salvation Army Colombia, Colombia

Third Global Gathering Planning Group

CHOROMANSKI Andrzej, Revd Dr, Catholic Church, Pontifical Council for Promoting Christian Unity, Vatican City

DIOP Ganoune, Revd Dr, Seventh-day Adventist Church, USA

GIBAUT John, Revd Canon Dr, Anglican Communion, United Kingdom

GOUNDIAEV Mikhail, Archpriest, Russian Orthodox Church, Switzerland

GRABER Anne-Cathy, Revd Dr, Mennonite World Conference, France

GRANBERG-MICHAELSON Wesley, Revd, World Communion of Reformed Churches, USA

HAN David Sang-Ehil, Prof Dr, Church of God (Cleveland), USA

HOWELL Richard, Revd Dr, World Evangelical Alliance, India

KOUKOURA Dimitra, Prof Dr, World Council of Churches, Greece

HOWELL Richard, Revd Dr, World Evangelical Alliance, India

JOHNSON Kathryn, Dr, Lutheran World Federation, USA

LUBAALE Nicta, Revd, Organization of African Instituted Churches, Kenya

MILLER Larry, Revd Dr, Global Christian Forum, France

PLÜSS Jean-Daniel, Dr, Fondation du Forum Chrétien Mondial, Switzerland

SCHIRRMACHER Thomas, Bishop Prof Dr, World Evangelical Alliance, Germany

WELLS David, Revd Dr, Pentecostal World Fellowship, Canada

Message Committee

GRANBERG-MICHAELSON Wesley Revd, World Communion of Reformed Churches, USA

HAN David Sang-Ehil, Prof Dr, Church of God (Cleveland), USA

MACMILLAN Christine, Commissioner, World Evangelical Alliance, Canada

OSITELU Rufus, The Most Revd Dr, The Church of the Lord (Prayer Fellowship) Worldwide, Nigeria

PEKRIDOU Katerina, Ms, Conference of European Churches, Belgium

RITSI Martin, Very Revd, Ecumenical Patriarchate/Orthodox Christian Mission Center, USA

SANTIAGO Helen, Dr, Latin American and Caribbean Pentecostal Forum, Puerto Rico

SHIRK LUCAS Katherine, Prof Dr, Institut Catholique de Paris, France

TAHAAFE-WILLIAMS Katalina, Revd Dr, World Council of Churches, Switzerland

Communications Team

ÁLVAREZ Diego, Mr, Lutheran World Federation, Colombia

CAIN Kim, Revd, Global Christian Forum, Australia

CAJÍAS Fernando, Mr, Episcopal Conference of Colombia, Colombia

GOROPEVSEK Timothy, Mr, World Evangelical Alliance, USA

HILLERT Albin, Mr, Church of Sweden/World Council of Churches, Sweden

KENNY Peter, Mr, Ecumenical News, Switzerland

KOSKELA Harri, Dr, Pentecostal World Fellowship, Finland

KUPCIS Ivars, Mr, World Council of Churches, Switzerland

MORFI Xanthi, Ms, World Council of Churches, France

OLANG Jim, Mr, Association of Evangelicals in Africa, Kenya

ROUSSINEAU Gabriel, Fr, Chemin Neuf Community, France

SANCHEZ Mayerly, Ms, World Vision Colombia, Colombia

SOOBRAYDO Gilbert, Mr, Chemin Neuf Community, France

Staff

ESSAMUAH Casely, Revd Dr, Global Christian Forum, USA

GROETING Patricia, Ms, Interpreter, Argentina

GULFO Gamaliel, Mr, Nurse, Colombia

JOSEPH Michael, Mr, Interpreter, Colombia

MÉAR Christine, Mrs, Interpreter, France

MILLER Eleanor, Mrs, Global Christian Forum, France

MILLER Larry, Revd Dr, Global Christian Forum, France

MORENO Magali, Ms, Global Christian Forum, Paraguay

NTIHINYUZWA, Joséphine, Mrs, Global Christian Forum, France

RAMÍREZ Raimy, Mrs, Global Christian Forum, Colombia

SINTADO Myriam, Ms, Interpreter, Switzerland,

SINTADO Carlos, Dr, Interpreter, Switzerland,

VAN BEEK Huibert, Mr, Global Christian Forum

WARNECKE Martin, Mr, World Evangelical Alliance, Germany

Stewards

BERNAL Cristian, Mr, Lutheran Church Colombia, Colombia

BONILLA Luisa, Ms, Mennonite Church Colombia, Colombia

COY Marian, Ms, Lutheran Church Colombia, Colombia

CUBILLOS Esteban, Mr, Mennonite Church Colombia, Colombia

GÓMEZ Ruth Vanessa, Ms, Lutheran Church Colombia, Colombia

LARA Daniel, Mr, Lutheran Church Colombia, Colombia

NATES Francisco, Mr, Mennonite Church Colombia, Colombia

PÉREZ Miyer, Mr, Mennonite Church Colombia, Colombia

PICO Jeimy Katherine, Ms, Lutheran Church Colombia, Colombia

PRECIADO Felipe, Mr, Mennonite Church Colombia, Colombia

PROAÑOS Felipe, Mr, Mennonite Church Colombia, Colombia

RAMÍREZ Paola, Ms, Presbyterian Church Colombia, Colombia

ROSERO Mayra, Ms, Mennonite Church Colombia, Colombia

SÁNCHEZ Michael, Mr, Mennonite Church Colombia, Colombia

VENEGAS Gabriela, Ms, Mennonite Church Colombia, Colombia

Youth Programme Participants

ALTIZER Ricky, Mr, Evangelical, USA

BAILEY Coleman, Mr, Church of God (Cleveland), USA (*Youth Delegate*)

COLÓN Eduardo, Mr, Catholic Church, Colombia

CRUZ Diana, Ms, World Student Christian Federation Colombia, Colombia

DUENSING Stacey, Revd, Reformed Church in America, USA (*Youth Delegate*)

ESSAMUAH Zinhle, Ms, Evangelical, USA

HAYALI Anmar, Mr, Together Church in the Netherlands, Netherlands

HOEKZEMA Trevin, Mr, Bay Area Community Church, USA

KROCHAK Andrij, Mr, Ecumenical Patriarchate, France (*Youth Delegate*)

LEITES Marcelo, Mr, World Student Christian Federation, Argentina (*Youth Delegate*)

LÓPEZ Magda, Ms, Young Women Christian Association, Colombia (*Youth Delegate*)

MURILLO Samuel, Revd, World Methodist Council, Mexico (*Youth Delegate*)

OLANG Jim, Mr, Association of Evangelicals in Africa, Kenya (*Youth Delegate*)

PEKRIDOU Katerina, Ms, Conference of European Churches, Belgium

RODRÍGUEZ Jeferson, Prof, Assemblies of God Colombia/ Latin American and Caribbean Pentecostal Forum, Colombia

SANTIZO Claudia, Ms, World Methodist Council, Guatemala (*Youth Delegate*)

SAXENA Samuel, Revd, World Evangelical Alliance, India (*Youth Delegate*)

SCHIRRMACHER Esther, Ms, World Evangelical Alliance, Germany (*Youth Delegate*)

TRIVIÑO Humberto, Captain, The Salvation Army, Colombia (*Youth Delegate*)

TSCHIRSCH Agustina, Ms, Baptist World Alliance, Argentina (*Youth Delegate*)

VIEIRA Raissa, Ms, World Communion of Reformed Churches, Brazil

WELLS Jonathan, Mr, Pentecostal World Fellowship, Canada (*Youth Delegate*)

ZURLO Gina, Dr, Center for the Study of Global Christianity, USA

Guests and Observers

ESSAMUAH Angela, Mrs, Bay Area Community Church, USA

ESSAMUAH Zikomo, Mr, Bay Area Community Church, USA

ESSAMUAH Zachary, Mr, Bay Area Community Church, USA

GASTELLU Adriana, Revd, Church of Sweden, Sweden

HAWXHURST Jean, Revd Dr, The United Methodist Church, USA

KINZER Mark, Rabbi Dr, Union of Messianic Jewish Congregations, USA

KURTÉN Kristina Sofia, Ms, Evangelical Lutheran Church of Finland, Finland

SELBACH Christopher, Mr, Brot für die Welt, Germany
STUCKY Peter, Revd, Mennonite Church Colombia, Colombia
VAN BEEK Maria, Mrs, Global Christian Forum, Switzerland

www.ingramcontent.com/pod-product-compliance
Lightning Source LLC
Chambersburg PA
CBHW071229290426
44108CB00013B/1343